CREATION EX NIHILO

A Theological and Philosophical Exploration

Dr. Maxwell R. Shimba

SHIMBA
PUBLISHING

TABLE OF CONTENTS

INTRODUCTION

Definition of Creation Ex Nihilo

The concept of Creation Ex Nihilo, Latin for "creation out of nothing," stands as one of the most profound and foundational doctrines in theistic philosophy and theology, particularly within the Judeo-Christian tradition. It asserts that the universe, including all matter and energy, was brought into existence by a transcendent, divine act, without the use of any pre-existing material. This idea distinguishes the Christian understanding of creation from other ancient creation myths and philosophical theories that often presuppose the existence of some primordial substance or chaos from which the cosmos was fashioned.

Historical Emergence of the Concept

The doctrine of Creation Ex Nihilo is not explicitly stated in the earliest texts of the Bible, yet it is implied and gradually developed within the broader narrative of Scripture. The opening verse of Genesis, "In the beginning, God created the heavens and the earth" (Genesis 1:1), has been interpreted by later theological reflection as an affirmation that God alone is the source of all that exists. The absence of any mention of pre-existing materials or forces in the creation narrative suggests that God's creative power is absolute and unbounded, capable of bringing the entire cosmos into being from nothing.

The concept became more explicitly formulated during the early centuries of the Christian Church as theologians sought to articulate a clear distinction between the Creator and the created order. This was particularly important in countering various heretical views, such as Gnosticism and Manichaeism, which posited an eternal dualism between matter and spirit, or between good and evil. In contrast, the doctrine of Creation Ex Nihilo affirmed the goodness of all creation, grounded in its divine origin, and underscored God's sovereignty over all things.

Philosophical Underpinnings

Philosophically, Creation Ex Nihilo raises significant questions about the nature of existence, causality, and the relationship between God and the universe. The idea that something can come from nothing challenges the intuitive notion that every effect must have a cause and that material things must come from other material things. However, in the context of divine creation, "nothing" is not to be understood as a mere absence or void, but rather as the complete non-existence of anything other than God. The act of creation, therefore, is not a transformation of something into something else, but the actualization of being where there was none before.

This doctrine also serves to emphasize the transcendence and omnipotence of God. If God can create ex nihilo, then His power is not limited by anything external to Himself. God does not require any pre-existing material to create; rather, all that exists depends entirely on His will and purpose. This concept not only underscores God's role as the ultimate cause of all things but also establishes a clear ontological distinction between God, who is uncreated and eternal, and the universe, which is created and contingent.

Theological Significance

Theologically, Creation Ex Nihilo has profound implications for understanding the nature of God, the world, and humanity's place within it. It affirms that the universe is not a necessary emanation of a divine being, but a free and deliberate act of God's will. This reinforces the idea that creation is inherently good, reflecting the character of its Creator and that all of reality has a purpose and meaning grounded in divine intention.

Moreover, this doctrine is essential for understanding the biblical narrative of salvation. The God who created the world ex nihilo is also the God who redeems it. Just as God brought the universe into existence without any pre-existing materials, so too can He bring new life and restoration out of situations that seem hopeless or beyond repair. The power of God to create from nothing is thus mirrored in the Christian hope of resurrection and new creation.

In summary, Creation Ex Nihilo is a doctrine that encapsulates the radical dependence of all creation on the Creator, the infinite power and freedom of God, and the inherent goodness and purposefulness of the created order. As we delve into the theological and philosophical dimensions of this concept, we will explore its historical development, its implications for understanding the nature of God and the universe, and its relevance in contemporary thought. This exploration will reveal how Creation Ex Nihilo serves as a cornerstone for much of Christian theology and a profound statement about the nature of reality itself.

Introduction: Historical and Contemporary Relevance

The doctrine of Creation Ex Nihilo—the belief that God created the universe out of nothing—has not only shaped theological discourse for centuries but also continues to hold significant relevance in contemporary religious, philosophical, and scientific discussions. This concept, deeply rooted in the Judeo-Christian tradition, has played a crucial role in defining the relationship between God and the cosmos, influencing not only how believers understand the origin of the universe but also how they perceive the nature of reality, divine sovereignty, and human existence. Its implications have resonated through the ages, adapting to new contexts while remaining a central tenet of theistic belief.

Historical Relevance

Historically, the doctrine of Creation Ex Nihilo emerged as a critical response to various ancient worldviews that proposed different models of creation. In the ancient Near East, for example, creation myths often involved gods fashioning the world from pre-existing chaotic matter or through battles with other deities, implying that the material of the universe existed independently of the divine will. Such myths can be found in the Babylonian Enuma Elish, where the god Marduk creates the world by defeating the chaos monster Tiamat and using her body to form the heavens and the earth.

In contrast, the Hebrew Scriptures presented a radically different narrative. The creation account in Genesis 1, while not explicitly mentioning the concept of creation from nothing, emphasized God's sovereign command in bringing forth light, life, and order from a formless void (Genesis 1:2). Over time, Jewish and early Christian theologians, such as the Apostle Paul and Church Fathers like Augustine, began to articulate more clearly the idea that God did not shape the world from pre-existing materials but rather called it into existence through His word alone. This development was crucial in distinguishing the biblical worldview from surrounding pagan cosmologies and in affirming the absolute sovereignty and transcendence of the God of Israel.

During the early centuries of the Christian Church, the doctrine of Creation Ex Nihilo became a key point of orthodoxy, especially in the face of emerging heresies that challenged the traditional understanding of creation. Gnostic and Manichean teachings, for instance, posited a dualistic universe in which matter was inherently evil and separate from a distant, unknowable deity. In response, the doctrine of Creation Ex Nihilo was further refined and defended as a way to affirm the goodness of the material world, as well as the intimate involvement of a benevolent and omnipotent Creator in all aspects of creation. The early ecumenical councils, such as the Council of Nicaea in 325 AD, would later reinforce this doctrine as part of the Church's creedal affirmations.

Throughout the medieval period, theologians like Thomas Aquinas continued to explore the implications of Creation Ex Nihilo within the framework of Christian metaphysics. Aquinas integrated Aristotelian philosophy with Christian doctrine, arguing that God, as the First Cause, must have created the world from nothing because nothing else existed prior to His creative act. This synthesis of faith and reason became a cornerstone of Scholastic theology, influencing not only religious thought but also the development of Western philosophy as a whole.

Contemporary Relevance

In the modern era, the relevance of Creation Ex Nihilo extends beyond purely theological circles, intersecting with philosophical and scientific discussions about the origin and nature of the universe. With the rise of scientific cosmology, particularly the Big Bang Theory, which posits that the universe had a beginning point from which it has been expanding, some see a correlation with the doctrine of Creation Ex Nihilo. While the scientific community generally refrains from making theological claims, the idea that the universe had an origin aligns intriguingly with the biblical notion of creation out of nothing.

Philosophically, the concept continues to be a topic of significant debate. Contemporary philosophers of religion engage with Creation Ex Nihilo in discussions about the nature of existence, causality, and the possibility of a universe without a cause. The question of why there is something rather than nothing remains one of the most profound inquiries in metaphysics, and Creation Ex Nihilo offers one possible answer, rooted in the idea of a necessary being—God—who freely chooses to create a contingent universe.

The doctrine also holds continued relevance in discussions about the nature of God. In an era where philosophical arguments for the existence of God often focus on the cosmological argument, Creation Ex Nihilo provides a theological basis for understanding God's relationship to the world. It affirms God's ultimate authority over all that exists, underscoring the belief that everything owes its existence to the divine will, which is not constrained by any external necessity or material.

Furthermore, Creation Ex Nihilo has practical implications for contemporary believers. It shapes how individuals understand their place in the universe, fostering a sense of dependence on God and a recognition of the giftedness of creation. It also influences Christian perspectives on environmental stewardship, human dignity, and the inherent value of all created things, given their origin in the divine will.

In a pluralistic world, the doctrine of Creation Ex Nihilo also serves as a point of dialogue and sometimes tension between different religious and philosophical traditions. As interfaith discussions become more prominent, understanding this concept's historical development and contemporary significance can facilitate deeper conversations about the nature of God, the universe, and human existence across various worldviews.

In conclusion, the doctrine of Creation Ex Nihilo remains as relevant today as it was in the early centuries of the Church. Its profound implications continue to shape theological discourse, philosophical inquiry, and scientific exploration. As we delve deeper into the intricacies of this doctrine, we will uncover its enduring significance and its capacity to address some of the most fundamental questions about the nature of reality and the divine.

Introduction: Purpose and Scope of the Book

The doctrine of Creation Ex Nihilo—the belief that the universe was created out of nothing by a sovereign and omnipotent God—stands as one of the most profound and debated concepts in both theology and philosophy. This book aims to provide a comprehensive exploration of Creation Ex Nihilo by examining its historical development, theological significance, and philosophical implications. The purpose of this book is to offer readers a deeper understanding of how this doctrine has shaped religious thought throughout the centuries and to explore its relevance in contemporary discussions.

Purpose of the Book

The primary purpose of this book is to delve into the concept of Creation Ex Nihilo from both theological and philosophical perspectives, offering a well-rounded analysis that appeals to scholars, theologians, philosophers, and interested lay readers alike. By examining the doctrine's origins, evolution, and implications, the book seeks to clarify how Creation Ex Nihilo serves as a cornerstone of theistic belief, particularly within the Judeo-Christian tradition.

Theologically, the book will explore how Creation Ex Nihilo has been understood and articulated within the Christian tradition, from its implicit presence in the biblical texts to its explicit formulation by the early Church Fathers, medieval theologians, and modern Christian thinkers. This exploration will highlight the doctrine's importance in defining God's relationship to the universe, affirming the goodness of creation, and shaping key Christian doctrines such as the nature of God, the problem of evil, and the concept of salvation.

Philosophically, the book will engage with the broader questions that Creation Ex Nihilo raises about existence, causality, and the nature of reality. It will examine the arguments for and against the possibility of creation from nothing, drawing on both classical and contemporary philosophical thought. Additionally, the book will address the intersection of this doctrine with modern scientific theories about the origin of the universe, offering a thoughtful dialogue between faith and reason.

Beyond academic inquiry, this book also aims to provide practical insights for contemporary believers. Understanding Creation Ex Nihilo can deepen one's appreciation for the divine act of creation and foster a greater sense of awe and reverence for the Creator. It also offers a framework for addressing modern existential questions about the meaning and purpose of life, the nature of the universe, and humanity's place within it.

Scope of the Book

To achieve its purpose, the book is divided into three main parts: Theological Perspectives, Philosophical Perspectives, and Integrative Perspectives. Each part is designed to build on the previous one, offering a comprehensive and coherent examination of Creation Ex Nihilo.

1. Theological Perspectives: This section will trace the development of the doctrine of Creation Ex Nihilo from its roots in biblical texts through its articulation by early Christian theologians and its subsequent refinement in medieval and modern theology. It will explore how this doctrine has been used to address various theological issues, including the

nature of God, the goodness of creation, and the problem of evil.

2. Philosophical Perspectives: This part of the book will engage with the philosophical questions raised by the concept of Creation Ex Nihilo. It will examine the metaphysical implications of creating something from nothing, the nature of causality, and the concept of nothingness. It will also explore how this doctrine interacts with modern scientific theories and what it means for our understanding of reality.

3. Integrative Perspectives: The final section of the book will bring together the theological and philosophical discussions, offering an integrative analysis of Creation Ex Nihilo. It will explore the common ground and differences between the two perspectives and discuss the relevance of this doctrine in contemporary thought. This section will also consider the future directions of theological and philosophical research on creation and the ongoing dialogue between faith and reason.

Throughout the book, readers will find a blend of historical analysis, theological reflection, and philosophical argumentation. The writing aims to be accessible while remaining rigorous, ensuring that readers from various backgrounds can engage with the material.

In conclusion, this book is designed to serve as both a scholarly resource and a reflective guide for anyone interested in the profound concept of Creation Ex Nihilo. By exploring its historical roots, theological significance, and philosophical implications, the book seeks to provide a comprehensive understanding of how this doctrine continues to shape religious and philosophical thought today.

DR. MAXWELL SHIMBA

CHAPTER 01

BIBLICAL FOUNDATIONS

Creation Ex Nihilo in Genesis 1

The opening chapter of the Bible, Genesis 1, is one of the most significant texts in the Judeo-Christian tradition, offering a profound narrative of the origins of the universe. The phrase "In the beginning, God created the heavens and the earth" (Genesis 1:1) introduces not only the biblical creation story but also the foundational concept of Creation Ex Nihilo—the belief that God created the universe out of nothing. While the term "ex nihilo" is not explicitly mentioned in the text, the implications of this doctrine are deeply embedded in the Genesis account, influencing centuries of theological reflection and interpretation.

The Structure and Content of Genesis 1

Genesis 1 is structured as a series of divine creative acts over the course of six days, culminating in the creation of humanity and the establishment of the seventh day as a day of rest. The chapter begins with a statement of divine creation: "In the beginning, God created the heavens and the earth" (Genesis 1:1). This verse serves as a summary of the entire creation narrative, introducing the idea that God is the sole creator of everything that exists.

The subsequent verses describe the state of the universe before God's creative work: "The earth was without form and void, and darkness was over the face of the deep. And the Spirit of God was hovering over the face of the waters" (Genesis 1:2). This description suggests a primordial chaos or formlessness, a state of disorder that is soon transformed by God's creative word. The repeated phrase "And God said..." followed by the creation of various elements—light, sky, land, vegetation, celestial bodies, animals, and finally humans—emphasizes the power of God's word in bringing the cosmos into existence.

The narrative progresses in a rhythmic and orderly fashion, with each day marked by a specific act of creation, a declaration that "it was good," and the evening and morning cycle. The culmination of the narrative is the creation of humanity, made in the image of God, and the declaration that the entire creation was "very good" (Genesis 1:31).

Implications of Creation Ex Nihilo in Genesis 1

Although Genesis 1 does not explicitly state that God created the universe out of nothing, several aspects of the text strongly imply this idea. The absence of any reference to pre-existing materials, the depiction of the universe as initially "formless and void," and the emphasis on the creative power of God's word all point to the doctrine of Creation Ex Nihilo.

1. The Absence of Pre-existing Material:

Unlike other ancient Near Eastern creation myths, such as the Babylonian Enuma Elish, which describe creation as the ordering of pre-existing chaos or the result of divine conflict, Genesis 1 presents God as creating without reference to any pre-existing material. The text does not suggest that God-shaped or molded the world from something that already existed. Instead, the narrative begins with a formless void, and it is through God's spoken word that order, substance, and life emerge. This absence of pre-existing material is a key indicator of the concept of Creation Ex Nihilo.

2. The Power of the Divine Word:

A central theme in Genesis 1 is the power of God's word to bring about creation. The repeated refrain "And God said…" followed by the immediate realization of what was spoken, underscores the idea that God's creative acts are effortless and sovereign. There is no struggle, no need for raw materials, and no limitations on what God can create. This portrayal aligns with the idea that God created everything out of nothing, as His word alone is sufficient to bring the universe into being. This understanding is later echoed in the New Testament, particularly in the Gospel of John, which begins by stating, "In the beginning was the Word, and the Word was with God, and the Word was God. All things were made through Him, and without Him was not anything made that was made" (John 1:1, 3).

3. The State of the Universe Before Creation:

Genesis 1:2 describes the pre-creation state as "without form and void," with darkness covering the "face of the deep." This depiction suggests a condition of emptiness and formlessness that is distinct from the later-ordered creation. The Spirit of God "hovering over the face of the waters" indicates a divine presence poised to bring order and life out of this chaotic state. The notion of formlessness and void, combined with the subsequent creation narrative, implies that everything that follows is the result of God's creative action, and nothing existed independently of God before this action.

Theological Significance of Creation Ex Nihilo in Genesis 1

The doctrine of Creation Ex Nihilo derived from Genesis 1 carries profound theological significance for the Judeo-Christian understanding of God, creation, and humanity.

1. God's Sovereignty and Omnipotence:

The idea that God created the universe out of nothing underscores His absolute sovereignty and omnipotence. Unlike the gods of other ancient religions who might have needed materials or were limited by external forces, the God of Genesis is depicted as having complete control over all that exists. He alone is the source of all being, and nothing exists independently of His will. This understanding of God's creative power has been foundational to the Christian doctrine of God, affirming that God is not part of the universe but its Creator, distinct from and sovereign over all creation.

2. The Goodness of Creation:

Genesis 1 repeatedly emphasizes that creation is "good," and after the creation of humanity, it is declared "very good." This affirmation of the goodness of creation is closely tied to the doctrine of Creation Ex Nihilo. If God created everything from nothing, then all that exists is a direct result of His will and reflects His character. The goodness of creation, therefore, is rooted in its divine origin. This theological affirmation counters any notion that the material world is inherently evil or corrupt, a view that would later be rejected in Christian responses to Gnosticism.

3. Humanity's Place in Creation:

The culmination of the Genesis 1 narrative is the creation of humanity in the image of God. This unique status of humans as image-bearers of God underscores their special role in creation. The doctrine of Creation Ex Nihilo emphasizes that humanity, like the rest of creation, is a product of God's will and design. However, being made in the image of God also implies a responsibility to reflect God's character in the stewardship of creation. Humanity's role is not to dominate or exploit but to care for the created order as God's representatives, honoring the divine purpose embedded in all of creation.

4. The Relationship Between Creator and Creation:

Creation Ex Nihilo establishes a clear distinction between God and the created order. God is uncreated, eternal, and self-sufficient, while the universe is created, temporal, and contingent upon God for its existence. This distinction is crucial for understanding the nature of the relationship between God and the world. While creation is dependent on God, God is not dependent on creation. This theological insight helps to safeguard against pantheism (the idea that God is identical with the universe) and deism (the idea that God created the universe but is not involved in its ongoing existence).

Implications for Christian Theology and Doctrine

The implications of Creation Ex Nihilo as presented in Genesis 1 extend beyond the narrative itself, influencing several key areas of Christian theology and doctrine.

1. Doctrine of God:

The doctrine of Creation Ex Nihilo contributes to a robust understanding of God's attributes, including His omnipotence, omniscience, and sovereignty. It affirms that God is the ultimate reality, the source of all that exists, and that His creative power is limitless. This understanding of God as Creator shapes other doctrines, such as the doctrine of providence, which holds that God not only created the world but also sustains and governs it.

2. Doctrine of Creation:

Creation Ex Nihilo affirms the inherent goodness of creation, as it is the product of a good and purposeful God. This doctrine has implications for how Christians view the material world, including the environment, human bodies, and the value of physical existence. It also influences Christian eschatology, the belief in a future new creation, which will be the fulfillment of God's original creative purpose.

3. Doctrine of Salvation:

The concept of Creation Ex Nihilo also has implications for the Christian understanding of salvation. Just as God brought the universe into existence from nothing, He is also able to bring about new creation through the work of Christ. The power of God to create from nothing serves as a foundation for the Christian hope in the resurrection and the renewal of all things.

4. Doctrine of Humanity:

The unique creation of humanity in the image of God, as presented in Genesis 1, underscores the special role of humans in God's creation. This doctrine affirms human dignity, value, and responsibility, and it provides a theological basis for Christian ethics, particularly in areas such as human rights, justice, and care for the environment.

Genesis 1, though ancient, presents a narrative that is foundational for understanding the concept of Creation Ex Nihilo. While the text does not explicitly use the term "ex nihilo," the implications are clear: God, by His sovereign will and powerful word, created the universe out of nothing. This understanding has profound theological significance, shaping key doctrines about God, creation, and humanity. As we continue to explore the development and implications of Creation Ex Nihilo, we will see how this foundational belief continues to influence Christian thought and practice throughout history and into the present day.

Old Testament Insights

The Old Testament, comprising the Hebrew Scriptures, provides a rich tapestry of narratives, laws, prophecies, and wisdom literature that together reveal a comprehensive understanding of God's relationship with creation. While the explicit doctrine of Creation Ex Nihilo—the belief that God created the universe out of nothing—is not formally articulated in the Old Testament, several passages and themes strongly suggest this concept. The Old Testament's portrayal of God as the sovereign Creator who brings the cosmos into existence by His will and word forms the foundation for the later theological development of Creation Ex Nihilo.

Creation Narratives Beyond Genesis 1

The creation account in Genesis 1 is the most well-known and direct discussion of God's creative work in the Old Testament, but it is not the only one. Other passages, particularly in the Psalms, the Prophets, and the wisdom literature, offer additional insights into the nature of creation and the role of God as Creator.

1. Genesis 2: A Complementary Perspective

The second chapter of Genesis provides a more anthropocentric account of creation, focusing on the formation of humanity and the Garden of Eden. While Genesis 2 emphasizes God's intimate involvement in creation—forming Adam from the dust of the ground and breathing life into him—it complements the more cosmic scope of Genesis 1. The idea of God creating humanity from the dust, a material that He presumably created earlier, further supports the notion that all creation, including the materials from which humanity is made, originates from God's creative act.

2. Job 38-41: God's Sovereignty Over Creation

The book of Job offers profound insights into God's relationship with creation, particularly in the speeches from the divine perspective found in chapters 38 to 41. Here, God challenges Job with a series of rhetorical questions that emphasize His supreme knowledge and power over all aspects of the natural world: "Where were you when I laid the foundation of the earth? Tell me, if you have understanding" (Job 38:4). These chapters portray God as the architect of the universe, the one who set the boundaries for the sea, and the one who commands the morning. The emphasis on God's authority over creation, without reference to any pre-existing material, aligns with the concept of Creation Ex Nihilo, suggesting that everything exists solely by God's command.

3. Psalm 33:6-9: Creation by the Word of God

Psalm 33 provides a poetic reflection on God's creative power, declaring, "By the word of the Lord the heavens were made, and by the breath of His mouth all their host" (Psalm 33:6). This psalm echoes the Genesis 1 narrative, emphasizing the power of God's word in bringing the universe into existence. The passage continues, "For He spoke, and it came to be; He commanded, and it stood firm" (Psalm 33:9). The immediacy and effectiveness of God's word in creation suggest that no pre-existing materials were required—creation occurred purely by divine decree. This reinforces the idea that God's creative power is absolute and unbounded, consistent with the doctrine of Creation Ex Nihilo.

4. Psalm 148: The Praise of All Creation

Psalm 148 calls on all of creation to praise the Lord, including the heavens, the earth, the sea creatures, and all living beings. This psalm reflects a worldview in which everything that exists owes its existence to God's creative act and is therefore called to worship Him. The repeated emphasis on God's command—"He commanded and they were created" (Psalm 148:5)—highlights the belief that creation is entirely dependent on God's will. The universality of this praise, extending to all elements of creation, underscores the totality of God's creative work, reinforcing the idea that all of existence comes from God alone.

5. Proverbs 8:22-31: Wisdom and Creation

In Proverbs 8, Wisdom is personified and described as being present with God during the creation of the world: "The Lord possessed me at the beginning of His work, the first of His acts of old" (Proverbs 8:22). While this passage does not directly describe the act of creation ex nihilo, it does emphasize that creation was a deliberate, ordered act by God, with Wisdom as His companion. The portrayal of Wisdom as a participant in the creation process suggests that creation was not random or chaotic but was brought into being with purpose and order, further supporting the idea of an intentional creation by God alone.

The Prophets and Creation

The prophetic books of the Old Testament also provide significant insights into the doctrine of creation, often linking God's creative power to His ability to redeem and judge.

1. Isaiah 40-45: God as Creator and Redeemer

The book of Isaiah, particularly chapters 40-45, presents a powerful affirmation of God's role as the Creator of the universe. Isaiah 40:28 declares, "The Lord is the everlasting God, the Creator of the ends of the earth. He does not faint or grow weary; His understanding is unsearchable." This passage, along with others in Isaiah, emphasizes God's sovereignty and uniqueness as the Creator. Isaiah 45:18 reinforces this: "For thus says the Lord, who created the heavens (He is God!), who formed the earth and made it (He established it; He did not create it empty, He formed it to be inhabited!): 'I am the Lord, and there is no other.'"

These passages highlight not only God's creative power but also His ongoing involvement in creation. The assertion that God alone is the Creator and that there is no other reinforces the idea that all things originated from God's creative act, without reliance on any external materials. This aligns with the concept of Creation Ex Nihilo and underscores the theological importance of this belief in the context of Israel's monotheistic faith.

2. Jeremiah 10:12-16: God's Creative Authority

Jeremiah 10 contrasts the living God with the idols worshipped by the nations, emphasizing that it is God who "made the earth by His power, who established the world by His wisdom, and by His understanding stretched out the heavens" (Jeremiah 10:12). This passage underscores the power and wisdom of God in creation, highlighting the futility of idolatry. The portrayal of God as the one who "stretched out the heavens" suggests that creation is an act of divine will and wisdom, rather than a mere manipulation of existing matter. This further supports the concept of Creation Ex Nihilo, where God's creative authority is seen as absolute and unmatched.

3. Amos 4:13: The Creator Who Judges

The prophet Amos also speaks of God as the Creator, particularly in Amos 4:13: "For behold, He who forms the mountains and creates the wind, and declares to man what is His thought, who makes the morning darkness, and treads on the heights of the earth—the Lord, the God of hosts, is His name!" Here, God's role as Creator is linked to His role as Judge, emphasizing that the one who created the natural world is also the one who governs it. The mention of God creating the wind—a seemingly intangible element—reinforces the idea that God's creative power extends to all aspects of existence, whether seen or unseen, and does not depend on pre-existing materials.

Theological Themes of Creation in the Old Testament

Several overarching theological themes related to creation emerge from the Old Testament, contributing to the development of the doctrine of Creation Ex Nihilo.

1. God's Unrivaled Sovereignty

The Old Testament consistently portrays God as the supreme and unrivaled Creator. This sovereignty is evident in the way creation is described: God speaks, and creation responds. There are no rival gods, no forces of chaos that challenge God's authority. This portrayal is in stark contrast to the mythologies of surrounding cultures, where creation often involved conflict among deities. The Old Testament's depiction of God as the sole Creator supports the idea that creation itself is entirely contingent on God's will and power, reinforcing the concept of Creation Ex Nihilo.

2. Creation as an Expression of God's Wisdom and Order

The Old Testament frequently associates creation with divine wisdom and order. Whether in the poetic descriptions of Job, the Psalms, or Proverbs, creation is depicted as a well-ordered and purposeful act. This wisdom-infused creation suggests that the universe is not the product of chance or pre-existing chaos but of a deliberate act of divine will. This perspective aligns with the idea of Creation Ex Nihilo, where God's wisdom is the source of all that exists.

3. The Goodness and Purpose of Creation

The Old Testament affirms the goodness of creation, a theme introduced in Genesis 1 and reiterated throughout the scriptures. The declaration that creation is "good" implies that it reflects the character and purpose of its Creator. This goodness is not limited to the material world but extends to the entire created order, including humanity's role within it. The concept of Creation Ex Nihilo underscores this goodness, as everything that exists originates from the will of a good and purposeful God.

4. Creation and Redemption

The Old Testament often links God's role as Creator with His role as Redeemer. This connection is particularly evident in the prophetic literature, where God's ability to create is presented as a basis for His ability to save and restore. The implication is that the God who brought the universe into existence from nothing is also capable of bringing about new creation and redemption. This theme anticipates the New Testament's use of Creation Ex Nihilo in the context of Christ's redemptive work and the promise of a new heaven and new earth.

The Old Testament, while not explicitly formulating the doctrine of Creation Ex Nihilo, provides a wealth of insights that strongly suggest this concept. Through its various narratives, poetic expressions, and prophetic declarations, the Old Testament portrays God as the sovereign Creator who brings the universe into existence by

His word and will, without reliance on any pre-existing materials. This portrayal lays the groundwork for the later theological articulation of Creation Ex Nihilo, a doctrine that would become central to Christian theology.

By exploring the Old Testament's insights into creation, we gain a deeper appreciation for the foundational role this doctrine plays in shaping our understanding of God, the world, and humanity's place within it. The Old Testament's depiction of creation as an act of divine sovereignty, wisdom, and goodness continues to resonate in theological discussions, offering a robust framework for engaging with the profound mystery of existence itself.

New Testament References

The New Testament builds upon the theological foundations laid in the Old Testament and further develops the concept of God as the Creator of all things. The doctrine of Creation Ex Nihilo—the belief that God created the universe out of nothing—is more explicitly affirmed in the New Testament, where it is closely connected to the identity and work of Jesus Christ. Through various passages, particularly in the writings of John, Paul, and the author of Hebrews, the New Testament reinforces and expands the idea that all of creation originates from the divine will, emphasizing the central role of Christ in the act of creation.

John 1:1-3 – The Word and Creation

The Gospel of John opens with a profound theological statement that directly connects the act of creation with the person of Jesus Christ, referred to as the Word (Logos):

> "In the beginning was the Word, and the Word was with God, and the Word was God. He was in the beginning with God. All things were made through Him, and without Him was not anything made that was made." (John 1:1-3, ESV)

This passage is one of the most explicit New Testament affirmations of Creation Ex Nihilo. John echoes the language of Genesis 1:1, "In the beginning," but he adds a crucial layer of interpretation by identifying the Word as both with God and as God. This identification firmly establishes the preexistence and divine nature of the Word, who is later revealed to be Jesus Christ (John 1:14).

John 1:3 is particularly significant in affirming the doctrine of Creation Ex Nihilo. The phrase "All things were made through Him, and without Him was not anything made that was made" emphasizes that every part of creation, without exception, owes its existence to the creative activity of the Word. This statement leaves no room for the existence of any independent or pre-existing materials from which the universe was formed. Instead, it underscores that everything—both the material and immaterial—came into being through the Word's creative power. This is a clear affirmation that creation was not a process of shaping pre-existing matter but an act of bringing all things into existence from nothing.

Moreover, the association of the Word with creation highlights the centrality of Christ in the creative work of God. The Logos is not a secondary agent but the very means through which God created the cosmos. This concept integrates the doctrine of Creation Ex Nihilo with the Christological focus of the New Testament, suggesting that the act of creation is intrinsically linked to the identity and mission of Jesus Christ.

Hebrews 11:3 – Faith and Understanding Creation

The Epistle to the Hebrews provides another key New Testament insight into the doctrine of Creation Ex Nihilo:

> "By faith we understand that the universe was created by the word of God, so that what is seen was not made out of things that are visible." (Hebrews 11:3, ESV)

This verse is crucial in articulating the relationship between faith and the understanding of creation. The author of Hebrews asserts that it is through faith that believers comprehend the true nature of the universe's origin—that it was created by the word of God. This statement reaffirms the power and efficacy of God's word in bringing the universe into existence, echoing the creative acts described in Genesis 1.

The latter part of the verse, "so that what is seen was not made out of things that are visible," directly supports the concept of Creation Ex Nihilo. The phrase implies that the visible, material world was not fashioned from pre-existing visible materials. Instead, it came into being through the divine word, from what was previously non-existent. This idea closely aligns with the belief that God created the universe from nothing, without relying on any pre-existing substance.

Hebrews 11:3 also emphasizes the role of faith in accepting the doctrine of Creation Ex Nihilo. The creation of the universe is presented as a truth that transcends empirical observation, accessible only through the conviction that God, by His word, brought everything into existence. This faith-based understanding reinforces the idea that the doctrine of creation is foundational to the Christian worldview, shaping how believers perceive the world and their place within it.

Colossians 1:15-17 – Christ as the Creator and Sustainer

In his letter to the Colossians, the Apostle Paul provides a profound theological reflection on the role of Christ in creation:

> "He is the image of the invisible God, the firstborn of all creation. For by Him, all things were created, in heaven and on earth, visible and invisible, whether thrones or dominions or rulers or authorities—all things were created through Him and for Him. And He is before all things, and in Him all things hold together." (Colossians 1:15-17, ESV)

This passage presents Christ as the preeminent agent of creation, affirming His divine status and His central role in the cosmos. The term "firstborn of all creation" does not imply that Christ is a created being but rather emphasizes His preeminence and authority over all creation. The subsequent verses clarify that Christ is the one through whom all things were created, both in the material and spiritual realms.

Paul's assertion that "all things were created through Him and for Him" reinforces the idea that Christ is not only the agent but also the purpose of creation. This statement ties the act of creation directly to Christ's divine nature and mission, suggesting that the entire universe exists to reflect His glory and to fulfill His purposes.

The phrase "in Him all things hold together" further emphasizes Christ's role as the sustainer of creation. This idea complements the doctrine of Creation Ex Nihilo by highlighting that the same divine power that brought the universe into existence from nothing continues to sustain and govern it. The existence of the universe is thus entirely dependent on Christ, from its initial creation to its ongoing preservation.

Paul's theology in Colossians 1 provides a holistic view of Christ's relationship to creation, integrating the doctrine of Creation Ex Nihilo with the broader themes of Christ's divinity, authority, and redemptive work. It affirms that creation is a deliberate act of divine will, executed through Christ, and that the universe continues to exist and function according to His sustaining power.

Revelation 4:11 – Creation as the Basis for Worship

The Book of Revelation, with its vivid imagery and apocalyptic themes, also affirms the doctrine of Creation Ex Nihilo, particularly in its portrayal of heavenly worship:

> "Worthy are you, our Lord and God, to receive glory and honor and power, for you created all things, and by your will they existed and were created." (Revelation 4:11, ESV)

This verse is part of a doxology sung by the twenty-four elders in the heavenly throne room, acknowledging God's sovereignty and creative power. The phrase "by your will they existed and were created" underscores the idea that creation is entirely dependent on the divine will. Nothing in creation exists independently or by chance; everything owes its existence to God's purposeful act of creation.

The emphasis on God's will as the basis for creation aligns with the doctrine of Creation Ex Nihilo, affirming that the universe was not the result of pre-existing materials or cosmic accidents but was brought into being by God's sovereign decree. This act of creation is presented as a primary reason for worship, highlighting the theological significance of recognizing God as the Creator of all things.

Revelation 4:11 thus reinforces the centrality of Creation Ex Nihilo in Christian worship and theology. It affirms that the acknowledgment of God as Creator is foundational to the Christian faith and is a key reason for giving glory, honor, and power to God.

Romans 4:17 – God as the Creator Who Gives Life

In his Epistle to the Romans, Paul makes a passing but significant reference to God's creative power:

> "…in the presence of the God in whom he believed, who gives life to the dead and calls into existence the things that do not exist." (Romans 4:17, ESV)

This verse, though focused on the faith of Abraham, contains a crucial affirmation of God's ability to create ex nihilo. The phrase "calls into existence the things that do not exist" explicitly supports the idea that God can bring forth reality from non-existence. This power is linked to God's ability to give life to the dead, further emphasizing His sovereignty over all aspects of creation and existence.

Paul's statement in Romans 4:17 reflects a deep theological understanding of God's creative power, affirming that creation itself is an act of divine will that brings something into being from nothing. This passage ties the concept of Creation Ex Nihilo to God's ongoing work of giving life and fulfilling His promises, demonstrating that the same power that created the universe continues to operate in the world.

Theological Implications of New Testament References

The New Testament's references to Creation Ex Nihilo carry profound theological implications, particularly in relation to the identity and work of Christ.

1. Christ as the Agent of Creation:

The New Testament consistently presents Christ as the central figure in the act of creation. Whether in John's identification of the Logos as the means through which all things were made, Paul's assertion that all things were created through and for Christ, or the doxologies in Revelation, the

New Testament affirms that Christ is the divine agent through whom God created the universe. This identification reinforces the doctrine of Creation Ex Nihilo by emphasizing that the entire cosmos, visible and invisible, originated through Christ's creative power.

2. Creation as an Act of Divine Will:

The New Testament highlights the idea that creation is a result of God's sovereign will, rather than a process involving pre-existing materials. This is particularly evident in Revelation 4:11, which emphasizes that all things exist by God's will. This concept underscores the absolute dependence of creation on

God aligns with the doctrine of Creation Ex Nihilo, affirming that the universe's existence is a product of God's deliberate and purposeful act.

3. The Relationship Between Creation and Redemption:

The New Testament often links creation with redemption, particularly in the writings of Paul. The same power that brought the universe into existence from nothing is also at work in the redemption and renewal of creation through Christ. This theological connection suggests that the doctrine of Creation Ex Nihilo is not only about the origins of the universe but also about God's ongoing work in bringing new life and restoration to a fallen world.

4. Faith and Understanding Creation:

Hebrews 11:3 emphasizes that understanding the nature of creation is an act of faith. The doctrine of Creation Ex Nihilo is presented as a truth that transcends empirical observation, accessible only through the conviction that God, by His word, brought the universe into existence. This emphasis on faith highlights the importance of the doctrine in shaping the Christian worldview and its implications for how believers perceive reality.

The New Testament provides a rich and explicit affirmation of the doctrine of Creation Ex Nihilo, particularly in its portrayal of Christ as the agent of creation. Through key passages in John, Hebrews, Colossians, and Revelation, the New Testament reinforces the idea that the universe was brought into existence by God's will and through Christ's creative power, without reliance on any pre-existing materials. This understanding of creation is foundational to Christian theology, shaping the doctrines of Christ, creation, and redemption, and offering profound insights into the nature of God and the cosmos.

As we continue to explore the doctrine of Creation Ex Nihilo, these New Testament references will serve as a crucial foundation for understanding the relationship between God, Christ, and the created order, and how this relationship informs the broader theological and philosophical discussions surrounding the origin and purpose of the universe.

CHAPTER 02

HISTORICAL THEOLOGY

Early Church Fathers' Views on Creation Ex Nihilo (e.g., Augustine, Origen)

The doctrine of Creation Ex Nihilo—the belief that God created the universe out of nothing—became a central tenet of Christian theology largely through the writings and teachings of the Early Church Fathers. These early theologians were instrumental in articulating and defending this doctrine against various philosophical and theological challenges. Among the most influential figures in this development were Origen and Augustine, whose writings laid the groundwork for a comprehensive Christian understanding of creation, rooted in the concept of God's absolute sovereignty and the contingency of all created things.

Origen (c. 184–253 AD)

Origen of Alexandria was one of the most prominent early Christian theologians, known for his extensive and systematic work in Christian theology, biblical exegesis, and philosophy. His views on creation were deeply influenced by the philosophical traditions of his time, particularly Platonism, yet he sought to integrate these ideas with the Christian faith.

Origen's Cosmology and Creation

Origen's understanding of creation was complex and multifaceted, deeply influenced by his engagement with Platonic thought. He argued that God's creation of the world was a free and deliberate act, rather than a necessary emanation from His being. However, Origen's views on the eternity of the world have led to much debate among scholars.

Origen suggested that God, being eternal and unchanging, has always been a Creator, and therefore, there was never a time when He did not create. This led to the controversial idea that there may have been an eternal succession of worlds, with the current world being one in a series of creations. However, Origen was careful to distinguish his view from the Platonic idea of eternal matter. For Origen, the world was not eternal in itself but was brought into existence by God's will. His writings indicate that he affirmed God as the ultimate cause of everything, and while he entertained the idea of an eternal creation, he did not conceive of matter as co-eternal with God.

In his work De Principiis (On First Principles), Origen emphasized the spiritual and immaterial nature of God's creative act, asserting that the visible world was preceded by a spiritual creation. This dual creation—first the spiritual, then the material—allowed Origen to maintain the transcendence of God while explaining the presence of the material world.

Origen and Creation Ex Nihilo

While Origen's cosmology included the idea of an eternal creation, he did not deny the possibility of Creation Ex Nihilo. In fact, Origen argued against the Gnostic and Manichaean views that posited an eternal dualism between matter and spirit or between good and evil. He contended that all things were created by God's will, including the material world, and that matter itself was good, contrary to the Gnostic belief in the inherent evil of the material.

Origen's affirmation of God's creative power over all things, including matter, aligns with the doctrine of Creation Ex Nihilo, even if he did not fully articulate it in the same way later theologians like Augustine would. Origen's contribution to the development of this doctrine lies in his emphasis on God's sovereignty and the goodness of creation, as well as his rejection of any form of dualism that would undermine the belief in God as the sole Creator.

Augustine of Hippo (354–430 AD)

Saint Augustine, one of the most influential Church Fathers, played a pivotal role in the development and articulation of the doctrine of Creation Ex Nihilo. His extensive writings on theology, philosophy, and biblical interpretation have left a lasting impact on Christian thought, particularly in the Western tradition.

Augustine's Understanding of Creation

Augustine's views on creation were shaped by his engagement with Neoplatonism, his rejection of Manichaeism, and his deep study of the Scriptures. Unlike Origen, Augustine firmly rejected the idea of an eternal creation and strongly affirmed the doctrine of Creation Ex Nihilo.

In his work Confessions, Augustine reflects on the nature of time and creation, famously asserting that time itself was created by God: "For You made the heaven and the earth in the beginning, and it was not in the beginning that You began to make heaven and earth. You did not make them in time, but you made time itself" (Confessions XI.13). For Augustine, this meant that there was no "before" creation in the temporal sense, as time itself came into existence with the act of creation.

Augustine and Creation Ex Nihilo

Augustine's most direct discussion of Creation Ex Nihilo is found in his work The City of God. In Book XI, Augustine explicitly argues that God created the world out of nothing: "God, then, made nothing evil, and He Himself is not evil. He made everything out of nothing" (The City of God XI.22). This assertion is a clear affirmation of the doctrine of Creation Ex Nihilo, emphasizing that everything that exists has its origin in God's creative will and that there was no pre-existing matter from which the universe was formed.

For Augustine, Creation Ex Nihilo was not just a theological concept but also a philosophical necessity. He argued that if matter were eternal, it would imply that something existed independently of God, which would undermine the Christian understanding of God's absolute sovereignty and the contingent nature of creation. Augustine's defense of Creation Ex Nihilo was therefore also a defense of monotheism against any form of dualism or polytheism that might suggest the existence of independent or co-eternal realities alongside God.

Theological Implications of Augustine's Doctrine of Creation

Augustine's articulation of Creation Ex Nihilo had profound implications for Christian theology. First, it affirmed the goodness of creation, countering the Manichaean belief in the inherent evil of the material world. Augustine argued that everything created by God is good, even if it is subject to corruption and decay as a result of human sin.

Second, Augustine's doctrine of Creation Ex Nihilo reinforced the idea of divine sovereignty. By asserting that everything, including time and matter, was created by God out of nothing, Augustine upheld the belief that God is the ultimate cause of all things and that nothing exists independently of His will. This idea was crucial in Augustine's broader theological framework, particularly in his understanding of providence, predestination, and the nature of evil.

Finally, Augustine's views on creation were closely tied to his understanding of salvation. Just as God created the world out of nothing, He is also able to bring about new creation through the work of Christ. Augustine saw the act of creation as the beginning of a divine plan that culminates in the redemption and restoration of the world through the Incarnation, death, and resurrection of Jesus Christ.

The Legacy of Origen and Augustine

The views of Origen and Augustine on creation, while distinct in certain respects, both contributed significantly to the development of the doctrine of Creation Ex Nihilo in Christian theology.

Origen's influence can be seen in his emphasis on the spiritual nature of creation and the rejection of dualistic cosmologies that posited an eternal conflict between matter and spirit. Although Origen's views on the eternity of creation led to some controversy, his affirmation of God as the Creator of all things laid important groundwork for later theological developments.

Augustine's more explicit articulation of Creation Ex Nihilo became a cornerstone of Western Christian theology. His rejection of the idea of eternal matter, combined with his affirmation of God's sovereignty and the goodness of creation, provided a robust defense of the doctrine against various philosophical and theological challenges. Augustine's integration of this doctrine into his broader theological system ensured its central place in the Christian understanding of God, creation, and salvation.

Together, Origen and Augustine helped to shape the early Christian understanding of creation, providing theological and philosophical insights that would influence the Church's teaching on this doctrine for centuries to come. Their contributions continue to be studied and debated by theologians and scholars, reflecting the enduring significance of their work in the development of Christian doctrine.

The early Church Fathers, particularly Origen and Augustine, played a crucial role in the development of the doctrine of Creation Ex Nihilo. Origen's engagement with Platonic thought and his rejection of dualistic cosmologies helped to lay the groundwork for a Christian understanding of creation as an act of God's will. Augustine, building on this foundation, provided a more explicit and philosophically rigorous defense of the doctrine, affirming that God created the world out of nothing and that all things exist by His sovereign will.

The legacy of these early theologians is evident in the way the doctrine of Creation Ex Nihilo has been integrated into the broader Christian theological tradition. Their work continues to influence contemporary discussions on the nature of creation, the relationship between God and the world, and the implications of this doctrine for Christian faith and practice. As we move forward in exploring the historical and theological development of Creation Ex Nihilo, the contributions of Origen and Augustine remain foundational, offering insights that are as relevant today as they were in the early centuries of the Church.

Medieval Perspectives

The Doctrine of Creation Ex Nihilo in Medieval Theology

The medieval period was a time of profound theological and philosophical development within the Christian tradition. During this era, the doctrine of Creation Ex Nihilo—the belief that God created the universe out of nothing—was further refined and articulated by some of the greatest minds in Christian history. Among these, Thomas Aquinas stands out as a key figure whose work synthesized Christian theology with the philosophy of Aristotle, providing a robust framework for understanding the nature of creation and God's relationship to the world. This chapter will explore the medieval perspectives on Creation Ex Nihilo, focusing particularly on the contributions of Thomas Aquinas, as well as the broader theological context in which this doctrine was developed.

Thomas Aquinas (1225–1274)

Thomas Aquinas, a Dominican friar and one of the most influential theologians and philosophers of the medieval period, played a pivotal role in shaping the Christian understanding of Creation Ex Nihilo. His magnum opus, the Summa Theologica, along with other writings, provided a comprehensive synthesis of Christian theology and Aristotelian philosophy, addressing key issues such as the nature of God, the act of creation, and the relationship between faith and reason.

Aquinas and the Nature of God

Aquinas begins his discussion of creation by first addressing the nature of God. In his Summa Theologica, Aquinas describes God as the "First Cause" and the "Necessary Being," emphasizing that God is the source of all that exists and that everything in creation is contingent upon Him. This foundational understanding of God's nature is crucial for Aquinas's articulation of Creation Ex Nihilo.

For Aquinas, God's essence is identical to His existence, meaning that God is pure act (actus purus) without potentiality, change, or limitation. This understanding of God as a fully actualized being with no potential for change or deficiency supports the idea that God is the ultimate cause of everything that exists. Consequently, creation must be seen as an act of God's will, originating from His perfect and infinite nature.

Aquinas argues that God, being omnipotent, has the power to bring something into existence from nothing. This power is unique to God because only an omnipotent being could create without relying on any pre-existing material. Thus, Aquinas affirms the doctrine of Creation Ex Nihilo as a logical consequence of God's omnipotence and the contingency of creation.

Creation as an Act of Divine Will

In Aquinas's theology, creation is not a necessary emanation from God, as in some Neoplatonic systems, but a free and deliberate act of God's will. Aquinas explicitly rejects the idea that God was compelled to create the world out of any necessity. Instead, he insists that creation is a product of God's free choice, motivated by His goodness.

Aquinas addresses the question of why God would choose to create anything at all if He is already perfect and self-sufficient. He argues that God's decision to create is rooted in His goodness. God's goodness is so abundant that it naturally inclines Him to share His existence with other beings. Thus, creation is an expression of God's goodness, not a fulfillment of any lack or need within God Himself. This view aligns with the doctrine of Creation Ex Nihilo, as it emphasizes that the world's existence is entirely dependent on

God's will and is not the result of any external necessity or pre-existing material.

Aquinas and the Doctrine of Creation Ex Nihilo

Aquinas's most direct discussion of Creation Ex Nihilo is found in the Summa Theologica, where he systematically addresses the nature of creation and the implications of God's creative act. Aquinas begins by affirming that God created the universe out of nothing, not from any pre-existing matter. He states:

> "God alone is properly the creator, because He alone brings things into existence out of nothing (creatio ex nihilo)" (Summa Theologica I, Q.45, Art.1).

This statement encapsulates Aquinas's understanding of creation as an act that is unique to God. He argues that while human beings can create in a limited sense by shaping or forming existing materials, only God can bring something into existence without any prior substance.

Aquinas further explains that creation is not a change in the strict sense because change involves the transformation of something that already exists. Instead, creation is the production of being itself, bringing something from non-being (nothing) into being. This idea is central to the doctrine of Creation Ex Nihilo, as it underscores the radical nature of God's creative act.

The Eternality of the World and Aquinas's Solution

One of the significant debates in medieval theology was the question of the world's eternality. Aristotle, whose works had been reintroduced to the Christian West in the 12th century, argued that the world was eternal, without beginning or end. This posed a challenge for Christian theologians, who affirmed the temporal beginning of the universe based on biblical revelation.

Aquinas engaged with Aristotle's arguments and sought to reconcile them with Christian doctrine. He acknowledged that, philosophically, one could argue for the possibility of an eternal world in the sense that God could have created a world that always existed. However, Aquinas insisted that, according to divine revelation, the world did indeed have a beginning in time. This beginning was the moment of creation, where God brought the universe into existence from nothing.

Aquinas's approach allowed him to maintain the compatibility of faith and reason. While he recognized the philosophical arguments for an eternal world, he upheld the biblical teaching of a temporal beginning, affirming that the doctrine of Creation Ex Nihilo is grounded in both reason and revelation.

Creation and the Conservation of the World

Another critical aspect of Aquinas's theology of creation is his understanding of God's ongoing relationship with the world. Aquinas argued that creation is not merely a past event but a continuous process. He introduced the concept of creatio continua (continuous creation), which holds that God not only created the world out of nothing but also sustains it in existence at every moment.

For Aquinas, the continued existence of the world depends entirely on God's will. If God were to withdraw His sustaining power, the universe would cease to exist. This idea reinforces the doctrine of Creation Ex Nihilo by emphasizing that creation's contingency is not just a feature of its origin but also of its ongoing existence. Everything that exists is continuously dependent on God, who alone has the power to create and sustain.

The Influence of Aquinas on Medieval Theology

Thomas Aquinas's synthesis of Christian theology with Aristotelian philosophy had a profound and lasting impact on medieval theology. His articulation of Creation Ex Nihilo became a cornerstone of Christian doctrine, influencing not only his contemporaries but also later theologians in the scholastic tradition.

Aquinas's careful distinction between creation and change, his affirmation of God's omnipotence, and his understanding of creation as an act of divine will provided a robust theological framework that addressed many of the philosophical challenges of his time. His work demonstrated that the doctrine of Creation Ex Nihilo was not only consistent with reason but also provided a more coherent explanation of the universe's origin than alternative philosophical systems.

Other Medieval Perspectives

While Aquinas was the most prominent figure in medieval theology, other theologians also contributed to the development of the doctrine of Creation Ex Nihilo. The broader scholastic tradition, which included figures like Bonaventure and Duns Scotus, continued to explore and refine this doctrine, often engaging with the philosophical challenges posed by Aristotelian thought and the writings of Muslim and Jewish philosophers.

Bonaventure (1217–1274)

Bonaventure, a contemporary of Aquinas and a leading figure in the Franciscan tradition, also addressed the doctrine of Creation Ex Nihilo in his theological writings. Like Aquinas, Bonaventure affirmed that God created the world out of nothing and that creation was an expression of God's goodness. However, Bonaventure placed a stronger emphasis on the idea of creation as a reflection of the Trinity.

He argued that the world was created to manifest the glory of the Triune God and that every creature bears a trace of the divine.

Bonaventure also engaged with the question of the world's eternality, arguing that while God could have created an eternal world, He chose to create a world with a temporal beginning. This choice reflects God's free will and His desire to manifest His glory in a way that is intelligible to creatures bound by time.

Duns Scotus (1266–1308)

Duns Scotus, another significant figure in medieval theology, approached the doctrine of Creation Ex Nihilo from a slightly different angle than Aquinas. Scotus emphasized the primacy of God's will in the act of creation, arguing that God's decision to create was entirely free and not determined by any external factors, including His nature. For Scotus, this emphasis on divine freedom underscored the absolute contingency of the created world and the radical nature of Creation Ex Nihilo.

Scotus also contributed to the discussion on the nature of being, arguing that there is a fundamental difference between the being of God and the being of creatures. This distinction reinforced the idea that creation is an act of bringing something entirely new into existence, rather than merely organizing pre-existing matter.

The medieval period was a time of significant development in the doctrine of Creation Ex Nihilo, with Thomas Aquinas standing out as a key figure in articulating and defending this doctrine within the framework of Christian theology. Aquinas's synthesis of Aristotelian philosophy and Christian doctrine provided a robust and systematic explanation of creation as an act of God's omnipotent will, bringing the universe into existence from nothing.

Aquinas's contributions, along with those of other medieval theologians like Bonaventure and Duns Scotus, helped to solidify the doctrine of Creation Ex Nihilo as a central tenet of Christian theology. Their work addressed key philosophical challenges, affirmed the contingency and dependence of the created world on God, and provided a theological foundation that continues to influence Christian thought to this day.

As we move forward in exploring the historical development of the doctrine of Creation Ex Nihilo, the contributions of these medieval theologians remain crucial for understanding how this doctrine has been articulated, defended, and refined throughout the history of Christian theology. Their insights continue to offer valuable perspectives on the nature of creation, the relationship between God and the world, and the implications of this doctrine for Christian faith and practice.

Reformation and Post-Reformation Views on Creation Ex Nihilo

The Reformation and Post-Reformation periods were times of significant theological development and debate within Christianity, marked by a renewed focus on Scripture, the authority of the Church, and the nature of salvation. During these periods, the doctrine of Creation Ex Nihilo—the belief that God created the universe out of nothing—continued to be an essential aspect of Christian theology. While the Reformers were primarily concerned with issues related to salvation, grace, and the authority of Scripture, they also addressed the doctrine of creation, reaffirming and sometimes reinterpreting earlier teachings in light of their theological concerns.

The Reformation: Martin Luther and John Calvin

The Protestant Reformation, spearheaded by figures like Martin Luther and John Calvin, was a movement that sought to reform the Catholic Church's practices and doctrines. While their primary focus was on issues like justification by faith, the sacraments, and church authority, the Reformers also maintained and articulated the traditional

Christian belief in Creation Ex Nihilo. They did so within the broader framework of their theological reforms, emphasizing God's sovereignty, the authority of Scripture, and the rejection of speculative philosophy in favor of biblical revelation.

Martin Luther (1483–1546)

Martin Luther, the German monk and theologian who initiated the Reformation, upheld the doctrine of Creation Ex Nihilo as an essential part of Christian belief. For Luther, the doctrine was closely linked to his understanding of God's sovereignty, the authority of Scripture, and the nature of faith.

Luther's views on creation are primarily found in his commentaries on Genesis, where he interprets the creation account in light of his theological principles. He strongly affirmed that God created the world out of nothing by His word, as described in Genesis 1. Luther emphasized that God's creative act was a demonstration of His omnipotence and sovereignty, reflecting His power to bring all things into existence by His command.

In his Lectures on Genesis (1535-1545), Luther repeatedly affirmed the doctrine of Creation Ex Nihilo, rejecting any notion that the world was formed from pre-existing materials or that creation was a necessary emanation from God. He insisted that the universe had a definite beginning in time, brought into being by God's will alone.

Luther also connected the doctrine of creation to his understanding of faith. He argued that belief in Creation Ex Nihilo requires faith because it goes beyond human reason and comprehension. For Luther, the doctrine of creation was not merely a philosophical concept but a fundamental article of faith grounded in the authority of Scripture. He stressed that Christians must accept this truth based on God's revelation, rather than attempting to understand it through speculative philosophy.

In addition, Luther's theology of creation was tied to his doctrine of providence. He believed that God not only created the world out of nothing but also continues to sustain and govern it. This belief in God's ongoing involvement in creation reinforced Luther's emphasis on God's sovereignty and the dependence of all things on His will.

John Calvin (1509–1564)

John Calvin, a French theologian and one of the most influential figures of the Reformation, also upheld the doctrine of Creation Ex Nihilo as a central tenet of Christian faith. In his magnum opus, Institutes of the Christian Religion, Calvin provided a detailed exposition of Christian doctrine, including his views on creation.

Calvin affirmed that God created the world out of nothing by His word, as revealed in Scripture. He rejected the idea that the world was eternal or that it was formed from pre-existing matter, arguing instead that all things were brought into existence by God's sovereign will. For Calvin, the doctrine of Creation Ex Nihilo was a testament to God's power and majesty, demonstrating that He alone is the source of all that exists.

In his commentary on Genesis, Calvin emphasized the importance of the biblical creation account as the foundation for understanding God's relationship with the world. He argued that the creation narrative in Genesis 1-2 reveals God's wisdom, power, and goodness, and that it provides the basis for the proper worship of God as the Creator.

Calvin's doctrine of creation was closely connected to his understanding of divine providence. He taught that God not only created the world out of nothing but also continually sustains and governs it. Calvin emphasized that God's providential care extends to all aspects of creation, from the movements of the stars to the smallest details of life on earth. This belief in God's ongoing involvement in creation reinforced Calvin's view of God's sovereignty and the dependence of all things on His will.

Calvin also addressed the philosophical implications of Creation Ex Nihilo. While he acknowledged that the doctrine raises complex metaphysical questions, he insisted that Christians must accept it based on the authority of Scripture. Calvin cautioned against relying too heavily on speculative philosophy to understand the mysteries of creation, emphasizing instead the importance of faith and the guidance of the Holy Spirit in interpreting God's revelation.

The Post-Reformation Period: Confessional Developments and Theological Refinement

Following the Reformation, the doctrine of Creation Ex Nihilo continued to be affirmed and developed within the various confessional traditions that emerged. The Post-Reformation period saw the rise of detailed confessional statements and theological works that sought to codify the teachings of the Reformation and address the challenges posed by new philosophical and scientific developments.

The Westminster Confession of Faith (1647)

One of the most significant confessional statements to emerge from the Post-Reformation period is the Westminster Confession of Faith, a Reformed confession of faith written in the mid-17th century by the Westminster Assembly in England. The Westminster Confession provides a clear and concise summary of Reformed theology, including the doctrine of creation.

The Westminster Confession explicitly affirms the doctrine of Creation Ex Nihilo in its first chapter, stating:

> "It pleased God the Father, Son, and Holy Ghost, for the manifestation of the glory of His eternal power, wisdom, and goodness, in the beginning, to create, or make of nothing, the world, and all things therein, whether visible or invisible, in the space of six days, and all very good" (Westminster Confession of Faith, Chapter IV).

This statement reaffirms the traditional Christian belief that God created the world out of nothing by His will. The Confession also emphasizes the Trinitarian nature of creation, asserting that the Father, Son, and Holy Spirit were all involved in the act of creation. This Trinitarian emphasis reflects the broader Reformed commitment to the doctrine of the Trinity and the belief that all of God's works are the unified actions of the three persons of the Godhead.

The Westminster Confession's affirmation of Creation Ex Nihilo is also closely linked to its doctrine of providence. The Confession teaches that God continues to uphold, direct, and govern all things in creation according to His sovereign will. This belief in God's ongoing involvement in creation reinforces the idea that the world is entirely dependent on God for its existence and sustenance.

The Lutheran Formula of Concord (1577)

The Formula of Concord, a Lutheran confessional document written in the late 16th century, also addresses the doctrine of creation. While the Formula of Concord does not provide as detailed an exposition of Creation Ex Nihilo as the Westminster Confession, it nevertheless affirms the traditional Christian belief that God created the world out of nothing by His word.

In the Epitome of the Formula of Concord, the doctrine of creation is included under the discussion of God's providence and governance of the world. The Formula of Concord emphasizes that God is the Creator and sustainer of all things and that He continues to uphold and govern the world by His power.

The Formula of Concord also addresses the issue of human reason and its role in understanding the doctrine of creation. The document cautions against relying too heavily on human reason to explain the mysteries of creation, emphasizing instead the importance of faith in accepting the truth of God's revelation. This emphasis on faith over reason reflects the broader Lutheran commitment to the principle of sola scriptura (Scripture alone) and the belief that God's word is the ultimate authority in matters of doctrine.

Theological Debates and Challenges in the Post-Reformation Period

The Post-Reformation period was also marked by theological debates and challenges related to the doctrine of creation, particularly in response to new philosophical and scientific developments. The rise of new philosophical systems, such as Cartesianism, and the emergence of early modern science posed challenges to the traditional Christian understanding of creation and prompted theologians to refine and defend the doctrine of Creation Ex Nihilo.

Cartesianism and the Doctrine of Creation

The philosophy of René Descartes (1596–1650), known as Cartesianism, introduced new ideas about the nature of reality, the relationship between mind and body, and the role of human reason in understanding the world. Descartes' emphasis on doubt and the use of reason to arrive at certain knowledge led to a shift in philosophical thinking, raising questions about the nature of creation and the existence of God.

While Descartes himself affirmed the existence of God and the doctrine of Creation Ex Nihilo, his philosophical system was interpreted by some as challenging traditional

Christian beliefs. Cartesian dualism, which posited a clear distinction between mind and matter, raised questions about the nature of God's creative act and the relationship between the spiritual and material realms.

Theologians in the Post-Reformation period responded to these challenges by reaffirming the doctrine of Creation Ex Nihilo and emphasizing the importance of Scripture and divine revelation in understanding the nature of creation. They argued that while reason and philosophy have their place in the study of creation, they must be subordinated to the authority of Scripture and guided by the principles of faith.

Early Modern Science and the Doctrine of Creation

The rise of early modern science in the 16th and 17th centuries also posed challenges to the traditional Christian understanding of creation. The discoveries of figures like Copernicus, Galileo, and Newton introduced new ideas about the nature of the universe, the movement of the planets, and the laws of physics, prompting theologians to reconsider the relationship between science and the doctrine of creation.

While some theologians saw these developments as a threat to the doctrine of Creation Ex Nihilo, others sought to harmonize the new scientific discoveries with Christian theology. They argued that the laws of nature and the discoveries of science were ultimately expressions of God's creative power and providence and that they could be understood as complementary to the doctrine of Creation Ex Nihilo.

The Post-Reformation period also saw the development of natural theology, which sought to understand the nature of God and creation through the study of the natural world. Natural theologians argued that the order and complexity of the universe provided evidence of God's existence and creative power, and they sought to demonstrate that the findings of science were consistent with the doctrine of Creation Ex Nihilo.

The Reformation and Post-Reformation periods were times of significant theological development and debate, during which the doctrine of Creation Ex Nihilo continued to be affirmed and refined. The Reformers, particularly Martin Luther and John Calvin, upheld the traditional Christian belief that God created the world out of nothing by His sovereign will, emphasizing the authority of Scripture and the centrality of faith in understanding this doctrine.

In the Post-Reformation period, the doctrine of Creation Ex Nihilo was further codified in confessional statements like the Westminster Confession of Faith and the Formula of Concord, which provided clear and concise summaries of Reformed and Lutheran theology. These confessional documents reaffirmed the doctrine of Creation Ex Nihilo as an essential aspect of Christian faith, linking it to the broader doctrines of providence, the Trinity, and divine sovereignty.

The Post-Reformation period also saw theological debates and challenges related to the doctrine of creation, particularly in response to new philosophical and scientific developments. Theologians of this period sought to defend and refine the doctrine of Creation Ex Nihilo in light of these challenges, emphasizing the importance of Scripture and divine revelation in understanding the nature of creation.

As we continue to explore the historical development of the doctrine of Creation Ex Nihilo, the contributions of the Reformers and Post-Reformation theologians remain crucial for understanding how this doctrine has been articulated, defended, and refined throughout the history of Christian theology. Their insights continue to offer valuable perspectives on the nature of creation, the relationship between God and the world, and the implications of this doctrine for Christian faith and practice.

CHAPTER 03

MODERN THEOLOGICAL INTERPRETATIONS

Contemporary Christian Theologians' Perspectives on Creation Ex Nihilo

The doctrine of Creation Ex Nihilo—the belief that God created the universe out of nothing—continues to be a central tenet of Christian theology in the modern era. However, contemporary Christian theologians have engaged with this doctrine in various ways, responding to new philosophical, scientific, and cultural challenges. This chapter will explore the perspectives of several influential contemporary theologians on Creation Ex Nihilo, examining how they have reaffirmed, reinterpreted, or expanded upon traditional understandings of this doctrine.

Karl Barth (1886–1968)

Karl Barth, one of the most significant theologians of the 20th century, profoundly influenced modern Christian thought with his emphasis on the sovereignty of God and the centrality of Christ. Barth's theology is characterized by a strong rejection of natural theology and an insistence on the primacy of divine revelation in understanding God and creation. His views on Creation Ex Nihilo are deeply rooted in his broader theological framework, which centers on the self-revelation of God in Jesus Christ.

Barth's Doctrine of Creation

In his Church Dogmatics, Barth devotes substantial attention to the doctrine of creation, which he sees as inseparable from the doctrine of God. Barth affirms the traditional Christian belief in Creation Ex Nihilo, emphasizing that the universe was brought into existence solely by God's sovereign will and creative word. He argues that creation is an act of divine freedom, not a necessity or emanation and that it is entirely dependent on God.

Barth strongly rejects any notion that creation is in any way co-eternal with God or that matter existed before God's creative act. He insists that God alone is eternal, and all of creation owes its existence to God's free and sovereign act of creation. For Barth, the doctrine of Creation Ex Nihilo is crucial because it affirms the radical distinction between God and the created order, preserving God's transcendence and the contingency of creation.

Christ-Centered Creation

One of the distinctive features of Barth's theology is his Christocentric approach to all doctrines, including creation. Barth argues that the doctrine of creation cannot be fully understood apart from the revelation of God in Jesus Christ. He sees Christ as the center and goal of all creation, asserting that creation's purpose and meaning are ultimately found in Christ.

In Barth's view, the act of creation is intimately connected to the covenant of grace established in Christ. He suggests that God's decision to create the world was already informed by His plan of salvation through Christ. This Christocentric focus leads Barth to reinterpret Creation Ex Nihilo as not merely the beginning of the physical universe but as the first step in God's redemptive plan, culminating in the Incarnation, life, death, and resurrection of Christ.

Barth's emphasis on the centrality of Christ in creation challenges traditional views that treat creation as a separate or preliminary doctrine. Instead, he presents creation as inherently tied to God's redemptive work, with the doctrine of Creation Ex Nihilo serving as a foundation for understanding the entirety of God's relationship with the world.

Jürgen Moltmann (1926–Present)

Jürgen Moltmann, a German Reformed theologian, is another significant contemporary figure whose work has had a substantial impact on modern Christian theology. Moltmann is known for his emphasis on eschatology, the theology of hope, and the suffering of God. His views on creation are closely linked to these themes, and he offers a unique perspective on Creation Ex Nihilo that incorporates ecological and eschatological concerns.

Creation as an Act of Love

Moltmann's theology emphasizes the relational nature of God and the idea that creation is an expression of God's love. He affirms the doctrine of Creation Ex Nihilo but reframes it within the context of God's desire for relationship and communion with creation. For Moltmann, creation is not merely an act of divine will but also an act of divine love, aimed at bringing into existence beings capable of entering into a loving relationship with God.

Moltmann also connects the doctrine of creation with his understanding of the Trinity. He suggests that the act of creation reflects the inner life of the Triune God, where the Father, Son, and Holy Spirit exist in a perfect relationship of love and communion. Creation, therefore, is an extension of this divine communion, with God inviting creation to share in the love that exists within the Godhead.

Creation and the Future

A central theme in Moltmann's theology is the idea of creation as an ongoing process that is oriented toward the future. He argues that creation is not a static reality but one that is moving toward its fulfillment in the eschaton, the ultimate realization of God's purposes. For Moltmann, the doctrine of Creation Ex Nihilo is not only about the past act of bringing the universe into existence but also about the future hope of a new creation.

Moltmann's eschatological perspective leads him to emphasize the importance of ecological responsibility and the care of creation. He argues that since creation is part of God's redemptive plan, Christians have a responsibility to care for the environment and work toward the renewal of the earth. This view challenges traditional interpretations of Creation Ex Nihilo that focus solely on the origin of the universe, expanding the doctrine to include the ongoing process of creation and its ultimate destiny.

Moltmann's integration of ecological concerns with the doctrine of Creation Ex Nihilo offers a timely and relevant perspective for contemporary theology. His emphasis on creation as an expression of divine love and as a process oriented toward the future provides a holistic understanding of creation that resonates with current environmental and eschatological issues.

Wolfhart Pannenberg (1928–2014)

Wolfhart Pannenberg, a German theologian known for his work on theology and science, provides another important contemporary perspective on Creation Ex Nihilo. Pannenberg's theology is characterized by his emphasis on history, the integration of theology with scientific knowledge, and the idea of creation as a dynamic and evolving process.

Creation and the Order of Time

Pannenberg approaches the doctrine of creation with a focus on the relationship between creation and time. He argues that creation is not only an act of God at the beginning of time but also a process that unfolds within time. Pannenberg sees history as the arena in which God's creative activity is realized, with creation moving toward its ultimate fulfillment in the eschaton.

Pannenberg affirms the traditional doctrine of Creation Ex Nihilo, emphasizing that the universe was brought into existence by God's sovereign will. However, he also stresses that creation is an ongoing process that involves the development and unfolding of the potentialities inherent in creation. For Pannenberg, creation is dynamic and open-ended, with the future playing a crucial role in understanding the meaning and purpose of the created order.

Theological Engagement with Science

One of Pannenberg's significant contributions to contemporary theology is his engagement with scientific knowledge, particularly in the areas of cosmology and evolutionary biology. He argues that theology and science, while distinct, can offer complementary insights into the nature of creation. Pannenberg sees the scientific account of the universe's origin and development as compatible with the doctrine of Creation Ex Nihilo, provided that the theological understanding of creation is not reduced to a purely scientific explanation.

Pannenberg's theology of creation incorporates insights from contemporary science while maintaining the distinctiveness of theological claims. He argues that the doctrine of Creation Ex Nihilo provides the metaphysical foundation for understanding the universe as a contingent and dependent reality, brought into existence by a transcendent Creator. This perspective allows Pannenberg to affirm the legitimacy of scientific explanations of the natural world while also upholding the theological affirmation of God as the ultimate source of all that exists.

Pannenberg's approach to Creation Ex Nihilo reflects a commitment to integrating theology with contemporary knowledge, providing a framework for dialogue between faith and science. His emphasis on the dynamic nature of creation and the importance of history and eschatology offers a forward-looking perspective that addresses both traditional theological concerns and modern scientific developments.

Catherine Keller (1953–Present)

Catherine Keller, a contemporary feminist theologian and scholar of process theology, offers a critical and innovative perspective on the doctrine of Creation Ex Nihilo. Her work challenges traditional interpretations of the doctrine and presents an alternative view that emphasizes relationality, process, and the interconnectedness of all creation.

Critique of Creation Ex Nihilo

Keller is known for her critique of the traditional doctrine of Creation Ex Nihilo, which she argues has been historically linked to patriarchal and hierarchical notions of power and domination. She suggests that the idea of creation out of nothing can reinforce a dualistic worldview that separates God from creation and legitimizes human domination over the natural world.

Instead of Creation Ex Nihilo, Keller proposes a reinterpretation of the biblical creation narratives that emphasizes creation as an ongoing process of becoming, rooted in the relationality and interdependence of all things. She draws on process theology, a school of thought that views reality as dynamic and evolving, with God's creative activity understood as a continuous process of interaction and mutual influence between God and creation.

Keller's critique of Creation Ex Nihilo is not a rejection of the doctrine itself but rather a challenge to traditional interpretations that she believes have led to harmful theological and ethical consequences. She advocates for a more inclusive and relational understanding of creation that recognizes the interconnectedness of all life and the ongoing participation of creation in the divine creative process.

Theopoetics and the Language of Creation

Keller's theological approach is often described as "theopoetics," a term that emphasizes the creative and imaginative aspects of theology. She argues that the language of creation should be understood not as a static description of a past event but as a dynamic and poetic expression of the ongoing relationship between God and the world.

In her work Face of the Deep: A Theology of Becoming, Keller offers a reinterpretation of the Genesis creation narrative that emphasizes the chaotic and generative potential of the "deep" (tehom) described in Genesis 1:2. She suggests that instead of viewing creation as a one-time act of bringing order out of chaos, it should be seen as an ongoing process of emergence and transformation, with the deep serving as a symbol of the creative potential inherent in all of creation.

Keller's theopoetic approach challenges traditional metaphysical categories and invites a more imaginative and open-ended understanding of creation. Her emphasis on relationality, process, and the interconnectedness of all things provides a fresh perspective on the doctrine of creation that resonates with contemporary concerns about ecology, justice, and the flourishing of life.

John Polkinghorne (1930–2021)

John Polkinghorne, a physicist turned Anglican priest and theologian, is known for his efforts to bridge the gap between science and theology. His work offers a perspective on Creation Ex Nihilo that engages with contemporary scientific understandings of the universe while affirming the traditional theological belief in God as the Creator.

Creation in an Evolving Universe

Polkinghorne's theology is deeply informed by his background in physics, particularly his understanding of the universe as a dynamic and evolving reality. He affirms the doctrine of Creation Ex Nihilo but emphasizes that creation should be understood as a continuous process, with God's creative activity being realized through the natural processes of the universe, including evolution.

For Polkinghorne, the idea of a static creation is inadequate in light of modern scientific discoveries. He argues that the universe is not a finished product but an ongoing project in which God's creative work is continuously unfolding. This view aligns with the concept of creatio continua (continuous creation), which holds that God is constantly involved in the process of creation, sustaining and guiding the development of the cosmos.

Divine Action and the Role of Chance

Polkinghorne also explores the relationship between divine action and the apparent randomness observed in the natural world, particularly in the context of quantum mechanics and evolutionary biology. He argues that God's creative activity is not limited to direct interventions but is also expressed through the natural processes and the inherent openness of the universe.

Polkinghorne suggests that the role of chance in the natural world can be understood as part of God's creative purpose, allowing for the emergence of novelty and the development of complex life. He rejects the idea that chance events undermine the doctrine of Creation Ex Nihilo, instead proposing that they reflect the freedom and creativity inherent in God's creation.

Polkinghorne's approach to Creation Ex Nihilo provides a framework for integrating scientific knowledge with theological reflection, offering a perspective that respects both the integrity of scientific inquiry and the traditional Christian belief in God as the Creator of all things.

Contemporary Christian theologians have engaged with the doctrine of Creation Ex Nihilo in diverse and innovative ways, reflecting the complex challenges and opportunities of the modern world. While figures like Karl Barth and Jürgen Moltmann have reaffirmed traditional understandings of the doctrine, they have also expanded its implications, emphasizing the centrality of Christ, the relational nature of creation, and the eschatological hope of a new creation.

Other theologians, such as Wolfhart Pannenberg and John Polkinghorne, have engaged with contemporary scientific knowledge, offering perspectives that integrate theology with insights from cosmology, evolution, and quantum mechanics. Their work demonstrates that the doctrine of Creation Ex Nihilo remains a vital and relevant aspect of Christian theology, capable of addressing the profound questions raised by modern science.

Finally, theologians like Catherine Keller have challenged traditional interpretations of Creation Ex Nihilo, advocating for a more relational and process-oriented understanding of creation that resonates with contemporary concerns about ecology, justice, and the interconnectedness of all life.

As we continue to explore the doctrine of Creation Ex Nihilo in the context of contemporary theology, these diverse perspectives offer valuable insights into the ongoing relevance and significance of this doctrine. They remind us that the doctrine of creation is not merely a static affirmation of the past but a dynamic and living tradition that continues to shape Christian thought and practice in profound and meaningful ways.

Differences Between Creation Ex Nihilo and Other Creation Theories

The doctrine of Creation Ex Nihilo—the belief that God created the universe out of nothing—has been a central tenet of Christian theology for centuries. However, this doctrine is not the only way in which the origin of the universe has been understood within religious, philosophical, and scientific traditions. Various other creation theories have been proposed throughout history, each offering a different perspective on the relationship between the Creator (or creators) and the created world. Among these theories, creation ex materia (creation from pre-existing matter) and creation ex deo (creation out of God's own being) are particularly significant, offering contrasting views that have influenced theological and philosophical discourse. This chapter explores the key differences between Creation Ex Nihilo and these other creation theories, highlighting the theological implications and the reasons for the Christian preference for Creation Ex Nihilo.

Creation Ex Nihilo: A Theological Foundation

Before delving into the differences between Creation Ex Nihilo and other creation theories, it is essential to understand what Creation Ex Nihilo entails and why it holds such a foundational place in Christian theology.

Ceation Ex Nihilo asserts that God, by an act of sovereign will, brought the entire universe into existence without using any pre-existing materials. This doctrine is rooted in the biblical narrative, particularly in passages such as Genesis 1:1 ("In the beginning, God created the heavens and the earth"), John 1:3 ("All things were made through Him, and without Him was not anything made that was made"), and Hebrews 11:3 ("By faith we understand that the universe was created by the word of God, so that what is seen was not made out of things that are visible").

The theological significance of Creation Ex Nihilo is profound. It underscores God's absolute sovereignty, omnipotence, and transcendence. By affirming that God created everything from nothing, this doctrine emphasizes that God is the ultimate source of all that exists and that nothing in creation exists independently of His will. Furthermore, it establishes a clear distinction between the Creator and the created order, preventing any confusion between the nature of God and the nature of the universe.

Creation Ex Materia: Creation from Pre-existing Matter

In contrast to Creation Ex Nihilo, the theory of creation ex materia posits that the universe was created from pre-existing, chaotic matter. This view is found in various ancient Near Eastern creation myths, as well as in some philosophical systems.

Ancient Near Eastern Myths

Many ancient Near Eastern cultures, including the Babylonians, Egyptians, and Greeks, held beliefs in creation ex materia. These myths often depict gods or divine beings shaping the cosmos from an existing substance or chaos. A prominent example is the Babylonian creation myth Enuma

Elish, where the god Marduk defeats the chaos monster Tiamat and uses her body to form the heavens and the earth. In this narrative, the universe emerges from a primordial, chaotic substance, with the gods acting as craftsmen who impose order on pre-existing materials.

In these myths, creation is often portrayed as a struggle between order and chaos, with the gods triumphing over chaotic forces to establish the world as it is known. The gods are not the creators of matter itself; instead, they shape and organize what already exists.

Greek Philosophy and Platonic Influence

The concept of creation ex materia also has roots in Greek philosophy, particularly in the thought of Plato. In Plato's Timaeus, the Demiurge, a divine craftsman, creates the universe by imposing form and order on a pre-existing, chaotic substance. According to Plato, the material world is shaped by the Demiurge based on the eternal Forms, which are perfect and unchanging ideals. The material world, however, is imperfect and subject to change because it is made from this chaotic, pre-existing matter.

Plato's idea of creation ex materia influenced later philosophical and theological systems, particularly in Gnosticism, where the material world is often seen as inherently flawed or evil because it is created from a chaotic substance. The Demiurge, in Gnostic thought, is often portrayed as a lesser or even malevolent being who creates the material world, which is in contrast to the higher, spiritual realm of the true God.

Differences Between Creation Ex Nihilo and Creation Ex Materia

The key differences between Creation Ex Nihilo and Creation Ex Materia revolve around the nature of the creative act, the status of matter, and the relationship between the Creator and the created world.

1. Nature of the Creative Act:

- Creation Ex Nihilo: In Creation Ex Nihilo, the creative act is understood as bringing something into existence from nothing. God does not require any pre-existing material to create the universe; His will and word alone are sufficient to call everything into being. This creative act is seen as a direct expression of God's omnipotence and sovereignty, emphasizing His absolute control over all aspects of existence.

- Creation Ex Materia: In contrast, creation ex materia involves shaping or organizing pre-existing matter. The creative act in this view is more akin to craftsmanship, where the deity imposes form and order on something that already exists. The deity in this scenario is not the ultimate source of all existence but rather a craftsman working with what is available. This perspective limits the deity's power, suggesting that the deity is not the origin of matter but only of its current form.

2. Status of Matter:

- Creation Ex Nihilo: The doctrine of Creation Ex Nihilo posits that matter itself is created by God and is therefore inherently good because it originates from the divine will. There is no dualistic separation between spirit and matter; instead, all of creation is seen as good, though it can be corrupted by sin. The emphasis on the goodness of creation stems from its origin in God's will, and this has significant implications for Christian anthropology, ethics, and eschatology.

- Creation Ex Materia: In creation ex materia, matter is often viewed as eternal or at least co-eternal with the deity. This can lead to a dualistic worldview, where matter is seen as distinct from and possibly inferior to the divine. In some philosophical systems, like Gnosticism, matter is even considered evil or corrupt, which contrasts sharply with the biblical view of the goodness of creation. The eternal existence of matter in this view also raises questions about the deity's sovereignty, as it suggests that something exists independently of the deity.

3. Relationship Between Creator and Creation:

- Creation Ex Nihilo: In Creation Ex Nihilo, the relationship between God and creation is one of absolute dependence. The universe exists solely because of God's will, and it continues to depend on God for its existence. This doctrine maintains a clear distinction between the Creator and the created order, emphasizing God's transcendence while also affirming His immanence in sustaining creation. Creation is seen as an act of divine grace, and the entire cosmos is understood as a gift from God.

- Creation Ex Materia: The relationship in creation ex materia is more complex, as it involves a deity working with pre-existing materials. The deity and the matter are co-existent, and the created world is seen as a product of both the deity's craftsmanship and the nature of the chaotic matter. This can blur the distinction between the Creator and creation, leading to views that see the material world as less directly connected to the divine. In some traditions, this results in a diminished view of the material world, or even a focus on escaping or transcending it.

Creation Ex Deo: Creation from God's Own Being

Another alternative to Creation Ex Nihilo is the theory of creation ex deo, which posits that the universe is created out of God's own substance or being. This idea is less common in classical Christian theology but has appeared in various religious and philosophical systems.

Pantheism and Panentheism

Creation ex deo is closely associated with pantheism and panentheism, two theological perspectives that see the divine as intimately connected with the universe.

- Pantheism: In pantheism, God and the universe are seen as identical; everything that exists is a manifestation of the divine. The material world is not separate from God but is understood as an expression of God's being. This view effectively eliminates the distinction between Creator and creation, leading to the belief that all of reality is divine.

- Panentheism: Panentheism, while similar to pantheism, maintains some distinction between God and the universe. In panentheism, the universe is seen as existing within God, who is greater than the universe but also immanent within it. The material world is part of God's being, but God's existence is not limited to the material world. This view allows for a more complex relationship between God and creation, where creation is seen as both part of and distinct from God.

Differences Between Creation Ex Nihilo and Creation Ex Deo

The differences between Creation Ex Nihilo and Creation Ex Deo center on the nature of God, the distinction between Creator and creation, and the implications for divine immanence and transcendence.

1. Nature of God:

- Creation Ex Nihilo: In Creation Ex Nihilo, God is wholly other than creation. God is the transcendent Creator who brings the universe into existence by an act of will, and nothing in creation is made from God's own substance. This maintains a strong distinction between God and the created order, emphasizing God's transcendence.

- Creation Ex Deo: In contrast, Creation Ex Deo suggests that the universe is made from God's own substance, leading to a view where the divine and the material are closely intertwined. This view can imply that creation shares in the divine nature, blurring the lines between God and the world. It raises questions about God's transcendence and the nature of the material world as part of God's being.

2. Distinction

Between Creator and Creation:

- Creation Ex Nihilo: The doctrine of Creation Ex Nihilo emphasizes the radical distinction between Creator and creation. God is the source of all being, and creation is wholly dependent on God, but it remains distinct from Him. This distinction is crucial for maintaining the integrity of both God's transcendence and the contingency of creation.

- Creation Ex Deo: Creation Ex Deo tends to blur the distinction between Creator and creation, leading to views where the material world is seen as an extension or expression of God's being. This can lead to theological challenges, such as pantheism, where the distinction between God and creation is effectively erased, or panentheism, where the distinction is maintained but with significant overlap between the divine and the material.

3. Divine Immanence and Transcendence:

- Creation Ex Nihilo: Creation Ex Nihilo allows for a balanced understanding of divine immanence and transcendence. God is transcendent as the Creator who is wholly other than creation, but He is also immanent in that He sustains and upholds creation. This view affirms God's closeness to the world without compromising His otherness.

- Creation Ex Deo: In Creation Ex Deo, the emphasis on God's immanence can overshadow His transcendence. If creation is made from God's own substance, it implies that God is inherently present in all aspects of the material world. While this can enhance the sense of God's immanence, it risks diminishing God's transcendence and leading to pantheistic or panentheistic interpretations.

Theological Implications and Christian Preference for Creation Ex Nihilo

The Christian preference for Creation Ex Nihilo over other creation theories is rooted in several key theological commitments that have shaped the development of Christian doctrine.

1. Affirmation of God's Sovereignty:

Creation Ex Nihilo underscores God's absolute sovereignty and omnipotence. By asserting that God created the universe out of nothing, this doctrine emphasizes that all of creation is entirely dependent on God and that nothing exists apart from His will. This is crucial for maintaining the Christian understanding of God as the ultimate source of all being and the ruler over all creation.

2. Goodness of Creation:

The doctrine of Creation Ex Nihilo affirms the inherent goodness of the created order, as it originates from God's will. This counters dualistic or negative views of matter, such as those found in creation ex materia or Gnostic thought, where the material world is often seen as flawed or evil. By affirming that all creation is good, Creation Ex Nihilo supports a holistic Christian understanding of the world and humanity's place within it.

3. Distinctiveness of the Creator-Creation Relationship:

Creation Ex Nihilo maintains a clear distinction between the Creator and creation, preserving God's transcendence while also affirming His immanence in sustaining the world. This distinction is essential for upholding the uniqueness of God as the source of all existence and for avoiding pantheistic or panentheistic interpretations that blur the lines between the divine and the material.

4. Compatibility with Biblical Revelation:

The Christian doctrine of Creation Ex Nihilo is deeply rooted in the biblical narrative, particularly in the Genesis creation account and the teachings of the New Testament. This alignment with Scripture is a key reason for its central place in Christian theology, as it reflects the biblical portrayal of God as the sovereign Creator who brings all things into existence by His word.

The doctrine of Creation Ex Nihilo stands in contrast to other creation theories, such as creation ex materia and creation ex deo, by emphasizing God's sovereignty, the goodness of creation, and the distinctiveness of the Creator-creation relationship. While these alternative theories have been influential in various religious and philosophical traditions, the Christian preference for Creation Ex Nihilo is grounded in its alignment with biblical revelation and its ability to uphold key theological commitments.

By affirming that God created the universe out of nothing, Creation Ex Nihilo provides a robust framework for understanding the nature of God, the origin of the world, and the relationship between the Creator and creation. As we continue to explore the implications of this doctrine, it remains a foundational aspect of Christian theology, offering a coherent and meaningful account of the world's origins and its ongoing dependence on the divine will.

The Role of Creation Ex Nihilo in Christian Doctrines

The doctrine of Creation Ex Nihilo—the belief that God created the universe out of nothing—holds a central place in Christian theology and has profound implications for several key Christian doctrines. Among these, the doctrines of divine sovereignty and providence are particularly significant. Creation Ex Nihilo provides the foundation for understanding God's absolute authority over all things, His ongoing relationship with creation, and the nature of His governance of the world. This chapter will explore the role of

Creation Ex Nihilo in these and other Christian doctrines, demonstrating how this foundational belief shapes the way Christians understand God, creation, and the unfolding of history.

Divine Sovereignty

One of the most critical aspects of Christian theology is the doctrine of divine sovereignty, which asserts that God is the supreme ruler and authority over all creation. This sovereignty is not limited or contingent upon anything outside of God Himself; rather, it is absolute and comprehensive. The doctrine of Creation Ex Nihilo is essential in affirming and explaining God's sovereignty.

God as the Ultimate Source of All That Exists

Creation Ex Nihilo teaches that the entire universe, including all matter, energy, space, and time, was brought into existence by God's will alone, without the use of any pre-existing materials. This belief underscores the idea that God is the ultimate source of everything that exists. There is nothing in creation that exists independently of God or that has its origin apart from Him.

This understanding is crucial for affirming God's sovereignty. If the universe were created from pre-existing matter or if there were any other source of existence apart from God, then God's sovereignty would be compromised.

Creation Ex Nihilo, however, maintains that all of reality is contingent upon God's creative will, reinforcing the belief that God has complete authority over all things.

Furthermore, because God is the Creator of everything that exists, He has the right and power to govern creation according to His purposes. This governance is not subject to any external constraints or limitations, as there is nothing outside of God that could challenge or restrict His rule. In this way, Creation Ex Nihilo establishes the basis for understanding God's sovereignty as both universal and uncontested.

The Creator-Creation Distinction

Creation Ex Nihilo also plays a vital role in maintaining the distinction between the Creator and creation, which is essential for a proper understanding of divine sovereignty. In Christian theology, God is understood to be wholly other than the created order. He is transcendent, existing outside of and independent from creation, yet He is also immanent, actively involved in sustaining and governing the world.

The distinction between Creator and creation, affirmed by Creation Ex Nihilo, helps to prevent any confusion or conflation between God and the universe. This is important because it safeguards against pantheism (the belief that God is identical with the universe) and panentheism (the belief that the universe is part of God but that God also transcends the universe). By maintaining that God created the universe out of nothing, Christian theology preserves the idea that God is distinct from His creation, even as He exercises sovereign control over it.

This distinction also underscores the dependency of creation on God. Since the universe was created ex nihilo, it has no independent existence or inherent power. It relies entirely on God for its origin, its continued existence, and its ultimate destiny. This absolute dependence further highlights God's sovereignty, as He alone sustains all that exists.

Divine Providence

The doctrine of divine providence refers to God's ongoing involvement in and care for creation. It encompasses God's preservation of the world, His governance of history, and His provision for the needs of His creatures. The doctrine of Creation Ex Nihilo is foundational to understanding divine providence, as it establishes the framework for God's continuous relationship with and governance of the created order.

God as Sustainer

Creation Ex Nihilo implies that God's creative act did not end with the initial creation of the universe. Instead, God continues to sustain all that He has made. If God were to withdraw His sustaining power, the universe would cease to exist. This ongoing act of sustenance is a key aspect of divine providence.

The idea that God sustains creation is rooted in passages such as Colossians 1:17, where Paul writes, "He is before all things, and in Him all things hold together." This verse highlights the belief that the existence and coherence of the universe depend entirely on God's will. Creation Ex Nihilo reinforces this by emphasizing that the universe, having been brought into existence from nothing, continues to rely on God for its preservation.

This sustaining work of God is often described as creatio continua, or continuous creation. While God's initial act of creation was a one-time event, His sustaining work is ongoing, ensuring that creation remains orderly and functional. This understanding of divine providence underscores the intimate and continuous relationship between God and creation, a relationship that is grounded in the doctrine of Creation Ex Nihilo.

God as Governor of History

The doctrine of providence also includes God's governance of history. According to Christian theology, God not only sustains the universe but also directs the course of history according to His purposes. This belief is closely tied to Creation Ex Nihilo, as it affirms that the entire created order, including the flow of time and the unfolding of events, is under God's sovereign control.

Creation Ex Nihilo supports the idea that history is not a random or chaotic process but is instead guided by God's will. Since God created the universe out of nothing, He is not constrained by any external forces or pre-existing conditions. This allows Him to direct history toward the fulfillment of His divine purposes, including the redemption and restoration of creation.

This view of divine governance is reflected in numerous biblical passages, such as Ephesians 1:11, which states that God "works all things according to the counsel of His will." The doctrine of Creation Ex Nihilo reinforces this by affirming that all things, including the course of history, are ultimately subject to God's sovereign will and plan.

God as Provider

Another aspect of divine providence is God's provision for His creation. This includes not only the physical needs of creatures but also their spiritual and moral well-being. The doctrine of Creation Ex Nihilo plays a role in understanding this provision, as it emphasizes God's benevolence and care for all that He has made.

In creating the universe out of nothing, God demonstrates His goodness and generosity. Creation itself is an act of divine grace, bringing into existence a world that reflects God's glory and provides a home for His creatures. God's provision is seen in the way He has ordered the natural world, ensuring that it is capable of sustaining life and meeting the needs of His creatures.

The belief that God continues to provide for His creation is rooted in the understanding that, because God is the Creator of all things, He has the power and desire to care for His creation. Jesus highlights this aspect of divine providence in passages like Matthew 6:26-30, where He speaks of God's care for the birds of the air and the lilies of the field, assuring His followers that they are of even greater value to God.

The doctrine of Creation Ex Nihilo reinforces the idea that God's provision is both comprehensive and reliable. Since God created the world out of nothing, He is fully capable of sustaining and providing for His creation. This belief provides a foundation for trust in God's care and encourages believers to rely on His provision in all aspects of life.

The Doctrine of the Imago Dei

The doctrine of Creation Ex Nihilo also plays a crucial role in understanding the Christian concept of the imago Dei—the belief that human beings are created in the image of God. This doctrine has significant implications for Christian anthropology, ethics, and the relationship between humanity and the rest of creation.

Humanity's Unique Status in Creation

The idea that human beings are made in the image of God is rooted in the Genesis creation narrative, where God says, "Let us make man in our image, after our likeness" (Genesis 1:26). This declaration emphasizes the unique status of humanity within the created order, distinguishing humans from other creatures.

Creation Ex Nihilo provides the context for understanding the significance of the imago Dei. By affirming that God created the entire universe out of nothing, the doctrine underscores the intentionality and purpose behind creation, including the creation of humanity. Human beings are not the result of a random or impersonal process; rather, they are the deliberate creation of a personal and sovereign God.

This belief in the divine origin of humanity affirms the inherent dignity and worth of every human being. Because humans are created in the image of God, they possess a unique value that is rooted in their relationship with the Creator. This understanding has profound implications for Christian ethics, particularly in areas such as human rights, social justice, and the sanctity of life.

The Imago Dei and Dominion

The doctrine of the imago Dei is also closely connected to the concept of dominion, which is the idea that human beings are given authority over the rest of creation. In Genesis 1:28, God blesses humanity and commands them to "fill the earth and subdue it, and have dominion over the fish of the sea and over the birds of the heavens and over every living thing that moves on the earth."

Creation Ex Nihilo provides the theological foundation for understanding this dominion as a form of stewardship rather than exploitation. Since God created the universe out of nothing, all of creation belongs to Him, and humans are entrusted with the responsibility to care for and manage it on His behalf. This stewardship is an expression of the imago Dei, reflecting God's own care and governance of the world.

The doctrine of Creation Ex Nihilo, therefore, shapes the Christian understanding of humanity's role within creation, emphasizing the need for responsible and ethical stewardship that honors the Creator and reflects His character.

The Doctrine of Salvation

The doctrine of Creation Ex Nihilo also has important implications for the Christian understanding of salvation. Just as God created the universe out of nothing, so too does He have the power to bring about new creation and redemption through Jesus Christ. This parallel between creation and salvation highlights the continuity of God's creative and redemptive work.

New Creation in Christ

The New Testament frequently speaks of salvation in terms of new creation. For example, Paul writes in 2 Corinthians 5:17, "Therefore, if anyone is in Christ, he is a new creation. The old has passed away; behold, the new has come." This language suggests that salvation is not merely a moral or spiritual improvement but a radical transformation that mirrors the original act of creation.

Creation Ex Nihilo provides the theological basis for understanding this new creation as a work of divine power and grace. Just as God brought the universe into existence from nothing, so too does He bring new life to those who are in Christ. This transformation is not something that humans can achieve on their own; it is entirely dependent on God's creative and redemptive power.

This connection between creation and salvation also emphasizes the idea that salvation is part of God's larger plan for the redemption and restoration of the entire created order. The same God who created the world out of nothing is actively working to renew and restore it, culminating in the promise of a new heaven and a new earth (Revelation 21:1).

Resurrection and the Power of God

The doctrine of Creation Ex Nihilo also plays a role in understanding the Christian hope of resurrection. Just as God created the physical universe out of nothing, He also has the power to raise the dead and bring about the resurrection of the body. This belief is central to Christian eschatology and is grounded in the understanding of God as the Creator.

Paul emphasizes this connection in 1 Corinthians 15, where he discusses the resurrection of the dead. He argues that the same power that raised Jesus from the dead will also raise believers to new life, transforming their mortal bodies into immortal ones. This transformation is an act of new creation, reflecting the same divine power that brought the universe into existence.

Creation Ex Nihilo thus reinforces the Christian hope of resurrection by affirming God's ability to bring life out of death and to create anew. This hope is not based on human effort or natural processes but on the sovereign power of God, who is the source of all life and being.

The Doctrine of Eschatology

Finally, the doctrine of Creation Ex Nihilo has significant implications for Christian eschatology—the study of the end times and the ultimate destiny of creation. Christian eschatology is rooted in the belief that the God who created the world out of nothing will also bring it to its final fulfillment and renewal.

The Promise of New Creation

The biblical narrative culminates in the promise of a new creation, where God will renew and restore all things. This promise is found in passages such as Isaiah 65:17 ("For behold, I create new heavens and a new earth") and Revelation 21:5 ("And he who was seated on the throne said, 'Behold, I am making all things new'"). This new creation is understood as the ultimate fulfillment of God's creative and redemptive purposes.

Creation Ex Nihilo provides the framework for understanding this eschatological hope. Just as God brought the original creation into existence out of nothing, so too will He bring about a new creation that is free from sin, death, and decay. This belief underscores the continuity between the original creation and the eschatological renewal, while also emphasizing the transformative power of God's creative word.

The doctrine of Creation Ex Nihilo also reinforces the idea that the new creation will be a sovereign act of God, not the result of human effort or natural evolution. It will be a fulfillment of God's promise, demonstrating His faithfulness and His power to bring about His purposes for creation.

The Final Judgment and Divine Sovereignty

Eschatology also includes the doctrine of the final judgment, where God will bring justice to the world and establish His kingdom in its fullness. Creation Ex Nihilo supports the belief in the final judgment by affirming God's absolute sovereignty over all creation. Since God is the Creator of all things, He has the right and authority to judge the world and to bring about its ultimate destiny.

This belief in the final judgment is rooted in the understanding that creation is not an end in itself but is directed toward a final purpose. Creation Ex Nihilo emphasizes that the universe has a beginning, and it will also have an end, determined by God's will. The final judgment is the moment when God will bring creation to its intended fulfillment, separating good from evil and establishing His righteous rule.

Creation Ex Nihilo thus provides a foundation for Christian eschatological hope, affirming that the God who created the world will also bring it to its ultimate completion in accordance with His divine plan.

The doctrine of Creation Ex Nihilo plays a central role in shaping several key Christian doctrines, including divine sovereignty, providence, the imago Dei, salvation, and eschatology. By affirming that God created the universe out of nothing, this doctrine underscores God's absolute authority, His ongoing relationship with creation, and His power to bring about new creation and redemption.

Creation Ex Nihilo provides the foundation for understanding God as the sovereign Creator who is distinct from but also intimately involved in the world He has made. It emphasizes the contingency of creation, the goodness of the created order, and the ultimate purpose of history as directed by God's will.

As we continue to explore the implications of Creation Ex Nihilo, it becomes clear that this doctrine is not merely a theological abstraction but a profound affirmation of God's power, love, and faithfulness. It shapes the way Christians understand their relationship with God, the world, and the future, offering a vision of creation that is both rooted in the past and oriented toward the ultimate fulfillment of God's purposes.

CHAPTER 04

IMPLICATIONS FOR CHRISTIAN FAITH

Creation Ex Nihilo and the Doctrine of God (Omnipotence, Omniscience)

The doctrine of Creation Ex Nihilo—the belief that God created the universe out of nothing—has profound implications for the Christian understanding of God, particularly in relation to His attributes of omnipotence and omniscience. These two attributes are foundational to the Christian conception of God as the all-powerful, all-knowing Creator and Sustainer of the universe. This chapter will explore how the doctrine of Creation Ex Nihilo underscores and illuminates these divine attributes, shaping the way Christians understand God's nature, His relationship with the world, and His involvement in the unfolding of history.

Omnipotence: God's Absolute Power

Omnipotence, the attribute that describes God's unlimited power, is one of the central aspects of the Christian understanding of God. The doctrine of Creation Ex Nihilo directly relates to and emphasizes God's omnipotence, demonstrating that God has the power to bring into existence everything that is, solely by His will and without the need for any pre-existing materials.

God's Power to Create from Nothing

The most direct implication of Creation Ex Nihilo for the doctrine of omnipotence is the affirmation that God possesses the ultimate creative power—the ability to bring something into existence from nothing. This power is unparalleled and unique to God. Unlike human beings, who can only create by manipulating or transforming existing materials, God's creative act is entirely original and independent of any external resources.

This creative power is reflected in biblical passages such as Genesis 1:1, "In the beginning, God created the heavens and the earth," and Psalm 33:9, "For He spoke, and it came to be; He commanded, and it stood firm." These verses highlight the effortless nature of God's creative act, emphasizing that His word alone is sufficient to bring the entire cosmos into existence. This notion of creation by divine command is foundational to understanding God's omnipotence, as it demonstrates that there are no limitations or constraints on His power.

By affirming that God created the universe out of nothing, Creation Ex Nihilo underscores the idea that God's power is absolute and not dependent on any external factors. This has significant theological implications, as it means that God is not limited by the material world or by any pre-existing conditions. His power is sovereign, extending over all of creation and capable of accomplishing anything He wills.

The Universality of God's Power

Creation Ex Nihilo also implies the universality of God's power. Since everything that exists was brought into being by God's creative act, there is nothing in the universe that is outside of His control or authority. This universal scope of God's power is a direct consequence of His role as the Creator, as described in passages like Isaiah 40:28, "The Lord is the everlasting God, the Creator of the ends of the earth. He will not grow tired or weary, and His understanding no one can fathom."

God's omnipotence means that He not only created all things but also sustains and governs them according to His will. There is no part of creation that is independent of God's power or that can resist His sovereign will. This belief is central to the Christian understanding of divine providence, which holds that God is actively involved in sustaining and directing the course of history and the natural world.

The universality of God's power also has important implications for Christian worship and devotion. Because God is the Creator of all that exists, He is worthy of all praise and worship. The recognition of God's omnipotence as revealed through Creation Ex Nihilo inspires awe, reverence, and trust in God's ability to fulfill His promises and to bring about His purposes in the world.

God's Power Over Chaos and Evil

Another important implication of Creation Ex Nihilo for the doctrine of omnipotence is the affirmation that God has power over chaos and evil. In many ancient Near Eastern creation myths, creation is depicted as a struggle between order and chaos, with the gods battling chaotic forces to establish the world. In contrast, the biblical account of creation presents God as having complete control over chaos, bringing order and life out of nothingness without any struggle or opposition.

The concept of God creating ex nihilo suggests that chaos and evil are not independent forces that challenge God's authority. Instead, they are part of the created order, subject to God's sovereign control. This understanding is crucial for Christian theology, as it affirms that God is not in conflict with any external forces but is the ultimate source of all order and goodness.

God's omnipotence, as revealed through Creation Ex Nihilo, also provides the basis for the Christian hope of redemption and the ultimate defeat of evil. Just as God had the power to create the universe out of nothing, He also has the power to bring about new creation, redeeming and restoring the world from the effects of sin and evil. This hope is encapsulated in the Christian belief in the resurrection and the promise of a new heaven and a new earth.

Omniscience: God's All-Knowing Nature

Omniscience, the attribute that describes God's complete and perfect knowledge, is another key aspect of the Christian understanding of God. The doctrine of Creation Ex Nihilo has significant implications for the doctrine of omniscience, as it affirms that God's knowledge is comprehensive, encompassing all of creation, both past, present, and future.

God's Knowledge of Creation

Creation Ex Nihilo implies that God's knowledge of the universe is both intimate and exhaustive. Since God is the Creator of all that exists, He possesses perfect knowledge of every aspect of creation. This knowledge is not limited to the material world but extends to the spiritual, intellectual, and moral dimensions of existence.

God's omniscience means that He knows every detail of the created order, from the vastness of the cosmos to the smallest particle. This idea is reflected in passages such as Psalm 139:1-4, where the psalmist declares, "O Lord, you have searched me and known me! You know when I sit down and when I rise up; you discern my thoughts from afar. You search out my path and my lying down and are acquainted with all my ways. Even before a word is on my tongue, behold, O Lord, you know it altogether."

The doctrine of Creation Ex Nihilo reinforces the belief that God's knowledge is not passive or observational but active and creative. God's knowledge is part of His creative power, meaning that He knows all things because He has brought them into existence. This comprehensive knowledge is not limited by time or space; God knows the entirety of creation, including its origins, its current state, and its ultimate destiny.

God's Knowledge of Time and History

Another important implication of Creation Ex Nihilo for the doctrine of omniscience is the affirmation that God's knowledge encompasses all of time and history. Since God created the universe out of nothing, including time itself, He is not bound by temporal limitations. God exists outside of time, and His knowledge is not constrained by the past, present, or future.

This understanding is reflected in Isaiah 46:9-10, where God declares, "I am God, and there is no other; I am God, and there is none like me, declaring the end from the beginning and from ancient times things not yet done, saying, 'My counsel shall stand, and I will accomplish all my purpose.'"

God's omniscience means that He knows the entire scope of history, from the moment of creation to the end of time. He knows every event, every decision, and every consequence, both in the natural world and in human history. This knowledge is not merely foreknowledge; it is part of God's sovereign will, as He directs the course of history according to His purposes.

Creation Ex Nihilo underscores the idea that history is not a random sequence of events but is under the direction of God's all-knowing and all-powerful hand. This belief provides a foundation for the Christian understanding of providence and the assurance that God's purposes will ultimately be fulfilled.

God's Knowledge of Human Hearts and Minds

The doctrine of omniscience also extends to God's knowledge of human hearts and minds. Creation Ex Nihilo affirms that God knows every individual intimately because He is their Creator. This includes not only external actions but also internal thoughts, desires, and motivations.

Jesus speaks to this aspect of God's omniscience in passages like Matthew 6:8, where He says, "Your Father knows what you need before you ask Him." This idea is further emphasized in 1 Samuel 16:7, where it is stated, "For the Lord sees not as man sees: man looks on the outward appearance, but the Lord looks on the heart."

God's omniscience, as it relates to human beings, is both comforting and challenging. It is comforting because it assures believers that God knows their needs, fears, and struggles and is able to provide for them according to His will. It is challenging because it reminds individuals that nothing is hidden from God, and they are fully accountable to Him for their thoughts and actions.

The connection between Creation Ex Nihilo and God's knowledge of human hearts and minds highlights the personal nature of God's relationship with His creation. God is not distant or detached; He is intimately involved in the lives of His creatures, knowing them better than they know themselves.

The Relationship Between Omnipotence and Omniscience

The doctrine of Creation Ex Nihilo not only affirms God's omnipotence and omniscience individually but also highlights the relationship between these two attributes. In Christian theology, God's power and knowledge are understood to be perfectly integrated, meaning that God's omnipotence is informed by His omniscience, and His omniscience is exercised through His omnipotence.

God's Sovereign Will and Knowledge

Creation Ex Nihilo emphasizes that God's will is the ultimate source of all that exists. This means that God's power to create is directly connected to His knowledge of what He creates. God's knowledge is not reactive or passive; it is active and creative, shaping the very fabric of the universe according to His sovereign will.

This integration of omnipotence and omniscience is reflected in passages like Jeremiah 32:17-19, where the prophet declares, "Ah, Lord God! It is you who have made the heavens and the earth by your great power and by your outstretched arm! Nothing is too hard for you. You show steadfast love to thousands, but you repay the guilt of fathers to their children after them, O great and mighty God, whose name is the Lord of hosts, great in counsel and mighty in deed, whose eyes are open to all the ways of the children of man."

Here, God's great power ("mighty in deed") is directly connected to His great wisdom ("great in counsel") and His comprehensive knowledge ("whose eyes are open to all the ways of the children of man"). The doctrine of Creation Ex Nihilo underscores this connection, affirming that God's creative power is exercised with perfect knowledge and wisdom.

The Assurance of God's Providence

The relationship between omnipotence and omniscience, as revealed through Creation Ex Nihilo, also provides the basis for the Christian understanding of divine providence. Because God is both all-powerful and all-knowing, believers can have confidence that He is able to direct their lives and the course of history according to His perfect will.

This assurance is rooted in the belief that God's power is not arbitrary or capricious; it is guided by His perfect knowledge and wisdom. God knows the needs of His creatures, the challenges they face, and the best way to bring about His purposes in their lives and in the world. This understanding of providence provides a foundation for trust in God's care and guidance, even in the midst of uncertainty and suffering.

The integration of omnipotence and omniscience in Creation Ex Nihilo also affirms that God's plans cannot be thwarted. Because God knows all things and has the power to bring His will to pass, believers can be confident that His purposes will ultimately be fulfilled. This belief provides hope and encouragement in the face of adversity, reminding Christians that God is in control and that His good and perfect will shall prevail.

Implications for Christian Faith and Practice

The doctrine of Creation Ex Nihilo, with its emphasis on God's omnipotence and omniscience, has profound implications for Christian faith and practice. It shapes the way Christians understand their relationship with God, their place in the world, and their response to the challenges of life.

Trust in God's Sovereignty

One of the most important implications of Creation Ex Nihilo for Christian faith is the call to trust in God's sovereignty. Because God is both all-powerful and all-knowing, believers are encouraged to place their trust in Him, knowing that He is in control of all things and that His plans are good.

This trust in God's sovereignty is particularly important in times of difficulty or uncertainty. When faced with challenges that seem insurmountable or situations that are beyond human control, the belief in God's omnipotence and omniscience provides a foundation for confidence and hope. Christians are called to rely on God's power and wisdom, trusting that He is able to work all things together for good (Romans 8:28).

Worship and Reverence

The doctrine of Creation Ex Nihilo also inspires worship and reverence for God. The recognition of God's omnipotence and omniscience as revealed through His creative act leads to a deeper sense of awe and wonder at His majesty. Worship becomes a response to the greatness of God, who is the Creator and Sustainer of all things.

This reverence for God is reflected in passages like Revelation 4:11, where the heavenly hosts declare, "Worthy are you, our Lord and God, to receive glory and honor and power, for you created all things, and by your will they existed and were created." The doctrine of Creation Ex Nihilo emphasizes that God is deserving of all praise and worship because He is the source of all that exists.

Ethical Responsibility

Finally, the doctrine of Creation Ex Nihilo has implications for Christian ethics and the way believers live in the world. The belief that God is the Creator of all things, and that His power and knowledge encompass every aspect of life, calls Christians to live in a way that honors God and reflects His character.

This ethical responsibility includes stewardship of creation, care for others, and the pursuit of justice and righteousness. Because God created the world and entrusted it to human beings, Christians are called to be responsible stewards of the environment and to care for the well-being of all people. The belief in God's omnipotence and omniscience also encourages believers to act with integrity, knowing that God sees and knows all things and that they are accountable to Him for their actions.

The doctrine of Creation Ex Nihilo plays a crucial role in shaping the Christian understanding of God's omnipotence and omniscience. By affirming that God created the universe out of nothing, this doctrine emphasizes God's absolute power, His comprehensive knowledge, and His sovereign control over all that exists. These attributes of God are foundational to Christian theology, influencing the way believers understand God's relationship with the world and their own place within it.

Creation Ex Nihilo highlights the integration of God's omnipotence and omniscience, demonstrating that God's power is exercised with perfect knowledge and wisdom. This understanding provides a basis for trust in God's providence, inspires worship and reverence, and calls Christians to live ethically in response to God's creative and sustaining power.

As we continue to explore the implications of Creation Ex Nihilo, it becomes clear that this doctrine is not only a statement about the origin of the universe but also a profound affirmation of the nature and character of God. It shapes the way Christians relate to God, understand the world, and live out their faith, offering a vision of God as the all-powerful, all-knowing Creator who is worthy of all praise and trust.

The Relationship Between God and Creation

The doctrine of Creation Ex Nihilo—the belief that God created the universe out of nothing—profoundly shapes the understanding of the relationship between God and creation within Christian theology. This relationship is characterized by a delicate balance of divine transcendence and immanence, sovereignty and intimacy, and creator-creature distinction and communion. In this chapter, we will explore the various dimensions of this relationship, including the theological foundations laid by Creation Ex Nihilo, the implications for God's ongoing involvement in creation, and how this relationship informs Christian worship, ethics, and eschatology.

Theological Foundations: Transcendence and Immanence

The doctrine of Creation Ex Nihilo establishes two fundamental aspects of the relationship between God and creation: God's transcendence and God's immanence. These two aspects are complementary and must be held in tension to fully understand how God relates to the world He created.

God's Transcendence

God's transcendence refers to the belief that God is wholly other than and infinitely greater than creation. Because God brought the universe into existence out of nothing, He is not a part of creation but stands above and beyond it. This means that God is not subject to the limitations of time, space, or matter, and He exists independently of the created order.

The transcendence of God is emphasized in passages like Isaiah 55:8-9, where God declares, "For my thoughts are not your thoughts, neither are your ways my ways, declares the Lord. For as the heavens are higher than the earth, so are my ways higher than your ways and my thoughts than your thoughts." This underscores the vast difference between the

Creator and the creation, highlighting God's majesty, holiness, and sovereignty.

The doctrine of Creation Ex Nihilo reinforces God's transcendence by affirming that everything that exists is contingent upon God's creative will. Nothing in creation exists independently of God, and nothing can compare to His greatness. This transcendence is a key aspect of Christian worship, as it inspires reverence, awe, and humility before the Creator.

God's Immanence

While God's transcendence emphasizes His otherness, God's immanence refers to His presence and active involvement within creation. Despite being wholly other than creation, God is not distant or detached from it. Instead, He is intimately involved in sustaining, guiding, and interacting with the world He made.

God's immanence is expressed in passages like Acts 17:27-28, where Paul tells the Athenians, "Yet he is actually not far from each one of us, for 'In him we live and move and have our being.'" This highlights the belief that God is present in all aspects of creation, upholding it by His power and interacting with it according to His will.

Creation Ex Nihilo underscores God's immanence by teaching that the same God who created the universe out of nothing continues to sustain and govern it. The world is not a self-sustaining entity but relies on God's ongoing presence and action. This immanence is evident in the concept of creatio continua (continuous creation), which holds that God is continually involved in preserving and directing the created order.

God's immanence is also central to the Christian understanding of providence—the belief that God actively cares for and provides for His creation. This includes not only the natural world but also human history, individual lives, and the unfolding of God's redemptive plan. God's immanence assures believers that He is near, involved, and concerned with the details of their lives.

The Creator-Creation Distinction and Communion

The doctrine of Creation Ex Nihilo establishes a clear distinction between the Creator and the creation while also allowing for a deep communion between them. This distinction and communion are essential for understanding the relationship between God and the world.

The Creator-Creation Distinction

One of the key implications of Creation Ex Nihilo is the affirmation that God is fundamentally different from creation. God is eternal, self-existent, and unchanging, while creation is temporal, contingent, and dependent. This distinction is crucial for maintaining the integrity of Christian theology, as it prevents the confusion of God with the world (pantheism) or the belief that the world is part of God's being (panentheism).

The distinction between Creator and creation is highlighted in Romans 1:20-21, where Paul writes, "For his invisible attributes, namely, his eternal power and divine nature, have been clearly perceived, ever since the creation of the world, in the things that have been made. So they are without excuse. For although they knew God, they did not honor him as God or give thanks to him, but they became futile in their thinking, and their foolish hearts were darkened." Here, Paul emphasizes that creation reveals God's attributes but is not to be equated with God Himself.

This distinction has important theological implications, particularly in relation to idolatry and worship. Because God is distinct from creation, He alone is worthy of worship, and the created order is not to be venerated or treated as divine. This understanding helps to safeguard the monotheistic faith of Christianity and ensures that worship is directed solely to the Creator.

The Communion Between Creator and Creation

Despite the distinction between Creator and creation, the doctrine of Creation Ex Nihilo also allows for a profound communion between God and the world. This communion is rooted in God's desire to be in relationship with His creation and is expressed in various ways throughout the biblical narrative.

The most significant expression of this communion is found in the Incarnation, where God the Son took on human flesh and entered into the created order. The Incarnation is the ultimate demonstration of God's immanence and His desire to be in relationship with humanity. In John 1:14, we read, "And the Word became flesh and dwelt among us, and we have seen his glory, glory as of the only Son from the Father, full of grace and truth." The Incarnation bridges the gap between Creator and creation, allowing for an intimate and personal relationship between God and humanity.

This communion is also evident in the doctrine of the Holy Spirit, who dwells within believers and empowers them to live in accordance with God's will. The presence of the Holy Spirit within creation is a sign of God's ongoing involvement and care, as well as His desire for a close and personal relationship with His people.

The relationship between Creator and creation is also characterized by God's covenantal interactions with humanity. Throughout the Bible, God establishes covenants with His people, promising to be their God and to bless them.

These covenants, such as those with Noah, Abraham, Moses, and David, demonstrate God's commitment to His creation and His desire for a relationship based on love, faithfulness, and obedience.

God's Ongoing Involvement in Creation

The doctrine of Creation Ex Nihilo emphasizes that God's relationship with creation is not limited to the initial act of creation but continues throughout history. This ongoing involvement is central to the Christian understanding of divine providence, governance, and redemption.

Providence: God's Sustaining and Governing of Creation

Providence refers to God's ongoing care for and governance of the world. The doctrine of Creation Ex Nihilo provides the foundation for understanding providence, as it affirms that the same God who created the universe out of nothing continues to sustain and direct it according to His will.

God's providence is reflected in passages like Colossians 1:16-17, where Paul writes, "For by him all things were created, in heaven and on earth, visible and invisible, whether thrones or dominions or rulers or authorities—all things were created through him and for him. And he is before all things, and in him all things hold together." This emphasizes that creation is not self-sufficient but relies on God's sustaining power.

Providence includes God's provision for the needs of His creatures, His governance of history, and His guidance of individual lives. The doctrine of Creation Ex Nihilo assures believers that God is actively involved in every aspect of creation, ensuring that His purposes are fulfilled and that His creation is cared for.

Redemption: God's Restorative Work in Creation

The relationship between God and creation also includes the theme of redemption. The doctrine of Creation Ex Nihilo emphasizes that the world was created good, but it has been marred by sin and brokenness. God's response to this brokenness is one of redemption and restoration.

The promise of redemption is central to the Christian narrative, beginning with God's covenant with Abraham and culminating in the life, death, and resurrection of Jesus Christ. In Christ, God initiates a new creation, bringing about the restoration of all things. This is expressed in 2 Corinthians 5:17, where Paul writes, "Therefore, if anyone is in Christ, he is a new creation. The old has passed away; behold, the new has come."

The doctrine of Creation Ex Nihilo highlights the continuity between the original creation and the new creation.

Just as God brought the universe into existence out of nothing, He has the power to bring about new life and restore what has been lost. This hope of redemption extends beyond individual salvation to the renewal of the entire created order, as described in passages like Revelation 21:1, "Then I saw a new heaven and a new earth, for the first heaven and the first earth had passed away, and the sea was no more."

Redemption is a key aspect of God's ongoing relationship with creation, demonstrating His commitment to the world He made and His power to bring about its ultimate restoration.

Implications for Christian Worship and Ethics

The relationship between God and creation, as informed by the doctrine of Creation Ex Nihilo, has significant implications for Christian worship and ethics. It shapes the way believers understand their relationship with God, their responsibility toward the created order, and their participation in God's redemptive work.

Worship: Honoring the Creator

The doctrine of Creation Ex Nihilo calls believers to worship God as the Creator and Sustainer of all things. This worship is characterized by reverence, gratitude, and awe for the God who brought the universe into existence out of nothing and continues to uphold it by His power.

Worship is not only an acknowledgment of God's greatness but also a response to His love and care for creation. Passages like Psalm 100:3-4 express this call to worship: "Know that the Lord, he is God! It is he who made us, and we are his; we are his people and the sheep of his pasture. Enter his gates with thanksgiving, and his courts with praise! Give thanks to him; bless his name!"

The relationship between God and creation also informs the content of worship, as believers are called to praise God for His creative and redemptive work. This includes recognizing the goodness of creation, the beauty of the natural world, and the hope of new creation in Christ.

Ethics: Stewardship and Responsibility

The doctrine of Creation Ex Nihilo also has ethical implications, particularly in relation to stewardship and responsibility toward the created order. Since God is the Creator of all things, human beings are called to be stewards of creation, caring for the environment and using its resources wisely and justly.

This responsibility is rooted in the belief that creation is a gift from God, entrusted to humanity for its care and preservation. Genesis 2:15 reflects this calling: "The Lord God took the man and put him in the garden of Eden to work it and keep it." This stewardship involves not only the responsible use of natural resources but also the protection of the environment, the promotion of justice, and the care for all living creatures.

The relationship between God and creation also calls believers to participate in God's redemptive work in the world. This includes acts of mercy, justice, and reconciliation, as well as efforts to restore and heal the brokenness of creation. By engaging in these activities, Christians reflect the character of God and contribute to the fulfillment of His purposes for creation.

The Eschatological Fulfillment of God's Relationship with Creation

The relationship between God and creation, as informed by Creation Ex Nihilo, ultimately points to the eschatological fulfillment of God's purposes for the world. Christian eschatology emphasizes the belief that God will bring about the renewal and restoration of creation, culminating in the new heaven and new earth.

The New Creation

The promise of new creation is a central theme in Christian eschatology, rooted in the belief that God's creative and redemptive work will ultimately lead to the restoration of all things. This hope is expressed in passages like Revelation

21:5, where God declares, "Behold, I am making all things new."

The doctrine of Creation Ex Nihilo provides the foundation for this hope by affirming that the same God who created the universe out of nothing has the power to bring about its ultimate renewal. This new creation is not merely a return to the original state of the world but a transformation that fulfills God's purposes and brings about the final reconciliation of all things.

The eschatological fulfillment of God's relationship with creation is characterized by the eradication of sin, suffering, and death, and the establishment of God's kingdom in its fullness. In this new creation, God's relationship with the world will be fully realized, and His glory will be revealed in and through all of creation.

The Final Communion Between God and Creation

The eschatological hope of new creation also includes the promise of final communion between God and creation. This communion is described in Revelation 21:3, where John writes, "And I heard a loud voice from the throne saying, 'Behold, the dwelling place of God is with man. He will dwell with them, and they will be his people, and God himself will be with them as their God.'"

This final communion represents the fulfillment of God's desire to be in relationship with His creation. It is the culmination of the covenantal promises made throughout the biblical narrative and the realization of God's redemptive plan for the world.

The relationship between God and creation, as established by Creation Ex Nihilo, finds its ultimate expression in this eschatological communion, where God's presence will be fully known and experienced by all of creation. This hope provides the foundation for Christian faith and practice, inspiring believers to live in anticipation of the new creation and to participate in God's work of redemption in the world.

The relationship between God and creation, as informed by the doctrine of Creation Ex Nihilo, is characterized by a dynamic interplay of transcendence and immanence, distinction and communion, and sovereignty and intimacy. This relationship shapes the way Christians understand God's ongoing involvement in the world, their responsibility toward creation, and their hope for the future.

Creation Ex Nihilo establishes the foundation for understanding God as the transcendent Creator who is distinct from creation yet intimately involved in sustaining and redeeming it. It calls believers to worship God as the source of all that exists, to live as responsible stewards of His creation, and to participate in His redemptive work.

Ultimately, the relationship between God and creation points to the eschatological fulfillment of God's purposes, where the world will be renewed and restored, and final communion between Creator and creation will be realized. This hope provides the framework for Christian faith and practice, inspiring believers to live in anticipation of the new creation and to reflect God's character in their relationships with the world and with one another.

Theological Implications for Understanding Evil and Suffering

The doctrine of Creation Ex Nihilo—the belief that God created the universe out of nothing—has significant implications for how Christians understand the presence of evil and suffering in the world. This chapter explores the theological implications of Creation Ex Nihilo for addressing these profound and difficult issues, examining how this doctrine shapes the Christian response to questions about the origin of evil, the nature of suffering, and God's role in the midst of a broken and suffering world.

The Problem of Evil and Suffering

The problem of evil and suffering is one of the most challenging issues in Christian theology. It raises questions about the nature of God, the purpose of creation, and the meaning of human existence. How can a good and omnipotent God, who created the universe out of nothing, allow evil and suffering to exist? This question has been at the heart of theological reflection for centuries and continues to be a central concern for believers and skeptics alike.

The Doctrine of Creation Ex Nihilo and the Goodness of Creation

A foundational aspect of the Christian understanding of creation is the affirmation that God's creation is inherently good. The doctrine of Creation Ex Nihilo supports this by emphasizing that everything God created was brought into existence by His will and is fundamentally good, as it originates from a perfectly good God. This belief is rooted in the biblical narrative of creation, particularly in Genesis 1, where God repeatedly declares that His creation is "good" (Genesis 1:4, 10, 12, 18, 21, 25) and ultimately "very good" (Genesis 1:31).

The Original Goodness of Creation

Creation Ex Nihilo implies that God created the universe without any inherent flaw or defect. The material world, human beings, and all living creatures were made good, reflecting the goodness of their Creator. This understanding is essential for Christian theology, as it affirms the value and dignity of creation and provides the basis for understanding the distortion of that goodness through sin and evil.

The original goodness of creation is also critical for addressing the problem of evil. If creation were inherently flawed or evil, then God could be implicated as the source of that evil. However, by affirming that creation was originally good, Christian theology maintains that evil is not a product of God's creative will but a distortion or corruption of the good creation that God intended.

The Fall and the Corruption of Creation

While Creation Ex Nihilo affirms the goodness of creation, Christian theology also acknowledges that the current state of the world is marred by sin, evil, and suffering. This corruption is traced back to the Fall, the event in which the first humans, Adam and Eve, disobeyed God and introduced sin into the world. The Fall is described in Genesis 3, where the serpent tempts Eve to eat the forbidden fruit, leading to the disobedience of both Eve and Adam.

The Fall represents a turning point in the biblical narrative, as it introduces a rupture in the relationship between God and creation. The consequences of the Fall are far-reaching, affecting not only human beings but the entire created order. The ground is cursed, death enters the world, and suffering becomes a part of human existence (Genesis 3:14-19).

From a theological perspective, the Fall is not the introduction of something entirely new into creation but a distortion of the original goodness that God intended. Evil, therefore, is not a substance or a created entity but a perversion of the good. This understanding is rooted in the concept of privatio boni (the privation of good), a term used by early Christian theologians like Augustine to describe evil as the absence or corruption of good rather than a positive reality.

The Origin of Evil: A Theological Reflection

Given that God created the universe out of nothing and declared it to be good, how did evil come into existence? This question is central to the problem of evil and has been the subject of extensive theological reflection.

Free Will and the Possibility of Evil

One of the most common explanations for the origin of evil in Christian theology is the concept of free will. God, in His goodness, created human beings with the capacity for free will—the ability to choose between good and evil. This freedom is an essential aspect of what it means to be made in the image of God (imago Dei) and reflects God's desire for a genuine relationship with His creatures.

However, the gift of free will also carries the possibility of choosing against God's will, which is what happened in the Fall. Adam and Eve's disobedience was an exercise of their free will, but it resulted in the introduction of sin and evil into the world. This perspective suggests that evil is not something God created but something that arose as a consequence of the misuse of human freedom.

While free will accounts for the presence of moral evil—evil that results from human actions—it also raises questions about natural evil, such as natural disasters and diseases, which are not directly caused by human choices. Some theologians argue that natural evil is a consequence of the Fall, with the corruption of human nature extending to the natural world. Others suggest that natural evil is part of the mystery of creation, existing within the parameters of a world that is still good but incomplete and awaiting its final redemption.

The Role of Satan and Demonic Forces

Another aspect of the theological reflection on the origin of evil involves the role of Satan and demonic forces. The Bible presents Satan as a fallen angel who rebelled against God and now works to oppose God's purposes and to lead humanity into sin. This understanding is rooted in passages like Isaiah 14:12-15, Ezekiel 28:12-17, and Revelation 12:7-9, which describe the fall of a powerful angelic being and his subsequent role as the adversary of God.

In this view, Satan and his demons are seen as agents of evil who seek to corrupt and destroy God's good creation. While they have significant influence in the world, they are not equal to God and do not possess the power to create. Instead, their power is parasitic, relying on the corruption and perversion of what is good.

The presence of Satan and demonic forces in the world complicates the problem of evil, as it introduces the idea of spiritual warfare between the forces of good and evil. However, the doctrine of Creation Ex Nihilo ensures that God remains sovereign over all things, including the forces of evil. Satan and his demons, while powerful, are ultimately creatures who exist only because God created them, and they are subject to God's final judgment.

Theodicy: Reconciling the Existence of God with the Presence of Evil

Theodicy is the theological endeavor to reconcile the existence of a good and omnipotent God with the presence of evil and suffering in the world. The doctrine of Creation Ex Nihilo plays a crucial role in various theodicies by providing a framework for understanding the nature of evil, the purpose of suffering, and God's response to both.

The Greater Good Theodicy

One approach to theodicy is the Greater Good Theodicy, which argues that God allows evil and suffering in the world because they serve a greater purpose that contributes to the ultimate good of creation. This perspective suggests that certain goods—such as the development of virtue, the deepening of faith, or the demonstration of God's justice and mercy—can only arise in a world where evil and suffering are possible.

Creation Ex Nihilo supports this theodicy by emphasizing that God's creation is purposeful and directed toward an ultimate end. Since God is sovereign and omnipotent, He is able to bring about His purposes even in the midst of evil and suffering. This perspective is reflected in Romans 8:28, where Paul writes, "And we know that in all things God works for the good of those who love him, who have been called according to his purpose."

While the Greater Good Theodicy offers a way to understand the presence of evil and suffering, it also raises challenging questions about the nature and extent of suffering in the world. Critics of this theodicy argue that it can sometimes seem to justify or trivialize suffering by suggesting that it is necessary for a greater good. However, proponents maintain that this perspective does not deny the reality of suffering but rather affirms that God is at work to bring about redemption and healing, even in the darkest situations.

The Soul-Making Theodicy

Another approach to theodicy is the Soul-Making Theodicy, which builds on the idea that evil and suffering are necessary for the development of moral and spiritual virtues. According to this view, the world is a "vale of soul-making," where human beings are given the opportunity to grow in character, wisdom, and love through their experiences of suffering and struggle.

This theodicy is often associated with the writings of Irenaeus, an early Church Father, and has been developed by modern theologians like John Hick. The Soul-Making Theodicy suggests that a world without challenges, difficulties, or the possibility of failure would not allow for the development of meaningful virtues like courage, compassion, and perseverance.

Creation Ex Nihilo undergirds this theodicy by affirming that God created the world with a purpose, and that purpose includes the moral and spiritual growth of human beings. The presence of evil and suffering is not a sign of God's failure or indifference but is part of the process through which human souls are refined and brought to maturity.

However, like the Greater Good Theodicy, the Soul-Making Theodicy faces criticisms, particularly concerning the extent and intensity of suffering in the world. Critics question whether the amount of suffering experienced by individuals and communities is truly necessary for soul-making or whether it challenges the idea of a benevolent Creator. Nevertheless, this theodicy provides a framework for understanding how suffering can contribute to personal and spiritual growth.

God's Response to Evil and

Suffering: The Cross and Resurrection

The Christian understanding of God's relationship to evil and suffering is ultimately centered on the person and work of Jesus Christ. The doctrine of Creation Ex Nihilo emphasizes that the God who created the universe out of nothing is the same God who entered into the created order to address the problem of evil and suffering through the Incarnation, Crucifixion, and Resurrection.

The Incarnation: God's Identification with Suffering

The doctrine of the Incarnation holds that God the Son took on human flesh and entered into the world as Jesus Christ. This act of divine condescension is a profound expression of God's solidarity with human suffering. In Jesus,

God experiences the full range of human suffering, including physical pain, emotional anguish, and spiritual desolation.

Isaiah 53:3-4, a passage often associated with the Suffering Servant, captures this identification with suffering: "He was despised and rejected by men, a man of sorrows and acquainted with grief; and as one from whom men hide their faces he was despised, and we esteemed him not. Surely he has borne our griefs and carried our sorrows; yet we esteemed him stricken, smitten by God, and afflicted."

The Incarnation demonstrates that God is not distant or detached from the realities of evil and suffering. Instead, He enters into the depths of human suffering, taking it upon Himself in order to bring about redemption. This identification with suffering is central to the Christian response to the problem of evil, as it reveals a God who is deeply involved in the struggles of His creation.

The Crucifixion: The Defeat of Evil

The Crucifixion of Jesus Christ is the focal point of God's response to evil. On the cross, Jesus bears the weight of sin and evil, taking upon Himself the consequences of humanity's rebellion against God. The cross represents the ultimate confrontation between good and evil, with Jesus willingly enduring suffering and death in order to overcome the powers of darkness.

Colossians 2:15 describes the victory of the cross: "He disarmed the rulers and authorities and put them to open shame, by triumphing over them in him." The cross is not only an act of atonement for sin but also a decisive victory over the forces of evil that have corrupted God's good creation.

Creation Ex Nihilo provides the backdrop for understanding the significance of the cross. Just as God created the universe out of nothing, He is able to bring about new creation through the sacrificial death of Jesus. The cross reveals that God's power is not limited by the presence of evil but is able to transform and redeem even the darkest aspects of creation.

The Resurrection: The Triumph of Life Over Death

The Resurrection of Jesus Christ is the culmination of God's response to evil and suffering. It is the ultimate demonstration of God's power to bring life out of death, and it serves as the guarantee of the final victory over evil. The Resurrection affirms that death, suffering, and evil do not have the final word; instead, they are defeated by the power of God's life-giving love.

1 Corinthians 15:54-57 captures the significance of the Resurrection: "When the perishable puts on the imperishable, and the mortal puts on immortality, then shall come to pass

the saying that is written: 'Death is swallowed up in victory. O death, where is your victory? O death, where is your sting?' The sting of death is sin, and the power of sin is the law. But thanks be to God, who gives us the victory through our Lord Jesus Christ."

Creation Ex Nihilo emphasizes that the God who created the universe out of nothing is also the God who brings about new creation through the Resurrection. The Resurrection is the firstfruits of the new creation, pointing to the ultimate restoration of all things when God will make all things new.

The Resurrection also provides hope and meaning in the face of suffering. It assures believers that their suffering is not in vain and that, through faith in Christ, they will share in the victory of the Resurrection. This hope sustains Christians as they navigate the challenges of life in a fallen world, confident in the promise of eternal life and the final defeat of evil.

The Eschatological Hope: The End of Evil and Suffering

The Christian hope is ultimately eschatological, looking forward to the time when God will bring about the full realization of His kingdom, where evil and suffering will be no more. This hope is rooted in the doctrine of Creation

Ex Nihilo, which affirms that God has the power to bring about the renewal of all things.

The New Creation

The eschatological hope of Christianity is the promise of a new creation, where God will restore the world to its intended state of goodness and wholeness. Revelation 21:1-4 describes this new creation: "Then I saw a new heaven and a new earth, for the first heaven and the first earth had passed away, and the sea was no more. And I saw the holy city, new Jerusalem, coming down out of heaven from God, prepared as a bride adorned for her husband. And I heard a loud voice from the throne saying, 'Behold, the dwelling place of God is with man. He will dwell with them, and they will be his people, and God himself will be with them as their God. He will wipe away every tear from their eyes, and death shall be no more, neither shall there be mourning, nor crying, nor pain anymore, for the former things have passed away.'"

Creation Ex Nihilo supports this eschatological vision by affirming that the same God who created the world out of nothing will also bring about its renewal. The new creation is not a replacement for the old but its fulfillment and transformation. In the new creation, evil and suffering will be eradicated, and God's original purpose for creation will be fully realized.

The Final Judgment

The eschatological hope also includes the promise of final judgment, where God will bring justice to the world by judging evil and vindicating the righteous. This judgment is a necessary part of the Christian understanding of the end of evil, as it affirms that God will hold accountable those who perpetrate evil and will establish His righteousness in the world.

Matthew 25:31-34, 41-46 describes the final judgment: "When the Son of Man comes in his glory, and all the angels with him, then he will sit on his glorious throne. Before him will be gathered all the nations, and he will separate people one from another as a shepherd separates the sheep from the goats. And he will place the sheep on his right, but the goats on the left. Then the King will say to those on his right, 'Come, you who are blessed by my Father, inherit the kingdom prepared for you from the foundation of the world.'... Then he will say to those on his left, 'Depart from me, you cursed, into the eternal fire prepared for the devil and his angels.'"

Creation Ex Nihilo underscores the finality and authority of God's judgment. As the Creator of all things, God has the right and the power to judge His creation. The final judgment is not arbitrary but is based on God's perfect justice and knowledge. It assures believers that evil will not go unpunished and that God's righteousness will ultimately prevail.

Living in Light of Creation Ex Nihilo: The Christian Response to Evil and Suffering

The doctrine of Creation Ex Nihilo not only provides theological explanations for the presence of evil and suffering but also shapes the Christian response to these realities. Christians are called to live in light of the truths revealed by this doctrine, responding to evil and suffering with faith, hope, and love.

Faith in God's Sovereignty

The doctrine of Creation Ex Nihilo calls Christians to trust in God's sovereignty, even in the midst of evil and suffering. Since God created the universe out of nothing, He is in control of all things, including the forces of evil. This faith in God's sovereignty provides a foundation for enduring suffering with patience and confidence, knowing that God is ultimately working for good.

Hope in the Resurrection and New Creation

The Christian response to evil and suffering is also characterized by hope—hope in the resurrection and the promise of new creation. The belief that God has defeated evil through the death and resurrection of Jesus Christ, and that He will ultimately restore all things, gives believers the strength to persevere through suffering and to look forward to the fulfillment of God's redemptive plan.

Love and Compassion in a Broken World

Finally, the doctrine of Creation Ex Nihilo calls Christians to respond to evil and suffering with love and compassion. Just as God entered into the suffering of the world through the Incarnation, Christians are called to be agents of God's love in the midst of a broken and suffering world. This includes acts of mercy, justice, and service, as well as efforts to alleviate suffering and to stand against evil in all its forms.

The doctrine of Creation Ex Nihilo has profound theological implications for understanding evil and suffering. It affirms the goodness of creation, the corruption of that goodness through sin, and God's redemptive response to evil through the person and work of Jesus Christ. It provides a framework for theodicy, offering explanations for the presence of evil and suffering while maintaining faith in God's sovereignty and goodness.

Ultimately, Creation Ex Nihilo points to the eschatological hope of new creation, where evil and suffering will be no more, and God's purposes for creation will be fully realized. In the meantime, Christians are called to live in light of this doctrine, responding to evil and suffering with faith, hope, and love, and participating in God's redemptive work in the world.

CHAPTER 05

PHILOSOPHICAL UNDERPINNINGS

Historical Origins of the Concept of Creation Ex Nihilo

The concept of Creation Ex Nihilo—the idea that the universe was created out of nothing by a divine being—has deep philosophical roots that extend far beyond its formal adoption in Christian theology. The historical origins of this concept are intertwined with ancient cosmological and metaphysical debates, as well as the religious and philosophical traditions that shaped early human thought about the nature of existence, the divine, and the universe. This chapter will explore the historical origins of the concept of Creation Ex Nihilo, tracing its development from ancient cosmologies to its crystallization in early Christian thought, and examining the philosophical influences that contributed to its emergence.

Ancient Cosmologies and Creation Myths

Long before the formalization of the doctrine of Creation Ex Nihilo, ancient cultures developed various cosmologies—systems of thought that explained the origin and structure of the universe. These cosmologies often reflected the religious and philosophical beliefs of their respective cultures, providing a framework for understanding the relationship between the divine and the world.

Mesopotamian Cosmology: Creation from Chaos

One of the earliest and most influential cosmological systems emerged in Mesopotamia, particularly in the region between the Tigris and Euphrates rivers. The Mesopotamian creation myths, such as the Enuma Elish, offer a view of the universe that begins with a primordial chaos. In these myths, the gods are depicted as organizing and bringing order to this chaotic substance, rather than creating the world out of nothing.

The Enuma Elish, for example, describes the god Marduk's victory over the chaos monster Tiamat, after which he uses her divided body to create the heavens and the earth. This narrative reflects a common ancient Near Eastern theme of creation as the imposition of order on pre-existing chaos, rather than an act of creation from absolute nothingness.

This Mesopotamian view of creation from chaos (often termed creation ex materia) would later stand in contrast to the emerging concept of Creation Ex Nihilo. However, it is important to recognize that these early myths laid the groundwork for later philosophical discussions about the nature of creation, matter, and the divine.

Egyptian and Greek Cosmologies: Creation and Eternal Matter

In ancient Egypt, creation myths similarly emphasized the emergence of order from a primordial, chaotic substance. The Egyptian god Atum, for instance, is said to have arisen from the waters of chaos (Nun) and to have created the world through an act of self-generation. Here, too, the emphasis is on the organization of pre-existing matter rather than creation from nothing.

In ancient Greece, the philosophical approach to cosmology began to diverge from mythological narratives, leading to more abstract considerations of the nature of matter and creation. The pre-Socratic philosophers, such as Thales, Anaximander, and Heraclitus, offered various theories about the fundamental substance or principle (archê) from which the cosmos emerged. While these early thinkers did not articulate a concept of creation from nothing, their ideas laid the groundwork for later metaphysical discussions.

One of the most influential Greek thinkers in this regard was Plato, whose work in the Timaeus presents a cosmological model where the Demiurge, a divine craftsman, orders the cosmos from pre-existing chaotic matter. Plato's view, known as creation ex materia, posits that while the material world is shaped and ordered by the Demiurge, it is not created out of nothing. Instead, the material world is an imperfect reflection of the eternal Forms, which are the true reality.

Plato's ideas would later influence both Jewish and Christian thought, particularly in the development of concepts related to the creation and the nature of the material world. However, it is crucial to note that Plato's emphasis on eternal matter and the distinction between the material world and the realm of Forms marked a significant departure from the notion of creation from absolute nothingness.

Jewish Thought and the Emergence of Creation Ex Nihilo

The concept of Creation Ex Nihilo began to take shape within the context of Jewish thought, particularly during the Hellenistic period. Jewish theologians and philosophers, influenced by both their own religious traditions and the surrounding Greek culture, began to develop ideas about the nature of God's creative power and the origins of the universe.

The Hebrew Bible: Creation in Genesis

The Hebrew Bible, particularly the book of Genesis, provides the foundational text for the Jewish and later Christian understanding of creation. The opening verse of Genesis, "In the beginning, God created the heavens and the earth" (Genesis 1:1), has been the subject of extensive interpretation and debate throughout history.

While Genesis 1 does not explicitly state that God created the world out of nothing, it emphasizes God's sovereign power over creation. The text describes God speaking the world into existence, bringing order out of chaos through His divine word. This act of creation by divine command suggests a level of authority and power that would later be interpreted as consistent with the idea of Creation Ex Nihilo.

Some scholars argue that the Genesis creation narrative reflects an implicit assumption of pre-existing chaotic matter (the "deep" or "waters" mentioned in Genesis 1:2). However, others contend that the text's emphasis on God's sovereignty and the absence of any rival powers or materials in the creation process point toward a proto-concept of Creation Ex Nihilo.

Second Temple Judaism and Hellenistic Influence

During the Second Temple period (roughly 516 BCE to 70 CE), Jewish thought was increasingly influenced by Hellenistic philosophy, particularly the ideas of Plato and other Greek thinkers. This period saw the development of various Jewish texts, including the Septuagint (the Greek translation of the Hebrew Bible) and the writings of Philo of Alexandria, that reflect a synthesis of Jewish theological concepts with Greek philosophical ideas.

Philo of Alexandria (c. 20 BCE – 50 CE) was a Hellenistic Jewish philosopher who sought to harmonize the teachings of the Hebrew Bible with Greek philosophy. In his writings, Philo emphasizes the transcendence and ineffability of God, and he interprets the Genesis creation account in a way that aligns with Platonic metaphysics. However, Philo also introduces the idea of God as the ultimate source of all being, a concept that begins to move closer to the notion of Creation Ex Nihilo.

Philo's emphasis on God as the source of all existence, combined with the Jewish monotheistic belief in a singular, all-powerful Creator, set the stage for the later development of Creation Ex Nihilo as a fully articulated doctrine. While

Philo himself did not explicitly teach Creation Ex Nihilo, his ideas about God's creative power and the nature of existence influenced subsequent Jewish and Christian thought.

The Apocryphal and Pseudepigraphal Writings

In addition to the writings of Philo, other Jewish texts from the Second Temple period, including the Apocryphal and Pseudepigraphal writings, also reflect evolving ideas about creation. These texts, though not considered canonical by all Jewish or Christian traditions, provide valuable insights into the development of theological concepts during this period.

For example, the Book of 2 Maccabees (written in the 2nd century BCE) contains a passage in which a mother encourages her son to trust in God's creative power, saying, "I beseech you, my child, to look at the heaven and the earth and see everything that is in them, and recognize that God did not make them out of things that existed" (2 Maccabees 7:28). This statement is one of the earliest explicit references to the idea of Creation Ex Nihilo in Jewish literature, indicating that the concept was gaining traction in certain circles.

These texts suggest that by the time of the Second Temple period, the idea of God creating the world out of nothing was becoming an increasingly accepted and articulated belief within some strands of Jewish thought. This development laid the groundwork for the concept's adoption and further elaboration in early Christian theology.

Early Christian Thought and the Formalization of Creation Ex Nihilo

The concept of Creation Ex Nihilo was fully formalized and adopted as a central doctrine within early Christian theology. This development was influenced by both the Jewish theological heritage and the intellectual climate of the Greco-Roman world, where Christianity emerged and spread.

The New Testament and Early Christian Writings

The New Testament, while not offering a systematic exposition of the doctrine of Creation Ex Nihilo, contains passages that strongly support the concept. For example, the Gospel of John opens with a cosmic vision of creation: "In the beginning was the Word, and the Word was with God, and the Word was God. He was in the beginning with God. All things were made through him, and without him was not anything made that was made" (John 1:1-3).

This passage emphasizes the pre-existence of the Word (Logos) and its role in creation, aligning with the idea that everything that exists was brought into being through divine action. Similarly, the epistle to the Hebrews states, "By faith we understand that the universe was created by the word of God, so that what is seen was not made out of things that are visible" (Hebrews 11:3). This statement strongly suggests a belief in Creation Ex Nihilo, indicating that the material world was not fashioned from pre-existing materials.

Early Christian writers, known as the Church Fathers, further developed and defended the doctrine of Creation Ex Nihilo in response to various theological and philosophical challenges. These challenges included Gnostic and Platonic ideas that posited an eternal dualism between the spiritual and material worlds, as well as alternative creation theories that suggested the pre-existence of matter.

The Church Fathers and the Defense of Creation Ex Nihilo

One of the earliest and most influential Christian theologians to articulate and defend the doctrine of Creation Ex Nihilo was Irenaeus of Lyons

(c. 130–202 CE). In his work Against Heresies, Irenaeus argues against the Gnostic belief that the material world was created by a lesser, inferior god out of pre-existing matter. Instead, Irenaeus insists that the one true God, who is both all-powerful and all-good, created the universe out of nothing.

Irenaeus' defense of Creation Ex Nihilo is rooted in his belief in the goodness of creation and the sovereignty of

God. By affirming that God created everything out of nothing, Irenaeus emphasizes that the material world is not inherently evil, as the Gnostics claimed, but is a good creation that reflects the nature of its Creator. This view became a cornerstone of orthodox Christian theology.

Another key figure in the development of the doctrine was Tertullian (c. 160–225 CE), a North African theologian who also opposed Gnostic and Platonic ideas. In his writings, Tertullian explicitly affirms Creation Ex Nihilo, arguing that God's ability to create out of nothing is a fundamental aspect of His omnipotence. Tertullian's work helped to further establish the doctrine as a central tenet of Christian belief.

The doctrine of Creation Ex Nihilo was later formalized in the creeds and confessions of the early Church, including the Nicene Creed (325 CE), which states, "We believe in one God, the Father Almighty, Maker of heaven and earth, and of all things visible and invisible." This creedal statement reflects the belief that God is the sole Creator of all that exists, both material and immaterial, and that He brought the universe into existence from nothing.

Philosophical Influences on the Concept of Creation Ex Nihilo

While the doctrine of Creation Ex Nihilo was primarily shaped by theological concerns, it was also influenced by the philosophical traditions of the ancient world. These influences helped to refine and articulate the concept, particularly in response to competing ideas about the nature of matter, creation, and the divine.

The Influence of Middle Platonism

Middle Platonism, a philosophical movement that emerged in the 1st century BCE and continued into the early Christian era, played a significant role in shaping early Christian thought about creation. Middle Platonists, like their predecessors, emphasized the existence of an eternal realm of Forms or Ideas, but they also introduced the concept of a divine Logos or Reason that mediated between the transcendent realm and the material world.

Christian theologians, including the author of the Gospel of John and early Church Fathers like Justin Martyr, adopted and adapted the concept of the Logos to describe the pre-existent Christ as the divine agent of creation. This adaptation allowed them to articulate a Christian understanding of creation that affirmed both the transcendence of God and His immanence in the world through the Logos.

However, Christian thinkers departed from Middle Platonism by rejecting the idea that matter was eternal. Instead, they insisted that God created matter itself out of nothing, a belief that distinguished Christian theology from both Platonic and Gnostic thought.

The Challenge of Greek Philosophy and the Development of Christian Metaphysics

The emergence of Creation Ex Nihilo also represented a significant departure from the prevailing Greek philosophical view that matter was eternal. For Greek philosophers like Plato and Aristotle, the idea that matter had always existed was a fundamental assumption that underpinned their metaphysical systems.

Plato, as mentioned earlier, proposed that the material world was formed from pre-existing chaotic matter by a divine craftsman (Demiurge), who imposed order on it according to the eternal Forms. Aristotle, while differing from Plato in many respects, also assumed the eternity of matter and posited that the universe was eternal, with no beginning in time.

Christian theologians, in developing the doctrine of Creation Ex Nihilo, challenged these assumptions by asserting that God's creative power extended to the very existence of matter itself. This assertion required the development of a new metaphysical framework that could account for the creation of the universe from nothing—a framework that emphasized the absolute dependence of all created things on God's will and power.

In this context, Christian thinkers began to explore the nature of existence, causality, and the relationship between the Creator and the created order. These explorations laid the groundwork for the later development of Christian metaphysics, particularly in the works of theologians like Augustine and Thomas Aquinas, who further articulated the philosophical underpinnings of Creation Ex Nihilo.

Conclusion: The Historical Evolution of Creation Ex Nihilo

The concept of Creation Ex Nihilo did not emerge fully formed but developed gradually over centuries of philosophical and theological reflection. Its historical origins can be traced to ancient cosmologies that emphasized the organization of pre-existing matter, but it was within the context of Jewish and early Christian thought that the idea of creation from nothing began to take shape.

Influenced by both religious traditions and philosophical ideas, early Christian theologians formalized the doctrine of Creation Ex Nihilo as a central tenet of Christian faith. This doctrine represented a significant departure from the prevailing Greek philosophical view of eternal matter and laid the foundation for a distinctively Christian understanding of creation, divine sovereignty, and the nature of existence.

As we continue to explore the philosophical perspectives on Creation Ex Nihilo, it is important to recognize that this concept has not only shaped theological discourse but has also had a profound impact on the development of Western metaphysics and cosmology. The historical origins of Creation Ex Nihilo reveal the complex interplay between religion and philosophy in the formation of one of the most fundamental doctrines of the Christian faith.

Philosophical Underpinnings

Influences from Greek and Roman Philosophy

The concept of Creation Ex Nihilo—the idea that the universe was created out of nothing by a divine being—did not develop in isolation but was profoundly shaped by the philosophical traditions of the ancient Greek and Roman worlds. These intellectual traditions provided the context in which early Christian thinkers articulated and defended the doctrine, responding to and interacting with the prevailing metaphysical and cosmological ideas of their time. This chapter explores the significant influences of Greek and Roman philosophy on the development of the concept of Creation Ex Nihilo, focusing on key philosophical schools, thinkers, and ideas that played a crucial role in shaping early Christian thought.

Platonic Philosophy and the Eternal Forms

One of the most influential philosophical systems that interacted with early Christian thought was Platonism, particularly the ideas articulated by Plato and his followers. Plato's philosophy, as expounded in dialogues such as Timaeus and Republic, introduced a dualistic worldview that distinguished between the eternal, unchanging realm of Forms (or Ideas) and the temporal, mutable world of material objects.

The Realm of Forms and the Demiurge

In Plato's Timaeus, the Demiurge (a divine craftsman) creates the cosmos by imposing order on pre-existing chaotic matter, using the eternal Forms as the perfect models or templates. This cosmology posits that while the Demiurge shapes the material world, the Forms are the true reality, existing independently of both the Demiurge and the material world. The material world, in turn, is seen as an imperfect and transient reflection of the eternal Forms.

This Platonic dualism had a profound impact on early Christian thought, particularly in how it framed discussions about the relationship between the material and the spiritual, the eternal and the temporal. However, while Christian thinkers were influenced by Plato's emphasis on the transcendence and perfection of the divine, they diverged significantly from his ideas about the nature of matter and creation.

The Influence of Middle Platonism

During the Hellenistic period, Plato's ideas were further developed and systematized by Middle Platonists, such as Philo of Alexandria, Albinus, and Plutarch. Middle Platonism emphasized the transcendence of the divine and introduced the concept of the Logos—a rational principle that orders the cosmos and mediates between the divine and the material world. Philo of Alexandria, a Jewish philosopher deeply influenced by Platonic thought, integrated the concept of the Logos into his interpretation of the Hebrew Scriptures, identifying the Logos with the divine wisdom that created and sustains the world.

Christian thinkers, particularly the author of the Gospel of John, adapted this concept of the Logos to express the Christian understanding of Christ as the divine Word through whom all things were created. In John 1:1-3, the Logos is identified with Christ, who is both the agent of creation and the embodiment of divine reason and wisdom: "In the beginning was the Word, and the Word was with God, and the Word was God. All things were made through him, and without him was not anything made that was made."

While Middle Platonism provided a conceptual framework for articulating the role of the Logos in creation, early Christian theologians diverged from Platonic thought by rejecting the idea of pre-existing matter. Instead, they affirmed that the Logos, as the divine Word, created the universe out of nothing, thereby introducing a fundamental departure from Platonic cosmology.

Aristotelian Philosophy and the Unmoved Mover

Aristotle, a student of Plato, developed a philosophical system that differed significantly from his teacher's ideas, particularly in his understanding of metaphysics and cosmology. Aristotle's philosophy, as outlined in works such as Metaphysics and Physics, emphasized the importance of empirical observation and the analysis of causes in explaining the natural world.

The Concept of the Unmoved Mover

In Aristotle's metaphysics, the concept of the Unmoved Mover (or Prime Mover) plays a central role. The Unmoved Mover is the ultimate cause of motion and change in the universe, but it is itself unchanging and immaterial. Aristotle describes the Unmoved Mover as a purely actual being, existing in a state of perfect actuality without potentiality, and as the final cause that all things in the universe seek to emulate.

Aristotle's Unmoved Mover is often understood as a purely intellectual entity that contemplates itself and does not engage directly with the material world. Unlike the Platonic Demiurge, the Unmoved Mover does not create the universe but serves as the ultimate source of motion and order. The universe, in Aristotle's view, is eternal and uncreated, existing alongside the Unmoved Mover as an eternal cosmos without a beginning in time.

The Influence of Aristotelian Thought on Early Christian Theology

While Aristotelian philosophy was initially less influential in early Christian thought compared to Platonism, it later became a significant intellectual force, particularly through the work of medieval scholastic theologians such as Thomas Aquinas. Aquinas, in his synthesis of Christian theology and Aristotelian philosophy, adapted the concept of the Unmoved Mover to support the doctrine of Creation Ex Nihilo.

Aquinas argued that God, as the Unmoved Mover, is the first cause of all things, not only in terms of motion but also in terms of existence. While Aristotle viewed the cosmos as eternal, Aquinas posited that the universe had a beginning and was brought into existence by God's creative will. This creative act, Aquinas argued, was an exercise of God's omnipotence, bringing the universe into existence from nothing.

By integrating Aristotelian metaphysics with Christian doctrine, Aquinas provided a robust philosophical defense of Creation Ex Nihilo, arguing that the existence of the universe is contingent upon God's creative will. This synthesis helped to solidify the concept of Creation Ex Nihilo within the framework of Christian metaphysics and cosmology.

Stoicism and the Immanent Divine

Stoicism, a Hellenistic philosophy that emerged in the early 3rd century BCE, offered a distinct perspective on the nature of the divine and the cosmos. Founded by Zeno of Citium, Stoicism emphasized the immanence of the divine in the material world and the idea that the universe is governed by a rational principle known as the Logos.

The Stoic Concept of the Logos

In Stoic thought, the Logos is understood as the rational and ordering principle that permeates the entire cosmos. Unlike the Platonic and Christian Logos, which is often associated with a transcendent, personal deity, the Stoic Logos is more closely associated with the rational structure of the universe itself. The Stoics believed that the universe was a living organism, imbued with the divine Logos, which ensured the harmony and order of all things.

Stoicism also emphasized the concept of pneuma (spirit or breath), which was seen as the life-giving force that animates all living beings and binds the cosmos together. This immanentist view of the divine contrasted with the more transcendent perspectives found in Platonism and early Christianity.

Stoicism's Influence on Early Christian Thought

While Stoicism's emphasis on the immanence of the divine differed from the Christian understanding of a transcendent Creator, elements of Stoic thought did influence early Christian theology. The Stoic concept of the Logos, for example, was adapted by early Christian writers to articulate the idea of Christ as the divine Word that both transcends and immanently orders the universe.

However, early Christian theologians also distinguished their views from Stoicism by affirming the personal nature of the Logos and the doctrine of Creation Ex Nihilo. Unlike the Stoics, who believed in an eternal cosmos governed by an immanent Logos, Christians asserted that the universe was created by a transcendent God who brought it into existence out of nothing.

The Christian adaptation of Stoic ideas, therefore, involved a significant re-interpretation of key concepts to fit within the framework of a theistic worldview that emphasized both the transcendence and immanence of God.

Epicureanism and the Rejection of Divine Creation

Epicureanism, founded by Epicurus in the late 4th century BCE, offered a materialistic and atomistic view of the universe that rejected the idea of divine creation. Epicurus and his followers believed that the universe was composed of indivisible particles called atoms, which moved through the void and combined to form all material objects.

The Materialistic Worldview of Epicureanism

Epicureans posited that the universe was eternal and uncreated, with no need for a divine creator. They argued that the motion and interaction of atoms were sufficient to explain the formation and dissolution of all things in the cosmos. Epicureanism also rejected the notion of divine intervention in the world, emphasizing that the gods, if they existed, were indifferent to human affairs and had no role in the creation or governance of the universe.

The Epicurean worldview was fundamentally at odds with the Christian doctrine of Creation Ex Nihilo, as it denied both the existence of a divine creator and the idea that the universe had a beginning in time. Epicureanism represented a challenge to theistic worldviews by offering a naturalistic explanation of the cosmos that did not rely on divine agency.

The Christian Response to Epicureanism

Early Christian theologians, particularly those engaged in apologetics, responded to the materialistic and atheistic implications of Epicureanism by affirming the doctrine of Creation Ex Nihilo. They argued that the existence of the universe and the order within it could not be adequately explained by random atomic motion but required the intentional action of a divine creator.

Christian apologists, such as Tertullian and Augustine, criticized the Epicurean rejection of divine providence and emphasized the importance of a theistic worldview that recognized God's active role in both creating and sustaining the universe. Augustine, in particular, argued that the existence of the universe and its contingent nature pointed to the necessity of a creator who brought it into being from nothing.

The rejection of Epicurean materialism became a key component of Christian apologetics, as theologians sought to defend the doctrine of Creation Ex Nihilo against naturalistic and atheistic explanations of the cosmos.

Neoplatonism and the Emanation of the One

Neoplatonism, a philosophical system that emerged in the 3rd century CE, represented a significant development in Platonic thought and had a profound influence on early Christian theology. Founded by Plotinus and further developed by philosophers such as Porphyry and Proclus, Neoplatonism offered a metaphysical system that emphasized the emanation of all reality from a single, transcendent source known as the One.

The Emanation of the One

In Neoplatonism, the One is the ultimate, ineffable principle that transcends all being and thought. From the One emanates the Nous (Divine Intellect), which in turn gives rise to the World Soul, and finally to the material world. This process of emanation is seen as a gradual descent from the perfect unity of the One to the multiplicity and imperfection of the material world.

Neoplatonism posits that the material world is a distant reflection of the divine, with each level of reality becoming progressively less perfect as it moves further from the One. While the material world is seen as a necessary consequence of the emanative process, it is not considered to be created in the same sense as in Christian theology.

Neoplatonism's Influence on Christian Thought

Neoplatonism had a significant impact on early Christian theology, particularly in its emphasis on the transcendence of the divine and the hierarchical structure of reality. Christian theologians, such as Augustine and Pseudo-Dionysius the Areopagite, were influenced by Neoplatonic ideas, particularly in their understanding of the relationship between God and creation.

However, while Neoplatonism provided valuable metaphysical concepts for Christian thinkers, there were important differences between the two systems. Unlike the Neoplatonic concept of emanation, which suggests a necessary outflow from the One, the Christian doctrine of Creation Ex Nihilo asserts that God freely and intentionally created the universe out of nothing. This creation is not a necessary consequence of God's nature but an act of divine will.

Christian theologians adapted Neoplatonic ideas to fit within the framework of Creation Ex Nihilo, emphasizing that while all things ultimately depend on God, they do so by virtue of God's creative act rather than through a process of emanation. This adaptation allowed Christian thinkers to maintain the transcendence and sovereignty of God while also affirming the goodness and purposefulness of creation.

Conclusion: The Synthesis of Greek and Roman Philosophy with Christian Theology

The development of the concept of Creation Ex Nihilo was deeply influenced by the philosophical traditions of the ancient Greek and Roman worlds. Early Christian theologians engaged with the ideas of Platonism, Aristotelianism, Stoicism, Epicureanism, and Neoplatonism, adapting and reinterpreting these philosophies to articulate a distinctively Christian understanding of creation, the divine, and the cosmos.

While these philosophical systems provided valuable insights and conceptual tools, early Christian thinkers also departed from them in significant ways, particularly in their rejection of the eternity of matter and the affirmation of a transcendent Creator who brought the universe into existence out of nothing. The synthesis of these philosophical influences with Christian theology resulted in a robust and coherent doctrine of Creation Ex Nihilo, which became a central tenet of Christian faith.

As we continue to explore the philosophical perspectives on Creation Ex Nihilo, it is important to recognize the complex and dynamic interplay between Greek and Roman philosophy and early Christian thought. This interplay not only shaped the development of Christian doctrine but also contributed to the broader intellectual tradition that has influenced Western metaphysics, cosmology, and theology for centuries.

Philosophical Underpinnings

Key Philosophical Arguments For and Against Creation Ex Nihilo

The doctrine of Creation Ex Nihilo—the belief that God created the universe out of nothing—has been the subject of extensive philosophical debate throughout history. This chapter explores the key philosophical arguments that have been advanced both in favor of and against the concept of Creation Ex Nihilo, examining how these arguments have shaped the understanding of the doctrine and its implications for metaphysics, theology, and cosmology.

Arguments in Favor of Creation Ex Nihilo

Proponents of Creation Ex Nihilo have advanced several philosophical arguments to support the idea that the universe was brought into existence by a divine being without the use of pre-existing materials. These arguments often appeal to the nature of divine omnipotence, the contingency of the universe, and the logical coherence of creation from nothing.

The Argument from Divine Omnipotence

One of the most important philosophical arguments in favor of Creation Ex Nihilo is based on the concept of divine omnipotence. According to this argument, if God is truly omnipotent—that is, all-powerful—then He must have the ability to create the universe out of nothing. The creation of the universe from nothing is seen as the ultimate demonstration of God's power, as it requires the ability to bring something into existence without any reliance on external materials or conditions.

This argument is grounded in the traditional theological understanding of God as the Creator who is sovereign over all things. Since God is not limited by anything outside of Himself, He has the power to create the universe simply by an act of will. The doctrine of Creation Ex Nihilo, therefore, affirms that God's omnipotence extends to the very act of creation, and that there are no constraints on His creative power.

This view is reflected in the writings of early Christian theologians like Augustine, who argued that Creation Ex Nihilo is necessary to maintain the integrity of divine omnipotence. Augustine emphasized that if God needed pre-existing materials to create the universe, His power would be limited and dependent on something outside of Himself. By affirming Creation Ex Nihilo, Augustine sought to uphold the belief in a God who is truly sovereign and independent.

The Argument from the Contingency of the Universe

Another key argument in favor of Creation Ex Nihilo is based on the contingency of the universe. This argument posits that the universe is not a necessary being but a contingent one, meaning that it could have been otherwise or might not have existed at all. The contingency of the universe implies that it depends on something outside of itself for its existence—namely, a necessary being that is the cause of its existence.

In this view, the universe does not exist by its own nature or necessity; instead, its existence must be explained by an external cause. Proponents of Creation Ex Nihilo argue that this external cause is God, who, as a necessary being, has the power to create the universe out of nothing. The contingency of the universe thus points to the need for a transcendent creator who brings the universe into existence by an act of will.

This argument is closely related to the cosmological argument for the existence of God, which seeks to explain the existence of the universe by positing a first cause or necessary being. The doctrine of Creation Ex Nihilo complements this argument by providing a coherent explanation of how a contingent universe can come into existence—namely, through the creative act of a necessary and omnipotent being.

The Argument from the Logical Coherence of Creation from Nothing

Supporters of Creation Ex Nihilo also argue that the concept is logically coherent and does not involve any contradictions or impossibilities. This argument addresses the concern that creation from nothing might be an inherently self-contradictory idea, since it seems to suggest that something can come from nothing, which might violate basic principles of logic and causality.

Proponents of Creation Ex Nihilo respond to this concern by emphasizing that the doctrine does not assert that something comes from nothing on its own, but rather that something is brought into existence by an all-powerful creator without the use of pre-existing materials. The key idea is that creation from nothing is not an uncaused event, but rather the result of a deliberate and purposeful act by a divine being.

This understanding of Creation Ex Nihilo preserves the principle of causality, as the cause of the universe's existence is God's creative will. The concept of creation from nothing is thus seen as logically coherent when understood in the context of divine causality. Philosophers like Thomas Aquinas have argued that Creation Ex Nihilo is a reasonable and consistent doctrine that aligns with the broader metaphysical principles of causality and the nature of existence.

Arguments Against Creation Ex Nihilo

Critics of Creation Ex Nihilo have raised several philosophical objections to the doctrine, challenging its coherence, its implications for the nature of God, and its compatibility with alternative metaphysical frameworks. These arguments often center on the perceived difficulties of reconciling the concept of creation from nothing with established philosophical principles.

The Argument from the Impossibility of Creation from Nothing

One of the most common philosophical objections to Creation Ex Nihilo is the argument that creation from nothing is impossible or incoherent. Critics argue that the idea of something coming from nothing violates the principle of ex nihilo nihil fit, which means "nothing comes from nothing." This principle is rooted in the idea that existence cannot arise from non-existence, and that every effect must have a cause that is itself something rather than nothing.

According to this objection, the concept of Creation Ex Nihilo implies that the universe emerged from a state of absolute nothingness, which seems to contradict the principle that something cannot come from nothing. Critics argue that if there was truly nothing before the creation of the universe, then there would have been no potentiality for anything to come into existence, making creation from nothing logically impossible.

In response to this objection, defenders of Creation Ex Nihilo argue that the doctrine does not claim that the universe came into existence from nothing in an uncaused or random manner. Instead, they emphasize that the universe was created by God, whose omnipotent will is the cause of the universe's existence. The key point is that "nothing" in this context refers to the absence of pre-existing materials, not the absence of a cause. God's creative act is seen as the sufficient cause of the universe, thereby preserving the principle of causality.

The Argument from the Eternity of Matter

Another philosophical challenge to Creation Ex Nihilo comes from the idea that matter is eternal and uncreated. This argument has its roots in ancient Greek philosophy, particularly in the thought of Plato and Aristotle, who posited that the material world or the underlying substance of the universe had always existed in some form.

According to this view, the universe is eternal and does not require a beginning in time or a creative act to explain its existence. Instead, the cosmos is seen as an eternal and self-sustaining reality, governed by natural laws and principles that have always been in operation. The idea of Creation Ex Nihilo is therefore seen as unnecessary or redundant, as it introduces a divine act of creation where none is needed.

Critics who advocate for the eternity of matter argue that the concept of creation from nothing adds an unnecessary layer of metaphysical complexity to the explanation of the universe's existence. They contend that if the universe can be understood as an eternal, self-sustaining system, there is no need to posit a creator who brings it into existence out of nothing.

In response, proponents of Creation Ex Nihilo argue that the idea of an eternal universe does not adequately explain the contingency and order of the cosmos. They maintain that the universe's existence and the specific arrangement of matter within it require an explanation that goes beyond the mere assumption of eternity. The doctrine of Creation Ex Nihilo provides this explanation by positing a transcendent creator who is the ultimate cause of the universe's existence and order.

The Argument from Divine Immutability and Simplicity

Another philosophical objection to Creation Ex Nihilo involves the implications of the doctrine for the nature of God, particularly in relation to divine immutability and simplicity. According to classical theism, God is understood to be immutable (unchanging) and simple (not composed of parts or subject to division). Critics argue that the concept of Creation Ex Nihilo challenges these attributes by introducing the idea that God undergoes a change or performs a new action—namely, the creation of the universe.

The argument from divine immutability holds that if God creates the universe at a particular point in time, this implies a change in God's state or activity, which seems incompatible with the idea of an immutable being. If God is truly unchanging, critics argue, then the act of creation would either have to be eternal (and thus not an act of creation from nothing) or it would introduce a temporal change in God, which contradicts the doctrine of immutability.

The argument from divine simplicity similarly challenges Creation Ex Nihilo by questioning whether the act of creation involves a division or differentiation within God. Critics argue that if God is simple, then there can be no distinction between God's essence and His actions, which raises questions about how a simple and unchanging being can perform the complex act of creation from nothing.

In response, defenders of Creation Ex Nihilo argue that God's creative act is not a temporal event that introduces change or division within God. Instead, they posit that God's act of creation is an eternal, timeless act that reflects God's will and power without compromising His immutability or simplicity. From this perspective, the creation of the universe is understood as a free and sovereign expression of God's nature, rather than a temporal change in God's state.

Synthesis and Conclusion

The philosophical debates surrounding Creation Ex Nihilo have produced a rich and complex body of arguments both in favor of and against the doctrine. Proponents of Creation Ex Nihilo emphasize the coherence of the concept within the framework of divine omnipotence, the contingency of the universe, and the logical structure of causality. They argue that the doctrine provides a robust explanation for the existence of the universe and upholds the traditional attributes of God as the sovereign Creator.

On the other hand, critics raise significant challenges to Creation Ex Nihilo, questioning its coherence in light of principles such as ex nihilo nihil fit, the eternity of matter, and the implications for divine immutability and simplicity. These objections highlight the philosophical difficulties involved in reconciling the concept of creation from nothing with established metaphysical principles.

Despite these challenges, the doctrine of Creation Ex Nihilo has remained a central tenet of Christian theology, and its philosophical defense has evolved in response to ongoing debates. The synthesis of philosophical arguments for and against Creation Ex Nihilo reflects the dynamic nature of metaphysical inquiry and the enduring importance of this concept in the broader discussion of the nature of existence, causality, and the divine.

As we continue to explore the philosophical perspectives on Creation Ex Nihilo, it is important to recognize that these debates are not merely abstract exercises but have profound implications for how we understand the origin and nature of the universe, the attributes of God, and the relationship between the Creator and creation. The ongoing dialogue between proponents and critics of Creation Ex Nihilo enriches our understanding of these fundamental issues and contributes to the development of a coherent and meaningful worldview.

METAPHYSICAL CONSIDERATIONS

The Concept of Nothingness and Its Philosophical Implications

The concept of nothingness—or the idea of absolute non-being—has been a subject of deep philosophical inquiry for centuries. It is intricately connected to metaphysical discussions about existence, creation, and the nature of reality. When exploring the doctrine of Creation Ex Nihilo, the idea of nothingness becomes particularly significant, as it raises profound questions about what it means for something to come into existence from nothing. This chapter delves into the philosophical concept of nothingness, examining its implications for metaphysics, theology, and our understanding of the universe.

Understanding Nothingness: Definitions and Challenges

Defining Nothingness

At its most basic level, nothingness is defined as the absence of anything—complete non-existence, the total lack of being. It is not merely the absence of a particular thing or a specific object, but the absence of all things, including matter, energy, space, and time. In this sense, nothingness is not a state that exists; it is the absence of any state at all.

This definition of nothingness immediately presents challenges for philosophical thought. Nothingness is, by definition, devoid of properties, attributes, or characteristics. It cannot be perceived, measured, or experienced, because it is the absence of everything that could be perceived, measured, or experienced. As a result, nothingness resists easy conceptualization, leading to a paradox: How can we talk about or think about nothingness when it is, by nature, beyond the reach of thought and language?

Philosophers have grappled with this paradox for centuries, exploring whether nothingness can be meaningfully discussed or whether it remains an inherently unknowable and undefinable concept. Some have argued that nothingness is a purely conceptual construct with no actual existence, while others have explored its role in metaphysical theories about the origin of the universe and the nature of reality.

The Challenge of Conceptualizing Nothingness

One of the central challenges in discussing nothingness is that it is often misunderstood or conflated with other concepts, such as emptiness, void, or potentiality. For example, the void in physical space might be thought of as "nothing," but in physics, even a vacuum is not truly nothing, as it contains quantum fields, potential energy, and the possibility of particle fluctuations.

True nothingness, in contrast, would lack even these minimal properties—it would be a state in which there is absolutely no existence, no potentiality, and no possibility of change or becoming. This extreme conception of nothingness is difficult, if not impossible, to fully grasp, as our cognitive and linguistic frameworks are built around the assumption of somethingness—entities, processes, and relationships that exist.

Philosophers have employed various strategies to approach the concept of nothingness, often by using negative language or apophatic (negative) theology. Apophatic approaches describe nothingness by negation, emphasizing what it is not rather than attempting to describe what it is. For instance, nothingness is often described as the absence of being, the negation of existence, or the total lack of any properties or potentialities.

Nothingness and the Doctrine of Creation Ex Nihilo

Creation from Nothing: The Role of Nothingness

The doctrine of Creation Ex Nihilo posits that the universe was brought into existence by a divine act, without the use of any pre-existing materials. In this context, nothingness plays a crucial role, as it is the "state" (or more accurately, the non-state) from which the universe emerged. However, this raises significant philosophical questions: How can something come from nothing? What does it mean to say that the universe was created from nothing?

Philosophers and theologians have proposed various ways to understand the relationship between nothingness and creation. One common approach is to emphasize the distinction between nothingness as a metaphysical concept and the divine act of creation as a transcendent event. In this view, nothingness is not a causal agent or a substrate from which the universe is formed; rather, it represents the total absence of any pre-existing conditions. The creative act of God is understood as the sole cause that brings the universe into existence, and this act does not rely on anything other than the divine will.

This perspective maintains that nothingness, in itself, has no power or potentiality. It is only through the creative act of a transcendent being (God) that something (the universe) can emerge from nothing. The divine act of creation is thus seen as a unique and unparalleled event that transcends ordinary causality and metaphysical principles.

The Metaphysical Implications of Creation from Nothing

The concept of nothingness in relation to Creation Ex Nihilo has significant metaphysical implications, particularly concerning the nature of causality, the possibility of change, and the ontological status of the universe.

One implication is the challenge it poses to the principle of sufficient reason, which states that everything must have a reason or cause for its existence. In the case of Creation Ex Nihilo, the reason or cause for the existence of the universe is found in the divine will, but this cause is not like any other cause in the natural world. It does not involve a transformation of pre-existing materials or a process of becoming; instead, it is an absolute and sovereign act that brings something into being from nothing.

This leads to questions about the nature of divine causality and how it differs from causality within the universe. If God's creative act is fundamentally different from natural causes, how can we understand or describe this act? What does it mean for something to be caused by a being that is wholly other and transcendent?

Another implication concerns the nature of time and temporality. If the universe was created from nothing, does this imply that time itself was created along with the universe? If so, what does it mean to say that there was "nothing" before the universe, if "before" presupposes a temporal framework? These questions point to the complex relationship between nothingness, time, and the act of creation.

The doctrine of Creation Ex Nihilo also raises questions about the ontological status of the universe. If the universe was created from nothing, does this mean that its existence is contingent or dependent on something outside of itself? The answer to this question has profound implications for how we understand the nature of reality, the possibility of change, and the permanence or impermanence of the cosmos.

Nothingness in Metaphysical Thought

Nothingness in Existentialist Philosophy

The concept of nothingness has played a significant role in existentialist philosophy, particularly in the works of thinkers like Jean-Paul Sartre and Martin Heidegger. For these philosophers, nothingness is not merely an abstract concept but a central aspect of human existence and experience.

Jean-Paul Sartre, in his seminal work Being and Nothingness, explores the idea of nothingness as a fundamental aspect of consciousness. According to Sartre, human beings are defined by their ability to negate, to say "no," and to conceive of possibilities that are not currently actualized. This capacity for negation introduces nothingness into human existence, as individuals are constantly confronted with the gap between what is and what could be.

Sartre argues that this experience of nothingness is closely tied to the concept of freedom. Human beings are free precisely because they can imagine and choose among possibilities that are not yet realized. However, this freedom also comes with a sense of anxiety or dread, as individuals must confront the nothingness of their own existence—the fact that their choices and actions are not determined by any external necessity but are instead contingent and self-determined.

Martin Heidegger, another existentialist philosopher, also explores the concept of nothingness in his work Being and Time. Heidegger argues that nothingness is not merely the absence of being but is intimately connected to the experience of being itself. For Heidegger, the encounter with nothingness is a fundamental aspect of human existence, particularly in moments of profound reflection or existential crisis. This encounter reveals the contingent and finite nature of being and forces individuals to confront the question of meaning and purpose in a world that is ultimately characterized by transience and impermanence.

In both Sartre and Heidegger's thought, nothingness is not simply an abstract metaphysical concept but a lived reality that shapes the human experience. It is through the confrontation with nothingness that individuals come to understand their own freedom, responsibility, and the fragility of existence.

Nothingness in Eastern Philosophy

The concept of nothingness also plays a significant role in various Eastern philosophical traditions, particularly in Buddhism and Daoism. In these traditions, nothingness is often understood not as a void or absence but as an essential aspect of reality that transcends dualistic thinking.

In Buddhism, the concept of Śūnyatā (often translated as "emptiness" or "voidness") is central to understanding the nature of existence. Śūnyatā does not refer to nothingness in the sense of non-existence but rather to the absence of inherent, independent self-existence in all phenomena. According to Buddhist philosophy, all things are empty of intrinsic essence because they are interdependent and impermanent. This understanding of emptiness is meant to free individuals from attachment and delusion, allowing them to realize the true nature of reality and attain enlightenment.

In Daoism, the concept of Wu (often translated as "nothingness" or "non-being") is similarly important. Daoist philosophy emphasizes the complementary relationship between being and non-being, suggesting that nothingness is not the opposite of existence but a necessary counterpart. In the Dao De Jing, Laozi writes, "Thirty spokes share the wheel's hub; it is the center hole that makes it useful. Shape clay into a vessel; it is the space within that makes it useful." This passage highlights the idea that nothingness, or emptiness, is what gives form and function to things. In Daoism, embracing nothingness and non-action (wu wei) is seen as a way to align oneself with the natural flow of the Dao (the Way).

These Eastern perspectives on nothingness offer a different approach from Western metaphysical thought, emphasizing the dynamic and relational nature of nothingness rather than viewing it as a mere negation or absence. They suggest that nothingness is an integral part of the structure of reality and can provide insights into the nature of existence, interdependence, and the limitations of dualistic thinking.

Theological Implications of Nothingness

Nothingness and Divine Transcendence

In the context of Creation Ex Nihilo, the concept of nothingness is closely tied to the idea of divine transcendence. The doctrine asserts that God created the universe out of nothing, which implies that God is not dependent on anything outside of Himself for the act of creation. This underscores the radical otherness of God and His transcendence over the created order.

Theologically, nothingness serves to highlight the distinction between Creator and creation. Creation is contingent and dependent, while God is necessary and self-sufficient. The concept of nothingness thus reinforces the idea that the universe is not an extension or emanation of God but a distinct entity brought into existence by God's sovereign will.

This understanding of nothingness also has implications for the doctrine of divine providence. If the universe was created from nothing, then its continued existence is entirely dependent on God's sustaining power. This reinforces the idea that God is intimately involved in the world, not only as its creator but as its sustainer and governor. The concept of nothingness, therefore, supports a theistic worldview in which God's transcendence and immanence are both affirmed.

Nothingness and the Problem of Evil

The concept of nothingness also has important implications for the problem of evil in theology. If the universe was created from nothing, then evil cannot be understood as a pre-existing force or substance that opposes God. Instead, evil is often interpreted as a privation of good—a lack or corruption of the goodness that God intended in creation.

This view of evil as a privation aligns with the idea that nothingness represents the absence of being and goodness. Just as nothingness is not a positive reality but the absence of reality, evil is not a created entity but the absence or distortion of the good. This understanding of evil as a privation helps to preserve the goodness and omnipotence of God, as it suggests that God did not create evil but allows it as a consequence of free will and the limitations of the created order.

However, this interpretation also raises challenging questions about the nature of nothingness and its relationship to evil. If evil is associated with nothingness or the absence of good, how do we understand the presence of evil in a world created by a good and omnipotent God? The concept of nothingness, therefore, plays a critical role in theological discussions about the origin of evil, the nature of free will, and the meaning of suffering.

Conclusion: The Philosophical Significance of Nothingness

The concept of nothingness occupies a central place in metaphysical and theological discourse, particularly in relation to the doctrine of Creation Ex Nihilo. While nothingness is difficult to conceptualize and often resists clear definition, it serves as a crucial element in understanding the nature of existence, causality, and the divine.

Philosophically, nothingness challenges our assumptions about being, causality, and the nature of the universe. It raises profound questions about how something can come from nothing, the relationship between nothingness and the divine, and the implications of nothingness for our understanding of reality. These questions have inspired a wide range of philosophical and theological responses, each offering different perspectives on the meaning and significance of nothingness.

Theologically, nothingness highlights the transcendence and sovereignty of God as the Creator who brings the universe into existence without reliance on anything outside of Himself. It also plays a role in discussions about the nature of evil, free will, and divine providence, offering a framework for understanding how a good and omnipotent God can create and sustain a contingent and imperfect world.

As we continue to explore the metaphysical considerations surrounding Creation Ex Nihilo, the concept of nothingness remains a critical and enigmatic element in the broader conversation about the nature of reality, the origin of the universe, and the relationship between the Creator and creation. The philosophical and theological implications of nothingness challenge us to think deeply about the mysteries of existence and the ultimate questions of life, being, and the divine.

The Nature of Time and Space in the Context of Creation

The nature of time and space is fundamental to our understanding of reality, and these concepts take on particular significance in the context of the doctrine of Creation Ex Nihilo—the belief that the universe was created by God out of nothing. The relationship between time, space, and creation has been a subject of profound philosophical and theological inquiry, raising questions about the origins of the universe, the nature of divine action, and the framework within which all physical existence takes place. This chapter explores the nature of time and space in the context of creation, examining their metaphysical implications and the challenges they present to our understanding of the cosmos and the divine.

Time and Space: Foundational Concepts

The Traditional Understanding of Time

Time is traditionally understood as a sequential progression of events, where moments follow one another in a linear fashion. This linearity gives rise to the distinction between past, present, and future. Philosophically, time has been viewed in two primary ways: as an absolute entity that exists independently of the events within it (often associated with Newtonian physics) and as a relational entity that is dependent on the occurrences and changes within the universe (a view more closely aligned with the philosophy of Leibniz and the theory of relativity).

In the context of the doctrine of Creation Ex Nihilo, the concept of time is particularly significant because it raises questions about whether time itself was created, or whether time existed before the creation of the universe. If time began with creation, then what does it mean to speak of "before" creation, when "before" is itself a temporal concept?

The Traditional Understanding of Space

Space, like time, is a fundamental concept in both metaphysics and physics. Traditionally, space has been understood as the dimension within which objects exist and events occur. It is the "arena" or "container" that allows for the extension and arrangement of matter.

Philosophical debates about space have similarly centered around whether it is an absolute entity (as in Newtonian physics) or a relational one, existing only as the set of relationships between objects (a view closer to that of Leibniz and later, Einstein). The nature of space in the context of creation raises questions about whether space was created along with the universe, or whether it is something that exists independently of creation.

Time, Space, and Creation Ex Nihilo

The Creation of Time and Space

The doctrine of Creation Ex Nihilo posits that the universe was created out of nothing by a divine act. This belief suggests that time and space themselves were part of the creation, rather than pre-existing conditions within which creation occurred. If time and space were created, then they are contingent realities, dependent on the divine will rather than independent frameworks.

The idea that time and space were created has significant implications for how we understand the nature of the universe and the relationship between God and creation. It implies that time and space are not eternal, but have a beginning—specifically, the moment of creation. This raises profound questions about the nature of time "before" creation and the possibility of a reality in which time and space do not exist.

If time and space are part of the created order, then God's relationship to time and space must be fundamentally different from that of created beings. God, as the creator of time and space, would transcend both, existing outside of time and space in a manner that is difficult, if not impossible, for human beings to fully comprehend.

The Implications of God's Timelessness

One of the key implications of the idea that time was created is that God is often understood to be timeless or eternal, existing outside the flow of temporal events. This concept of divine timelessness suggests that God is not subject to temporal succession—He does not experience time as a series of moments, nor is He constrained by past, present, or future.

The concept of divine timelessness has been a central theme in classical theism, particularly in the works of thinkers like Augustine, Boethius, and Thomas Aquinas. According to this view, God perceives all of time simultaneously, in an "eternal now." From the divine perspective, all moments are present and fully known, and God's actions are not bound by temporal limitations.

However, the idea of divine timelessness also raises philosophical questions about how God interacts with the temporal world. If God is outside of time, how can He act within time? How can He respond to the actions of temporal beings, and how does His timeless existence relate to the dynamic, changing nature of the created universe?

Some theologians and philosophers have proposed that God's timelessness does not preclude His interaction with time but instead allows for a different kind of relationship between the Creator and creation. God's actions within time are seen as part of His eternal will, and the effects of these actions unfold within the temporal framework that He created.

The Beginning of Time: Philosophical and Theological Perspectives

The Big Bang and the Beginning of Time

The question of the beginning of time has been a central topic in both philosophy and modern cosmology. The scientific theory most commonly associated with the beginning of time is the Big Bang theory, which posits that the universe began as an extremely hot and dense singularity approximately 13.8 billion years ago. According to this theory, time and space themselves emerged from this initial singularity, marking the beginning of the observable universe.

The Big Bang theory aligns with the idea that time and space are part of the created order and that they have a finite beginning. From a theological perspective, the Big Bang is often seen as compatible with the doctrine of Creation Ex Nihilo, as it suggests that the universe had a definite starting point and that time and space are not eternal.

However, the concept of the Big Bang also raises questions about what, if anything, existed "before" the Big Bang. If time began with the Big Bang, then the notion of "before" becomes problematic, as it implies a temporal framework that does not exist. This leads to the idea that the universe's beginning is a boundary of time itself—a moment beyond which time does not extend.

Philosophically, this raises questions about the nature of causality and the conditions that led to the emergence of the universe. If time and space did not exist before the Big Bang, then the cause of the universe's existence must be something outside of time and space, pointing to a transcendent cause—such as God—who exists independently of the temporal and spatial dimensions.

The Kalam Cosmological Argument

One of the philosophical arguments that addresses the beginning of time is the Kalam Cosmological Argument, which has its roots in medieval Islamic philosophy and has been popularized in contemporary philosophy by thinkers like William Lane Craig. The Kalam argument is structured as follows:

1. Everything that begins to exist has a cause.

2. The universe began to exist.

3. Therefore, the universe has a cause.

The second premise, that the universe began to exist, is supported by both philosophical reasoning and scientific evidence, such as the Big Bang theory. The argument concludes that the universe must have a cause that is not itself part of the temporal and spatial order—namely, a transcendent, eternal cause, which many identify as God.

The Kalam Cosmological Argument emphasizes the idea that time and space are finite and contingent realities that depend on an external cause for their existence. This argument supports the doctrine of Creation Ex Nihilo by suggesting that the universe, including time and space, was brought into existence by a divine act.

The Kalam argument also addresses potential objections related to the infinite regress of causes. If time is infinite, it would imply an infinite series of past events, which the argument claims is metaphysically impossible. By asserting that time has a beginning, the Kalam argument seeks to avoid the paradoxes associated with an actual infinite and to establish the need for a first cause that is itself uncaused and outside of time.

Space, Place, and the Creation of the Universe

The Nature of Space in Creation

The nature of space in the context of creation is closely tied to questions about the relationship between the Creator and the created order. If space is part of the created universe, then it is a contingent reality that depends on God for its existence. This view contrasts with the idea of absolute space, which exists independently of any objects or events within it.

In the doctrine of Creation Ex Nihilo, space is often understood as a relational concept—a set of relationships between created entities rather than an independent entity in its own right. This relational view of space suggests that space is not a pre-existing "container" into which the universe was placed, but rather a framework that emerged along with the created order.

This understanding of space has implications for how we think about the presence of God in relation to the universe. If space is a created reality, then God is not "in" space in the same way that physical objects are. Instead, God transcends space, existing beyond the spatial dimensions while also being present to the entirety of creation. This idea is often expressed through the concept of divine omnipresence, which holds that God is present everywhere in creation, not by being spatially distributed but by sustaining and upholding all things.

The Concept of Place in Theology

The concept of "place" in theology has been a topic of discussion since ancient times, particularly in the context of God's relationship to the created order. The question of whether God has a "place" within the universe, or whether He exists beyond space and time, has significant implications for how we understand divine presence and action.

In classical theism, God is often described as "placeless" or "beyond place," meaning that He is not confined to a particular location or spatial dimension. This view emphasizes God's transcendence and His ability to act within the universe without being limited by the constraints of space.

However, the concept of place also raises questions about how God interacts with the created world. If God is not bound by space, how does He relate to specific places or events within the universe? Theologically, this is often addressed through the idea of divine immanence—the belief that God is intimately involved in the world and is present in all places through His sustaining power.

The relationship between place and divine action is also reflected in various religious practices and beliefs, such as the idea of sacred spaces or holy sites where God's presence is believed to be especially manifest. These concepts suggest that while God transcends space, He can also be particularly present in certain places or moments, acting in ways that are meaningful within the spatial and temporal dimensions of creation.

Time, Eternity, and the Eschatological Fulfillment

The Nature of Eternity

In theological discourse, eternity is often understood as the state of being outside of time—an existence that is not bound by temporal succession or change. God's eternity is frequently described as an "eternal now," in which all moments are fully present and there is no distinction between past, present, and future.

The concept of eternity raises important questions about the relationship between time and divine action. If God exists in an eternal now, how does He interact with a temporal world that experiences events in sequence? This question has led to various theological interpretations, including the idea that God's eternal will encompasses all of time and that His actions within time are expressions of His timeless purpose.

The nature of eternity also has implications for human understanding of eschatology—the study of the end times and the ultimate destiny of creation. In Christian theology, the eschatological fulfillment involves the renewal of creation and the realization of God's kingdom, often described as a transition from temporal existence to eternal life.

Time and the Eschatological Fulfillment

The relationship between time and eternity is central to eschatological thought, particularly in the context of the ultimate fulfillment of creation. The doctrine of Creation Ex Nihilo suggests that time is a created reality that has a beginning, and eschatological beliefs often hold that time will also have an end—a culmination in which the temporal order is transformed into a state of eternal fulfillment.

This eschatological fulfillment is often described as the "new creation" or the "new heaven and new earth" (Revelation 21:1), where the limitations and suffering of temporal existence are overcome and creation is brought into perfect harmony with the divine will. In this context, time is understood as a finite journey leading toward an eternal destination.

The transition from time to eternity raises philosophical questions about the nature of change, continuity, and the experience of time in the eschatological state. If time is fulfilled and transformed, what becomes of the temporal experiences and memories of created beings? How does the transition to eternity affect the identity and continuity of individuals and the created order?

These questions reflect the profound mystery of the relationship between time and eternity, a mystery that lies at the heart of both theological and philosophical inquiry. The doctrine of Creation Ex Nihilo provides a framework for understanding the beginning of time, while eschatological beliefs point to the ultimate fulfillment of time in the divine purpose.

Conclusion: The Metaphysical Significance of Time and Space in Creation

The nature of time and space in the context of creation is a topic of deep metaphysical significance, touching on fundamental questions about the origin, structure, and destiny of the universe. The doctrine of Creation Ex Nihilo provides a framework for understanding time and space as contingent realities that were brought into existence by a divine act, rather than as eternal or independent entities.

This understanding has profound implications for how we think about the relationship between God and creation, the nature of divine action, and the ultimate fulfillment of the temporal order. The concepts of time and space are not merely abstract ideas but are central to our experience of reality and our understanding of the cosmos.

As we continue to explore the metaphysical considerations of time and space, it becomes clear that these concepts are not static but dynamic, constantly interacting with our perceptions of existence, causality, and the divine. The relationship between time, space, and creation invites us to reflect on the mysteries of the universe and the ways in which the temporal and the eternal intersect in the divine plan.

The Issue of Causality and the First Cause Argument

The question of causality—how things come into being and what causes them to exist—has been a central concern in both philosophy and theology for millennia. The First Cause Argument, also known as the cosmological argument, is one of the most enduring philosophical arguments for the existence of God, focusing on the need for an initial cause or "first mover" that set everything else into motion. This chapter explores the nature of causality, the development of the First Cause Argument, and its significance in the context of the doctrine of Creation Ex Nihilo.

The Concept of Causality

Defining Causality

Causality refers to the relationship between cause and effect, where one event (the cause) brings about another event (the effect). It is a fundamental principle in both metaphysics and science, underlying our understanding of how the world works. The basic idea of causality is that every event or state of affairs has a cause, and this cause is itself the effect of a prior cause, creating a chain of events that stretches back in time.

Philosophers have distinguished between different types of causes, often building on Aristotle's four causes:

1. Material Cause: The substance or material from which something is made.

2. Formal Cause: The form or pattern according to which something is made.

3. Efficient Cause: The agent or process that brings something into existence.

4. Final Cause: The purpose or end for which something is made.

The focus of the First Cause Argument is primarily on the efficient cause—the cause that brings about the existence of something. In discussing the origin of the universe, the argument asks what the efficient cause of the universe itself is and whether there can be an infinite regress of causes, or if there must be a first, uncaused cause.

The Principle of Sufficient Reason

Closely related to the concept of causality is the Principle of Sufficient Reason, which states that everything that exists must have a reason or cause for its existence. This principle underlies many philosophical arguments, including the First Cause Argument, by insisting that the existence of the universe cannot be uncaused or without explanation. If everything in the universe has a cause, then the universe as a whole must also have a cause, leading to the search for an ultimate explanation.

The Principle of Sufficient Reason is often invoked to challenge the idea that the universe could simply exist without a cause. Proponents of the First Cause Argument argue that the existence of the universe requires a sufficient reason that is external to the universe itself—namely, a first cause that is not itself caused by anything else.

The First Cause Argument: Historical Development

Plato and Aristotle: The Origins of the Argument

The origins of the First Cause Argument can be traced back to ancient Greek philosophy, particularly in the works of Plato and Aristotle. Both philosophers grappled with the question of what causes the existence of the cosmos and whether there must be an ultimate cause or principle that explains everything else.

In Plato's dialogue Timaeus, the cosmos is described as being created by a divine craftsman (the Demiurge) who imposes order on pre-existing chaotic matter. While Plato does not explicitly develop a First Cause Argument, his work raises questions about the ultimate source of order and existence in the universe.

Aristotle, however, made a more direct contribution to the development of the First Cause Argument. In his work Metaphysics, Aristotle introduces the concept of the "Unmoved Mover"—a first cause that is itself uncaused and is responsible for the motion and change in the universe. The Unmoved Mover is pure actuality, without potentiality, and serves as the ultimate explanation for the existence of motion and causality in the cosmos.

Aristotle's Unmoved Mover is not a creator in the sense of bringing the universe into existence from nothing, but rather the ultimate source of motion and order. This idea laid the groundwork for later philosophical developments, particularly in the medieval period, where the concept of a first cause would be more explicitly connected to the creation of the universe.

Medieval Philosophy: The Argument's Christian Context

The First Cause Argument was further developed and refined by medieval philosophers, particularly within the context of Christian theology. Thinkers such as Augustine, Anselm, and Aquinas sought to reconcile the philosophical insights of the Greeks with the Christian doctrine of Creation Ex Nihilo.

St. Thomas Aquinas, in particular, is well-known for his articulation of the First Cause Argument in his Five Ways—five proofs for the existence of God presented in his Summa Theologica. The second of these ways, the Argument from Efficient Causes, closely follows the reasoning of the First Cause Argument:

1. There is an order of efficient causes in the world.

2. Nothing can be the cause of itself (for this would imply that it existed prior to itself, which is impossible).

3. Therefore, there cannot be an infinite regress of causes because without a first cause, there would be no subsequent causes, and hence nothing would exist.

4. Therefore, there must be a first efficient cause, which is uncaused and necessary for the existence of all other causes. This first cause is what everyone understands to be God.

Aquinas' argument builds on Aristotle's concept of the Unmoved Mover but adapts it to a Christian framework, identifying the first cause not only as the source of motion and order but as the Creator of the universe itself. Aquinas argues that without a first cause, nothing else could exist, and this first cause must be a necessary being—one whose existence is not contingent on anything else.

The First Cause Argument became a cornerstone of Christian apologetics, offering a philosophical defense of the belief in a Creator who is the ultimate cause of all that exists. It also provided a way to reconcile the concept of divine omnipotence with the observable order and causality in the natural world.

Modern and Contemporary Developments

Critiques of the First Cause Argument

While the First Cause Argument has been influential, it has also faced significant philosophical critiques, particularly in the modern period. Some of the most prominent critiques come from thinkers who question the assumptions underlying the argument, such as the need for a first cause or the impossibility of an infinite regress of causes.

One of the most famous critiques comes from the Scottish philosopher David Hume. In his Dialogues Concerning Natural Religion, Hume challenges the idea that every event must have a cause and questions whether the concept of causality can be applied to the universe as a whole.

Hume argues that just because we observe causality within the universe does not mean that the universe itself must have a cause. He also suggests that the idea of a first cause might be no more logically necessary than the idea of an infinite regress.

Immanuel Kant, another major figure in modern philosophy, also critiqued the First Cause Argument. In his Critique of Pure Reason, Kant argues that the concept of causality applies only to the realm of experience—what he calls the "phenomenal" world. According to Kant, we cannot extend the principle of causality to the "noumenal" world, the realm of things as they are in themselves, which includes the ultimate nature of the universe. For Kant, the First Cause Argument oversteps the limits of human reason by attempting to apply concepts derived from experience (such as causality) to the universe as a whole.

These critiques raise important questions about the validity of the First Cause Argument and whether it can provide a definitive proof of the existence of God. They challenge the idea that the universe must have a cause in the same way that events within the universe do, and they question whether human concepts of causality can adequately explain the origins of the cosmos.

The Kalam Cosmological Argument

In response to these critiques, some contemporary philosophers have sought to reformulate the First Cause Argument in ways that address the concerns of thinkers like Hume and Kant. One of the most well-known contemporary versions of the First Cause Argument is the Kalam Cosmological Argument, which has been championed by philosopher William Lane Craig.

The Kalam Cosmological Argument is structured as follows:

1. Everything that begins to exist has a cause.

2. The universe began to exist.

3. Therefore, the universe has a cause.

The Kalam argument differs from Aquinas' version by explicitly focusing on the idea that the universe began to exist, drawing on both philosophical reasoning and scientific evidence (such as the Big Bang theory) to support this claim. By emphasizing the beginning of the universe, the Kalam argument seeks to avoid the problem of an infinite regress of causes and to establish the necessity of a first cause.

Proponents of the Kalam argument argue that the universe cannot have an infinite past, as an actual infinite cannot exist in reality. They also argue that the cause of the universe must be an uncaused, timeless, spaceless, and immaterial being with the power to create—a being that corresponds to the traditional conception of God.

The Kalam Cosmological Argument has reinvigorated the debate over the First Cause Argument, particularly by engaging with contemporary scientific theories about the origins of the universe. It represents an attempt to bridge the gap between classical metaphysical arguments and modern cosmological understanding.

Theological Implications of the First Cause Argument

The First Cause as Creator

The First Cause Argument, particularly as developed by Aquinas and other medieval theologians, has significant theological implications. By identifying the first cause with God, the argument supports the doctrine of Creation Ex Nihilo—the belief that God created the universe out of nothing. This first cause is not just an impersonal force but is understood as a personal, intelligent Creator who deliberately brought the universe into existence.

This understanding of the first cause aligns with the classical attributes of God in Christian theology, including omnipotence, omniscience, and aseity (self-existence). The first cause is seen as a necessary being, whose existence is not contingent on anything else, and who is the source of all contingent beings.

The First Cause Argument also provides a framework for understanding the relationship between God and the created order. By positing God as the ultimate cause of all that exists, the argument emphasizes the dependency of the universe on God and the idea that God is continually sustaining and upholding creation.

The First Cause and Divine Simplicity

The concept of the first cause also has implications for the doctrine of divine simplicity—the idea that God is not composed of parts or attributes but is a single, indivisible being. In classical theism, God's simplicity is closely related to His status as the first cause, as it implies that God's essence is identical with His existence. God does not have being; He is being itself.

This understanding of divine simplicity reinforces the idea that God, as the first cause, is fundamentally different from all other beings, which are contingent and composite. The first cause is the ultimate source of all being, and as such, God's existence is not dependent on anything else. This also ties into the idea of divine immutability—the belief that God does not change, because change would imply a lack or potentiality, which cannot apply to a necessary and simple being.

The theological implications of the First Cause Argument, therefore, extend beyond the question of creation to encompass broader doctrines about the nature of God and His relationship to the universe.

Conclusion: The Enduring Significance of the First Cause Argument

The issue of causality and the First Cause Argument continues to be a central topic in both philosophy and theology. Despite the challenges and critiques it has faced, the First Cause Argument remains a powerful and influential way of reasoning about the origins of the universe and the existence of God.

The argument's significance lies not only in its logical structure but also in its ability to bridge the gap between metaphysical inquiry and theological doctrine. It provides a way of thinking about the universe that acknowledges both the need for a cause and the limits of human understanding when it comes to the ultimate source of existence.

In the context of the doctrine of Creation Ex Nihilo, the First Cause Argument supports the idea that the universe was brought into existence by a transcendent, uncaused cause—a cause that is identified with God. This understanding reinforces the view that the universe is not self-sustaining or eternal but is contingent upon a Creator who exists beyond time and space.

As philosophical and scientific developments continue to evolve, the First Cause Argument remains a dynamic and contested area of inquiry. It challenges us to consider the fundamental questions of existence, causality, and the nature of the divine, and it invites ongoing reflection on the relationship between reason, faith, and the origins of the universe.

CHAPTER 07

CONTEMPORARY PHILOSOPHICAL DEBATES

Analysis of Modern Philosophical Arguments for and Against Creation Ex Nihilo

The doctrine of Creation Ex Nihilo—the belief that God created the universe out of nothing—continues to be a central topic of debate in contemporary philosophy. This chapter provides an analysis of the modern philosophical arguments for and against Creation Ex Nihilo, exploring how recent developments in metaphysics, cosmology, and theology have shaped the ongoing discourse. The discussion will examine both the strengths and weaknesses of these arguments, highlighting the complexity and nuance that characterize the contemporary debate.

Modern Arguments in Favor of Creation Ex Nihilo

The Kalam Cosmological Argument

One of the most prominent modern arguments in favor of Creation Ex Nihilo is the Kalam Cosmological Argument. Revived and popularized by philosopher William Lane Craig, this argument builds on classical philosophical ideas while incorporating contemporary scientific insights, particularly from cosmology.

The Kalam Cosmological Argument is structured as follows:

1. Everything that begins to exist has a cause.

2. The universe began to exist.

3. Therefore, the universe has a cause.

Craig and other proponents argue that the cause of the universe must be timeless, spaceless, and immaterial—an entity that can bring about the existence of the universe without being part of the physical world. This entity is typically identified with God, who, according to the doctrine of Creation Ex Nihilo, created the universe out of nothing.

Strengths of the Kalam Argument:

1. Alignment with Modern Cosmology: The second premise of the Kalam Argument—that the universe began to exist—is supported by contemporary cosmological theories, such as the Big Bang theory, which suggests that the universe

had a definite starting point approximately 13.8 billion years ago. This scientific evidence bolsters the argument that the universe is not eternal and that it requires an explanation for its origin.

2. Philosophical Coherence: The argument maintains philosophical coherence by appealing to the Principle of Sufficient Reason, which states that everything that begins to exist must have a cause. The Kalam Argument avoids the problem of an infinite regress of causes by positing a first cause that is itself uncaused, thus providing a clear and logical explanation for the existence of the universe.

3. Integration of Metaphysics and Theology: The Kalam Argument successfully integrates metaphysical reasoning with theological principles, offering a framework that is both philosophically rigorous and theologically meaningful. It supports the idea of a transcendent Creator who is the ultimate cause of all that exists, aligning with the traditional theistic understanding of God.

Weaknesses and Criticisms:

1. Questioning the Causal Principle: Critics of the Kalam Argument, such as philosopher Quentin Smith, have challenged the first premise—that everything that begins to exist must have a cause. They argue that this principle may not necessarily apply to the universe as a whole, especially

when considering quantum mechanics, where events can occur without clear causation. This critique raises questions about whether the causal principle can be universally applied.

2. Challenges to the Concept of a Beginning: Some philosophers, like Graham Oppy, have questioned the idea that the universe had a beginning in the way the Kalam Argument suggests. They argue that even if the universe had a beginning, this does not necessarily imply that it was caused in the manner proposed by theists. Oppy suggests that the universe could have begun in a self-contained manner without the need for a transcendent cause.

3. Complexity of the Cause: Even if the Kalam Argument successfully demonstrates the need for a cause, critics argue that it does not necessarily lead to the conclusion that this cause is the God of classical theism. The nature and attributes of the cause remain open to interpretation, and some argue that the cause could be something other than a personal, theistic God.

The Argument from Contingency

Another modern argument in favor of Creation Ex Nihilo is the Argument from Contingency, which builds on the idea that everything in the universe is contingent—that is, it depends on something else for its existence. This argument posits that because the universe is composed of contingent entities, it must ultimately depend on a necessary being whose existence is not contingent. This necessary being is identified with God, who, according to the doctrine of Creation Ex Nihilo, brought the universe into existence without relying on any pre-existing materials.

Strengths of the Argument from Contingency:

1. Philosophical Depth: The Argument from Contingency draws on deep metaphysical principles, particularly the distinction between contingent and necessary beings. It provides a comprehensive explanation for the existence of the universe by appealing to a necessary being that underlies all contingent existence.

2. Avoidance of Infinite Regress: Like the Kalam Argument, the Argument from Contingency avoids the problem of an infinite regress of contingent causes by positing a necessary being that is self-existent and does not require a cause. This offers a clear and logical stopping point for the chain of causation.

3. Compatibility with Theism: The argument aligns closely with theistic views of God as a necessary being who is the source of all existence. It supports the idea that the universe is dependent on God for its existence and that God, as a necessary being, is the only entity that can explain the existence of contingent beings.

Weaknesses and Criticisms:

1. Challenge of Defining Necessity: One of the main criticisms of the Argument from Contingency is the challenge of defining what it means for a being to be "necessary." Critics argue that the concept of a necessary being is difficult to substantiate and may not be as clear-cut as proponents suggest. There is also debate over whether the existence of the universe truly requires a necessary being or if it could be explained in other ways.

2. Alternative Explanations: Some philosophers propose alternative explanations for the existence of the universe that do not rely on a necessary being. For example, naturalistic theories suggest that the universe could be self-sustaining or that it could have emerged from a quantum vacuum without the need for a transcendent cause.

3. The Nature of the Necessary Being: Even if the Argument from Contingency successfully establishes the existence of a necessary being, critics argue that this being does not necessarily have to be the God of classical theism. The attributes of this necessary being remain open to interpretation, and some argue that it could be something other than a personal, theistic God.

Modern Arguments Against Creation Ex Nihilo

The Argument from Quantum Mechanics

One of the most significant modern arguments against Creation Ex Nihilo comes from developments in quantum mechanics, particularly the idea that certain events in the quantum realm appear to occur without clear causation. For example, in quantum field theory, particles can emerge spontaneously from a quantum vacuum, a phenomenon that some interpret as a challenge to the idea that everything that begins to exist must have a cause.

Strengths of the Argument from Quantum Mechanics:

1. Empirical Evidence: The argument is supported by empirical evidence from quantum physics, which shows that events at the quantum level do not always conform to classical notions of causality. This challenges the universality of the causal principle and suggests that the universe could have emerged from a quantum vacuum without a need for a transcendent cause.

2. Compatibility with Naturalism: The argument from quantum mechanics aligns with a naturalistic worldview that seeks to explain the origins of the universe through physical processes rather than invoking a supernatural cause. It provides a framework for understanding the universe that is consistent with contemporary scientific theories.

3. Reduction of the Need for a First Cause: If quantum mechanics can explain the emergence of the universe without a clear cause, this reduces the need for a first cause and challenges the notion that the universe requires a divine creator. This argument supports the idea that the universe could be self-sustaining and does not require an external cause.

Weaknesses and Criticisms:

1. Interpretation of Quantum Mechanics: Critics of this argument, including some philosophers of science, argue that the interpretation of quantum mechanics as supporting causeless events is not universally accepted. They suggest that quantum mechanics might still involve causality, albeit in a non-classical form, and that the apparent lack of causation might reflect the limitations of current understanding rather than a true absence of cause.

2. Limitations of Quantum Mechanics: Some critics argue that quantum mechanics, as it is currently understood, may not be applicable to the entire universe, particularly when discussing the origins of the cosmos. The laws of quantum mechanics apply to subatomic particles, but it is not clear how they scale up to the macroscopic level or to the universe as a whole.

3. The Nature of the Quantum Vacuum: The quantum vacuum is not "nothing" in the metaphysical sense but is a state with its own properties, including energy fields and potentiality. Critics argue that equating the quantum vacuum with "nothing" is misleading and does not address the deeper metaphysical question of why anything exists at all.

The Argument from Eternal Universe Theories

Another modern argument against Creation Ex Nihilo comes from theories that propose the universe is eternal and has no beginning. These theories suggest that the universe could exist as an infinite series of events or as a self-contained, cyclical process without the need for a transcendent cause.

Strengths of the Argument from Eternal Universe Theories:

1. Alternative Models: Theories such as the cyclical universe model or the multiverse theory offer alternative explanations for the existence of the universe that do not rely on a beginning or a first cause. These models suggest that the universe, or a series of universes, could exist eternally in some form, thereby eliminating the need for a Creator.

2. Philosophical Support: Some philosophers, such as Graham Oppy, argue that the concept of an eternal universe is philosophically viable and does not require the introduction of a necessary being or first cause. They suggest that the

universe could be self-sustaining and that the principle of sufficient reason does not necessarily apply to the universe as a whole.

3. Consistency with Scientific Theories: Some eternal universe theories are consistent with certain interpretations of modern cosmology, such as the idea of a multiverse or an oscillating universe. These theories offer a naturalistic explanation for the existence of the universe that does not invoke supernatural causation.

Weaknesses and Criticisms:

1. Challenges to Infinite Regress: One of the main criticisms of eternal universe theories is the challenge of infinite regress. Philosophers such as William Lane Craig argue that an infinite series of past events is metaphysically impossible because it would imply the existence of an actual infinite, which cannot exist in reality. This argument supports the idea that the universe must have had a beginning, thereby requiring a first cause.

2. Lack of Empirical Evidence: While some eternal universe theories are consistent with certain cosmological models, they often lack direct empirical evidence. For example, the multiverse theory, while theoretically possible, has not been empirically verified and remains a speculative idea within cosmology.

3. Philosophical Inconsistencies: Critics argue that some eternal universe theories face philosophical inconsistencies, particularly in explaining the fine-tuning of the universe and the existence of order and complexity. The idea that the universe has existed eternally without any explanation for its specific properties or structure is seen by some as unsatisfactory and incomplete.

Synthesis and Conclusion

The contemporary philosophical debates surrounding Creation Ex Nihilo reveal a rich and complex landscape of ideas, arguments, and counterarguments. On one hand, proponents of Creation Ex Nihilo, through arguments like the Kalam Cosmological Argument and the Argument from Contingency, provide robust defenses of the idea that the universe requires a cause and that this cause is best understood as a transcendent, necessary being—namely, God. These arguments draw on both classical metaphysical principles and contemporary scientific insights to make their case.

On the other hand, critics of Creation Ex Nihilo, including those who appeal to quantum mechanics and eternal universe theories, challenge the need for a first cause and question the universality of traditional causal principles. These arguments offer alternative explanations for the existence of the universe that do not rely on a divine creator, appealing to naturalistic and scientific frameworks.

The ongoing debate reflects the enduring relevance of the question of creation and causality, as well as the interplay between philosophy, theology, and science in addressing the fundamental mysteries of existence. While the doctrine of Creation Ex Nihilo continues to be a central tenet of theistic belief, it is also a doctrine that remains open to rigorous scrutiny and debate in the contemporary philosophical arena.

As the discourse evolves, both proponents and critics of Creation Ex Nihilo continue to refine their arguments, engage with new developments in science and metaphysics, and seek to provide answers to the age-old questions about the origins of the universe and the nature of reality. This dynamic and ongoing conversation ensures that the issue of Creation Ex Nihilo will remain a vital topic of inquiry for philosophers, theologians, and scientists alike.

The Impact of Scientific Theories on the Concept of Creation Ex Nihilo

The doctrine of Creation Ex Nihilo—the belief that God created the universe out of nothing—has long been a central tenet of Judeo-Christian theology. However, the advent of modern scientific theories, particularly in cosmology, has profoundly influenced the way this concept is understood, debated, and defended. This chapter explores the impact of key scientific theories, such as the Big Bang Theory and Multiverse Theory, on the concept of Creation Ex Nihilo. We will examine how these theories challenge, support, or redefine traditional theological perspectives and consider their implications for contemporary philosophical and theological discussions.

The Big Bang Theory and Creation Ex Nihilo

Overview of the Big Bang Theory

The Big Bang Theory is one of the most widely accepted scientific explanations for the origin of the universe. According to this theory, the universe began approximately 13.8 billion years ago from an extremely hot and dense singularity—a point of infinite density and temperature. This singularity expanded rapidly, leading to the formation of space, time, and all the matter and energy in the universe.

The Big Bang Theory is supported by a wide range of empirical evidence, including the cosmic microwave background radiation, the observed redshift of distant galaxies (indicating the universe's expansion), and the abundance of light elements such as hydrogen and helium. These observations have led to the general acceptance of the Big Bang as the most plausible explanation for the universe's beginnings.

The Big Bang and Creation Ex Nihilo: Points of Convergence

The Big Bang Theory has significant implications for the concept of Creation Ex Nihilo, particularly in how it aligns with the idea that the universe had a beginning. Before the development of the Big Bang Theory, many scientists and philosophers believed in an eternal, unchanging universe—a view that seemed at odds with the notion of a universe created out of nothing. However, the Big Bang Theory suggests that the universe did indeed have a beginning, which can be seen as supportive of the doctrine of Creation Ex Nihilo.

Convergence of Science and Theology:

1. A Universe with a Beginning: The Big Bang Theory supports the idea that the universe is not eternal but had a definite starting point. This aligns with the theological claim that the universe was created by God at a specific moment in time, rather than existing eternally. For many theists, the Big Bang can be interpreted as the moment of creation—the point at which God brought the universe into existence from nothing.

2. Causality and the First Cause: The idea that the universe had a beginning also raises questions about causality and the need for a first cause. If the universe began with the Big Bang, what caused the Big Bang itself? For proponents of

Creation Ex Nihilo, the answer is that God is the first cause—the uncaused cause that brought the universe into existence. This interpretation supports the traditional theistic view that the universe's existence is contingent upon a transcendent creator.

3. Philosophical and Theological Integration: The Big Bang Theory has led to renewed interest in integrating scientific and theological perspectives. Many contemporary theologians and philosophers see the Big Bang as a scientific confirmation of the idea that the universe is not self-sustaining but depends on an external cause. This has led to a more harmonious relationship between science and theology, where the Big Bang is viewed as compatible with, and even supportive of, the doctrine of Creation Ex Nihilo.

Challenges Posed by the Big Bang Theory

While the Big Bang Theory offers points of convergence with Creation Ex Nihilo, it also presents certain challenges and raises questions that have sparked debate within philosophical and theological circles.

Challenges to Traditional Causality:

1. The Singularity and the Limits of Causality: One of the most significant challenges posed by the Big Bang Theory is the nature of the singularity itself. The conditions at the singularity—where density and temperature are infinite—are

beyond the explanatory power of current physical theories, including general relativity. As a result, the singularity represents a boundary to our understanding of causality. Some argue that because the laws of physics break down at the singularity, it is not clear whether traditional notions of cause and effect apply. This raises questions about how we can meaningfully speak of a cause (such as God) bringing about the Big Bang.

2. Quantum Cosmology and Spontaneous Creation: Some interpretations of quantum cosmology suggest that the universe could have emerged spontaneously from a quantum vacuum without a cause, challenging the idea that the Big Bang requires a transcendent cause. This interpretation draws on principles from quantum mechanics, where events can occur without deterministic causation. If the universe could emerge from a quantum vacuum, this might challenge the necessity of invoking a divine creator as the cause of the universe's existence.

3. The Nature of Time: The Big Bang Theory also raises questions about the nature of time, particularly the idea that time itself began with the Big Bang. If time began with the Big Bang, then the concept of a "before" the Big Bang becomes problematic. This challenges traditional theological notions of God's creation of the universe "before" time began

and raises complex questions about how to understand the relationship between God, time, and the act of creation.

Multiverse Theory and Its Implications

Overview of the Multiverse Theory

The Multiverse Theory is a speculative idea in modern cosmology that suggests our universe is just one of many (perhaps infinitely many) universes that exist. These universes together form what is known as the "multiverse." The concept of a multiverse arises from various scientific theories, including string theory, inflationary cosmology, and the many-worlds interpretation of quantum mechanics.

According to some versions of the Multiverse Theory, these different universes might have different physical constants, laws, and structures, potentially leading to a vast diversity of cosmic environments. The multiverse is often proposed as a way to explain certain fine-tuning observations in our universe—conditions that seem perfectly calibrated to allow for the existence of life.

The Multiverse and Challenges to Creation Ex Nihilo

The Multiverse Theory presents several challenges to the traditional concept of Creation Ex Nihilo, particularly by offering a naturalistic explanation for the existence of our universe and its fine-tuning.

Challenges Posed by the Multiverse:

1. Undermining the Need for a Creator: One of the primary challenges posed by the Multiverse Theory is that it potentially undermines the need for a divine creator. If there are countless universes, each with different properties, the existence of our universe, with its particular physical constants, might not require special explanation. Instead of attributing the fine-tuning of our universe to divine design, the Multiverse Theory suggests that we simply happen to live in one of the many universes where the conditions are right for life to exist.

2. Redefining the Origin of the Universe: The Multiverse Theory challenges the notion that the Big Bang was the singular event that brought everything into existence. If our universe is just one of many, then the Big Bang might be seen as a localized event within a broader multiverse context, rather than the absolute beginning of all existence. This raises questions about whether the concept of Creation Ex Nihilo can apply to a multiverse scenario, where "creation" might involve the generation of multiple universes rather than a single, all-encompassing event.

3. Naturalistic Explanations for Fine-Tuning: The Multiverse Theory provides a naturalistic explanation for the apparent fine-tuning of the universe, which is often cited as evidence for a creator. In a multiverse, the vast number of

universes with varying conditions would make it statistically likely that at least some universes would have the right conditions for life. This challenges the argument that the fine-tuning of our universe requires divine intervention or a purposeful act of creation.

Responses to the Multiverse Challenge

Proponents of Creation Ex Nihilo and theism have responded to the challenges posed by the Multiverse Theory in various ways, arguing that the concept of a multiverse does not necessarily negate the need for a creator.

Responses to Multiverse Challenges:

1. The Contingency of the Multiverse: Some theists argue that even if the Multiverse Theory is true, the multiverse itself would still require an explanation. The existence of a multiverse—whether finite or infinite—would still be contingent and would therefore require a cause. Proponents of this view argue that God could be the creator not just of our universe, but of the entire multiverse, bringing all possible universes into existence out of nothing.

2. Limits of Empirical Evidence: Critics of the Multiverse Theory often point out that the multiverse is currently a speculative hypothesis with limited empirical evidence. Because other universes, if they exist, are likely beyond our observational capabilities, the multiverse remains

a theoretical construct rather than a confirmed scientific fact. Some argue that it is premature to use the multiverse as a definitive challenge to the doctrine of Creation Ex Nihilo.

3. The Fine-Tuning Argument: Some proponents of theism suggest that the fine-tuning argument remains compelling even in the context of a multiverse. They argue that the existence of a life-permitting universe still requires an explanation, and that a multiverse does not necessarily eliminate the need for a designer. For example, the multiverse itself could be seen as a system designed by God, with the potential for generating life-permitting universes as part of a divine plan.

4. Philosophical Considerations: Some philosophers question whether the Multiverse Theory truly resolves the problem of fine-tuning or the need for a first cause. They argue that the multiverse merely shifts the question of origins to a higher level, without providing a final explanation for why anything exists at all. The existence of a multiverse, they suggest, might still require a necessary being or ultimate cause, which could be identified with God.

Other Scientific Developments and Their Impact

Quantum Cosmology

Quantum cosmology is an area of theoretical physics that applies principles from quantum mechanics to the early universe, particularly in the moments immediately following the Big Bang. Some quantum cosmological models suggest that the universe could have emerged from a quantum vacuum or that space and time could have been created through quantum processes.

Impact on Creation Ex Nihilo:

Quantum cosmology challenges traditional notions of causality and creation, particularly by suggesting that the universe could arise spontaneously without a cause. However, this does not necessarily negate the need for a creator; some theists argue that God could be the author of the quantum laws and conditions that allowed the universe to emerge.

The Anthropic Principle

The Anthropic Principle is the observation that the universe appears to be fine-tuned for the existence of life, particularly human life. There are two main versions: the Weak Anthropic Principle (WAP), which states that the universe must allow for the existence of observers (since we are here to observe it), and the Strong Anthropic Principle (SAP), which suggests that the universe is designed in such a way that it necessarily leads to the emergence of life.

Impact on Creation Ex Nihilo:

The Anthropic Principle has been used both to support and challenge the idea of Creation Ex Nihilo.

Proponents argue that the fine-tuning of the universe is evidence of a purposeful creator who designed the cosmos to support life. Critics, particularly those who support the multiverse hypothesis, argue that the fine-tuning can be explained by the existence of multiple universes, some of which happen to have the right conditions for life.

Conclusion: The Dynamic Relationship Between Science and Theology

The relationship between modern scientific theories and the doctrine of Creation Ex Nihilo is complex and multifaceted. While some scientific developments, such as the Big Bang Theory, have been seen as supportive of the idea that the universe had a beginning and thus aligns with the concept of creation from nothing, other theories, like the Multiverse Theory, present significant challenges to traditional theological perspectives.

The ongoing dialogue between science and theology highlights the dynamic nature of these debates. As scientific understanding continues to evolve, so too do the philosophical and theological interpretations of concepts like creation, causality, and the nature of the universe. While some see the Multiverse Theory and quantum cosmology as undermining the need for a creator, others argue that these theories simply push the question of origins to a higher level, where the existence of a multiverse or quantum processes might still require an ultimate cause or explanation.

Ultimately, the impact of scientific theories on the concept of Creation Ex Nihilo underscores the importance of interdisciplinary dialogue. It invites theologians, philosophers, and scientists to work together in exploring the profound questions of existence, the origins of the universe, and the relationship between the natural world and the divine. This dialogue ensures that the concept of Creation Ex Nihilo remains a vital and relevant topic of inquiry in both the scientific and theological realms.

Interaction Between Science and Philosophy in Understanding Creation

The relationship between science and philosophy has always been integral to our understanding of the cosmos, particularly when it comes to the profound question of creation. The interaction between these two disciplines offers a rich and complex dialogue that has shaped and reshaped our conceptions of how the universe came into being and what it means for existence itself. This chapter explores the interaction between science and philosophy in understanding creation, examining how these fields influence each other and contribute to a deeper comprehension of the origins and nature of the universe.

The Philosophical Foundations of Scientific Inquiry

Philosophy as the Groundwork for Scientific Exploration

Philosophy has long provided the foundational concepts and methods that underpin scientific inquiry. Before science emerged as a distinct discipline, natural philosophy was the primary means by which scholars sought to understand the world. Philosophical questions about the nature of reality, causality, and the existence of the universe laid the groundwork for the development of scientific theories.

Key Philosophical Contributions:

1. The Concept of Causality: The philosophical exploration of causality has been crucial for scientific inquiry. The idea that every effect must have a cause is a fundamental principle in both metaphysics and science. This principle drives scientific investigations into the origins of phenomena, including the origin of the universe itself. The First Cause Argument, a philosophical concept, has influenced scientific theories that seek to explain the initial conditions of the cosmos.

2. The Nature of Reality: Philosophical debates about the nature of reality, including discussions about materialism, dualism, and idealism, have informed scientific approaches to

understanding the physical world. These debates have shaped the ways in which scientists conceptualize space, time, matter, and energy, all of which are essential components in the study of cosmology.

3. Epistemology: The philosophy of knowledge, or epistemology, has provided the tools for evaluating the validity and scope of scientific theories. Questions about what can be known, how we can know it, and the limits of human understanding are central to both philosophy and science. Epistemology informs the scientific method, guiding how hypotheses are formed, tested, and validated.

The Shift from Natural Philosophy to Modern Science

The transition from natural philosophy to modern science occurred during the Scientific Revolution, when empirical observation and experimentation became the primary means of investigating the natural world. Figures like Galileo, Newton, and Descartes were instrumental in this shift, blending philosophical reasoning with empirical evidence to develop new theories about the cosmos.

This shift did not eliminate the influence of philosophy but rather transformed it. Philosophical concepts continued to play a crucial role in shaping scientific theories, particularly in areas where empirical data was sparse or ambiguous. For example, the philosophical concept of space as an absolute framework influenced Newtonian physics, while debates about the nature of causality informed the development of quantum mechanics and relativity.

The Role of Science in Philosophical Discussions of Creation

Scientific Theories and the Question of Creation

Modern scientific theories have profoundly impacted philosophical discussions of creation, particularly through advancements in cosmology, physics, and astronomy. These theories provide empirical evidence and conceptual frameworks that challenge, support, or refine traditional philosophical and theological ideas about the origin of the universe.

Key Scientific Theories Influencing Philosophical Thought:

1. The Big Bang Theory: The Big Bang Theory is perhaps the most significant scientific development in relation to the concept of creation. It provides a model in which the universe has a definite beginning, suggesting that space and time emerged from an initial singularity. This theory has influenced philosophical debates about the nature of time, causality, and the existence of a first cause.

2. Quantum Mechanics: Quantum mechanics, with its principles of uncertainty and probability, challenges classical

notions of determinism and causality. The idea that particles can emerge from a quantum vacuum without a clear cause has sparked philosophical discussions about the nature of existence and the possibility of creation from nothing. Quantum cosmology, in particular, explores how quantum principles might apply to the early universe, offering new perspectives on creation.

3. The Multiverse Theory: The Multiverse Theory posits that our universe is one of many, each potentially governed by different physical laws. This theory has significant philosophical implications for the concept of creation, particularly in challenging the uniqueness of our universe and the idea of a single, divine creator. The multiverse also raises questions about the nature of reality and the limits of human knowledge.

Science as a Tool for Philosophical Exploration

While science provides empirical data and theoretical models, it also serves as a tool for philosophical exploration. Scientific discoveries often prompt philosophical questions that go beyond the scope of empirical evidence, leading to deeper inquiries into the nature of existence, causality, and the meaning of creation.

Examples of Science Informing Philosophy:

1. The Nature of Time and Space: Scientific theories about the nature of time and space, particularly in the context of relativity and quantum mechanics, have prompted philosophical debates about whether time and space are fundamental aspects of reality or emergent properties. These discussions explore whether time and space existed "before" the Big Bang or if they are entirely dependent on the existence of the universe.

2. Causality and Determinism: The implications of quantum mechanics for causality and determinism have led to philosophical debates about free will, the nature of causation, and the possibility of a deterministic universe. These discussions intersect with theological concepts of divine foreknowledge and the nature of God's interaction with the universe.

3. The Fine-Tuning Argument: The observation that the physical constants of the universe are finely tuned to allow for the existence of life has philosophical implications for discussions about design and purpose. Some philosophers argue that this fine-tuning suggests the existence of a designer (often identified with God), while others propose naturalistic explanations, such as the multiverse.

The Philosophical Critique of Scientific Theories
The Limits of Scientific Explanation

Philosophers have long debated the limits of scientific explanation, particularly when it comes to metaphysical questions about the nature of existence and the origin of the universe. While science provides powerful tools for understanding the physical world, it may not be able to fully address certain fundamental questions that lie at the intersection of metaphysics and theology.

Key Philosophical Critiques:

1. The Problem of Infinite Regress: One critique of purely scientific explanations for the origin of the universe is the problem of infinite regress. If every event or state of affairs requires a cause, then what caused the initial conditions of the Big Bang? Some philosophers argue that scientific theories cannot fully explain the ultimate origin of the universe without positing a first cause, which leads back to philosophical and theological considerations.

2. The Nature of Scientific Theories: Some philosophers argue that scientific theories are inherently limited in their ability to provide ultimate explanations because they are based on empirical observation and mathematical models. These theories describe how the universe behaves but may not fully explain why it exists in the first place. This critique suggests that metaphysical questions

about creation require philosophical reasoning that goes beyond empirical science.

3. Epistemological Limits: The question of what can be known and how it can be known is central to the philosophy of science. Some philosophers argue that certain aspects of reality, such as the nature of consciousness or the existence of God, may lie beyond the reach of scientific inquiry. These epistemological limits suggest that science alone may not be sufficient to address all questions about creation and existence.

The Interaction Between Science and Theology

The interaction between science and theology is a key area where philosophy plays a mediating role. Philosophical analysis can help clarify the assumptions, implications, and limitations of both scientific and theological claims, facilitating a more nuanced dialogue between the two.

Philosophical Mediation Between Science and Theology:

1. Theological Interpretations of Scientific Theories: Philosophers of religion often engage with scientific theories to explore their theological implications. For example, the Big Bang Theory has been interpreted by some theologians as consistent with the doctrine of Creation Ex Nihilo, while

others see it as raising new challenges for traditional views of God and creation.

2. Philosophical Reconciliation of Conflicts: When scientific theories appear to conflict with theological doctrines, philosophers can help reconcile these differences by examining the underlying assumptions and exploring alternative interpretations. This can lead to a more integrated understanding of creation that respects both scientific insights and theological principles.

3. Expanding the Scope of Inquiry: Philosophy encourages an expanded scope of inquiry that includes not only empirical evidence but also metaphysical and existential questions. This broader perspective allows for a more comprehensive exploration of creation, encompassing both the physical origins of the universe and the deeper questions of meaning and purpose.

The Future of Science-Philosophy Interaction in Understanding Creation

Emerging Scientific Theories and Philosophical Questions

As scientific research continues to advance, new theories are likely to emerge that will further impact philosophical discussions of creation. For example, developments in quantum gravity, string theory, and the study of dark matter and dark energy may offer new insights into the nature of the universe and its origins. These theories will undoubtedly raise new philosophical questions about causality, the nature of reality, and the possibility of multiple or parallel universes.

Potential Areas of Future Inquiry:

1. The Role of Consciousness: The relationship between consciousness and the physical universe is an area of ongoing research in both science and philosophy. Understanding how consciousness arises and whether it plays a role in the creation or evolution of the universe could have profound implications for our understanding of existence and the nature of reality.

2. The Concept of Emergence: The idea that complex systems and properties can emerge from simpler components is a key concept in both science and philosophy. Exploring how emergence applies to the creation of the universe could offer new perspectives on the relationship between simplicity and complexity, as well as the nature of causality and design.

3. The Integration of Science, Philosophy, and Theology: As our understanding of the universe continues to evolve, there may be increasing opportunities for integrating scientific, philosophical, and theological perspectives into a more holistic view of creation. This could lead to new models

of reality that incorporate insights from multiple disciplines and address both empirical and metaphysical questions.

The Continuing Dialogue Between Science and Philosophy

The interaction between science and philosophy in understanding creation is not a one-way street; it is a dynamic dialogue in which each discipline informs and enriches the other. As new scientific discoveries challenge established philosophical ideas, philosophers respond by reexamining those ideas and developing new frameworks for understanding the world. Similarly, philosophical questions often inspire new scientific inquiries, leading to further advancements in our understanding of the universe.

This ongoing dialogue ensures that our understanding of creation remains a vibrant and evolving field of study, where science and philosophy work together to explore the deepest questions about existence, causality, and the origins of the cosmos.

The interaction between science and philosophy in understanding creation is a testament to the complexity and richness of human inquiry. While science provides powerful tools for exploring the physical universe, philosophy offers the conceptual frameworks and critical analysis necessary to address the deeper metaphysical and existential questions that arise from scientific discoveries.

Together, science and philosophy form a complementary partnership in the search for knowledge and understanding. By engaging in a continuous dialogue, these disciplines help us to approach the mystery of creation with both empirical rigor and philosophical depth, leading to a more comprehensive and meaningful understanding of the universe and our place within it.

CHAPTER 08

CREATION EX NIHILO AND EXISTENTIAL QUESTIONS

The Significance of Creation for Human Identity and Purpose

The doctrine of Creation Ex Nihilo—the belief that God created the universe out of nothing—has profound implications not only for our understanding of the cosmos but also for fundamental questions of human identity and purpose. This chapter explores the existential significance of Creation Ex Nihilo, examining how this concept shapes our perceptions of who we are, why we exist, and what our ultimate purpose might be. Through this lens, we can better understand the deep connections between theological doctrines, philosophical inquiry, and the search for meaning in human life.

Theological Foundations of Human Identity

Creation and the Imago Dei

In Judeo-Christian theology, the doctrine of Creation Ex Nihilo is closely linked to the belief that human beings are created in the Imago Dei—the image of God. According to the biblical narrative, God created humanity as the pinnacle of creation, endowing humans with unique qualities that reflect His nature. This belief has significant implications for how human identity is understood.

Key Aspects of the Imago Dei:

1. Dignity and Worth: The belief that humans are made in the image of God implies that every person possesses inherent dignity and worth. This dignity is not contingent on any external factors such as social status, achievements, or abilities, but is rooted in the divine act of creation. The idea that humans are created by God out of nothing, and in His image, suggests that our value is intrinsic and immutable, grounded in our relationship to the Creator.

2. Rationality and Creativity: Being made in the image of God also implies that humans share certain attributes with the divine, particularly rationality and creativity. Just as God exercised His will and intellect in creating the universe, so too

are humans endowed with the capacity for reason, problem-solving, and creativity. This connection to the divine creator emphasizes the human role as co-creators in the world, responsible for shaping and stewarding creation.

3. Relationality: The Imago Dei also points to the relational nature of human existence. Just as God is understood to be a relational being (in Christian theology, this is often articulated through the doctrine of the Trinity), so too are humans created to live in relationships—with God, with each other, and with the rest of creation. This relational aspect of identity highlights the importance of community, love, and interconnectedness as central to human life.

The Significance of Being Created

The doctrine of Creation Ex Nihilo emphasizes that human beings, like the rest of the universe, are not self-sustaining but are created and sustained by God. This understanding has several implications for how we perceive our identity and our place in the world.

Dependence and Contingency:

1. Contingent Existence: The belief that humans are created out of nothing underscores our contingent nature. We are not necessary beings; our existence depends entirely on the will of God. This sense of contingency can lead to a profound humility, as it reminds us that we are not the authors

of our own existence. Instead, we are part of a larger, divinely orchestrated plan, and our lives have meaning and purpose within that context.

2. Divine Purpose: If human beings are created by God, then our existence is not random or accidental. Instead, it is purposeful, rooted in the divine will. This belief can provide a strong sense of direction and meaning, as it suggests that our lives are part of a broader narrative in which each person has a role to play. The idea that we are created with purpose challenges the notion of existential nihilism and affirms the significance of our actions and decisions.

3. Relationship with the Creator: The doctrine of Creation Ex Nihilo implies that our identity is intrinsically linked to our relationship with God. We are not autonomous beings but are connected to our Creator in a fundamental way. This relationship provides the foundation for our sense of self and our understanding of who we are. It also invites us to seek out and cultivate that relationship, recognizing that our ultimate fulfillment is found in communion with the divine.

Philosophical Implications for Human Purpose

Existential Questions in the Light of Creation

The doctrine of Creation Ex Nihilo addresses some of the most profound existential questions that humans face: Who am I? Why am I here? What is the meaning of life? By situating these questions within the context of a divinely created universe, the doctrine offers a framework for understanding human purpose and meaning.

Existence and Essence:

1. Essence Precedes Existence: In traditional theistic frameworks, particularly those influenced by Creation Ex Nihilo, it is often said that "essence precedes existence." This means that God, in creating human beings, imbued them with a specific nature and purpose before they came into existence. Unlike in existentialist philosophy, where "existence precedes essence" (implying that humans must create their own meaning), the doctrine of Creation Ex Nihilo suggests that our purpose and identity are given by God.

2. The Search for Meaning: The belief that we are created with a purpose provides a foundation for the search for meaning. Rather than seeing life as a blank slate on which we must inscribe our own values and purposes, the doctrine suggests that meaning is something to be discovered, not invented. This discovery process involves understanding our relationship with God, our role in the world, and the moral and spiritual goals that we are called to pursue.

3. Purpose and Fulfillment: The doctrine of Creation Ex Nihilo implies that true fulfillment is found in aligning our lives with the purposes for which we were created. This might

include living in accordance with moral and ethical principles, cultivating relationships, contributing to the well-being of others, and seeking to understand and follow the divine will. In this view, human purpose is not arbitrary but is rooted in the very act of creation.

The Problem of Suffering and Evil

The existence of suffering and evil in a world created by a good and omnipotent God is one of the most challenging questions for both philosophy and theology. The doctrine of Creation Ex Nihilo offers a context for addressing these issues, though it does not provide easy answers.

Theodicy and Human Purpose:

1. The Role of Free Will: One common theodicy (justification of God's goodness in the face of evil) suggests that God created humans with free will, which is necessary for moral responsibility and genuine love. However, free will also allows for the possibility of evil and suffering. The doctrine of Creation Ex Nihilo implies that God's act of creation included the creation of beings with the freedom to choose, and this freedom is essential to our identity and purpose, even if it entails the risk of suffering.

2. Suffering as a Context for Growth: Some philosophical and theological perspectives suggest that suffering can have a purpose within God's creation, serving

as a context for personal and spiritual growth. The idea that we are created with a purpose implies that our experiences, including suffering, can contribute to our development and fulfillment of that purpose. This view does not trivialize suffering but seeks to understand it within a larger narrative of creation and redemption.

3. Evil as a Privation: Another theological response to the problem of evil, rooted in the doctrine of Creation Ex Nihilo, is the idea that evil is not a created substance but a privation of good—a distortion or absence of the good that God intended. This perspective aligns with the belief that everything God created is inherently good, and that evil results from the misuse of free will or the corruption of creation. Understanding evil as a privation rather than a created entity can shape how we respond to and understand suffering in our lives.

Human Identity in a Created Universe

The Significance of Human Stewardship

The doctrine of Creation Ex Nihilo not only defines human identity in relation to God but also assigns humans a specific role within the created order: that of stewards of creation. This role has profound implications for how we understand our purpose in the world.

Stewardship and Responsibility:

1. Caring for Creation: The belief that God created the universe out of nothing and entrusted it to human care implies a responsibility to protect and nurture the environment. As stewards, humans are called to manage the earth's resources wisely, ensuring that they are preserved and used in ways that reflect God's original intent. This responsibility is integral to human identity and purpose, emphasizing the role of humans as caretakers of the planet.

2. Ethical Implications: The concept of stewardship extends beyond environmental concerns to include social and ethical responsibilities. Humans, as part of a divinely created order, are called to promote justice, peace, and the well-being of all creatures. This ethical dimension of stewardship highlights the interconnectedness of all life and the importance of living in harmony with others and the natural world.

3. Innovation and Creativity: As stewards, humans are also encouraged to exercise their creativity and ingenuity in ways that contribute to the flourishing of creation. This might include scientific advancements, technological innovations, and cultural developments that enhance the quality of life and reflect the creative nature of the divine. The doctrine of Creation Ex Nihilo supports the idea that human creativity is

a reflection of the divine image and that it should be used to further God's purposes in the world.

The Ultimate Purpose of Human Existence

In the context of Creation Ex Nihilo, the ultimate purpose of human existence is often understood in terms of relationship—relationship with God, with others, and with creation. This relational understanding of purpose offers a holistic view of human identity that integrates spiritual, moral, and social dimensions.

Relational Purpose:

1. Union with God: The ultimate purpose of human existence, according to many theological perspectives, is union with God. The doctrine of Creation Ex Nihilo suggests that humans were created not just to exist, but to exist in relationship with their Creator.

This relationship is seen as the source of true fulfillment and the ultimate goal of human life. Practices such as prayer, worship, and ethical living are understood as means of deepening this relationship and aligning oneself with God's will.

2. Community and Love: The relational aspect of human purpose extends to relationships with others. Humans are created to live in community, to love and support one another, and to contribute to the common good. This

communal dimension of purpose reflects the belief that humans are not isolated individuals but are part of a larger, interconnected whole. Acts of compassion, justice, and service are seen as expressions of this communal purpose.

3. Participation in God's Creative Work: Finally, the doctrine of Creation Ex Nihilo implies that humans are called to participate in God's ongoing creative work. This includes not only stewardship of the environment but also the creation of culture, the pursuit of knowledge, and the promotion of justice. By contributing to the flourishing of creation, humans fulfill their purpose as co-creators with God, working to bring about the fullness of God's original intent for the world.

Conclusion: Creation Ex Nihilo and the Search for Meaning

The doctrine of Creation Ex Nihilo offers a profound framework for understanding human identity and purpose. It suggests that our existence is not arbitrary but is rooted in the intentional act of a loving and purposeful Creator. This belief shapes how we understand who we are, why we exist, and what our ultimate goals should be.

In a world often characterized by uncertainty and existential questioning, the doctrine of Creation Ex Nihilo provides a source of meaning and direction. It affirms the intrinsic value of every human being, the importance of living in relationship with God and others, and the significance of contributing to the flourishing of creation.

As we continue to explore the implications of this doctrine, we are invited to reflect on our own lives and consider how we might align our actions and choices with the purpose for which we were created. In doing so, we find not only a sense of identity and belonging but also a deeper understanding of the meaning of existence and the ultimate goal of human life.

The Impact on Ethics and Moral Values

The doctrine of Creation Ex Nihilo—the belief that God created the universe out of nothing—has profound implications for ethics and moral values. By grounding human existence in a divinely created order, this doctrine shapes how we understand concepts such as good and evil, justice, human rights, and our responsibilities toward others and the environment. This chapter explores the ethical and moral impact of Creation Ex Nihilo, examining how this doctrine influences moral reasoning, informs ethical principles, and guides human behavior.

The Foundations of Moral Values in Creation

The Moral Order and Divine Authority

The doctrine of Creation Ex Nihilo implies that the moral order is rooted in the will and nature of God, the

Creator. Since God is the source of all that exists, He is also the source of moral values and principles. This divine grounding gives moral values their ultimate authority and universality.

Key Aspects of the Moral Order:

1. Objective Moral Values: The belief in a divinely created order suggests that moral values are objective—they are not merely subjective preferences or social constructs but are grounded in the very nature of reality as ordained by God. This means that concepts of right and wrong, good and evil, have an absolute foundation in the divine will. Ethical principles are not arbitrarily determined by individuals or cultures but reflect the moral law established by the Creator.

2. Divine Command Theory: One approach to understanding the relationship between Creation Ex Nihilo and ethics is through Divine Command Theory. According to this view, moral obligations are determined by God's commands, which are rooted in His character and will. Because God is the Creator, His commands carry the highest moral authority, and humans are morally obligated to follow them. This perspective sees ethical behavior as a response to the moral order established by God through the act of creation.

3. The Goodness of Creation: The doctrine of Creation Ex Nihilo also implies that creation itself is inherently good, as it reflects the goodness of the Creator. This has ethical implications, suggesting that moral behavior involves respecting, preserving, and enhancing the goodness of creation. Acts that harm or degrade creation are seen as violations of the moral order and, by extension, of God's will.

Human Dignity and Rights

The doctrine of Creation Ex Nihilo underpins the concept of human dignity and the idea that all people possess inherent worth. If humans are created by God, they are not mere accidents of nature but are intentional beings with a unique status within the created order. This belief has significant implications for how we understand human rights and our ethical obligations toward one another.

Implications for Human Dignity:

1. Inherent Worth: The belief that every person is created by God suggests that all humans possess inherent worth and dignity. This dignity is not dependent on social status, abilities, or achievements but is rooted in the fact that each person is made in the image of God (Imago Dei). This theological foundation supports the idea that every human being deserves respect, protection, and the opportunity to flourish.

2. Universal Human Rights: The concept of inherent dignity also provides a basis for the idea of universal human rights. If all people are created by God and possess equal worth, then they are entitled to certain fundamental rights, such as the right to life, freedom, and justice. These rights are not granted by governments or societies but are intrinsic to human nature as created by God. This understanding of human rights is closely linked to the ethical principle of justice, which demands that these rights be respected and upheld for all people.

3. Moral Responsibility: Along with dignity and rights, the doctrine of Creation Ex Nihilo implies that humans have moral responsibilities toward one another. These responsibilities include caring for the vulnerable, promoting justice, and working to ensure that all people can live in dignity. The belief that humans are created by God with a purpose suggests that fulfilling these moral responsibilities is part of what it means to live a good and meaningful life.

Ethical Principles Derived from Creation Ex Nihilo

The Principle of Stewardship

One of the key ethical principles that arises from the doctrine of Creation Ex Nihilo is the principle of stewardship. This principle is based on the idea that the world and all its resources are not human possessions but are entrusted to humanity by God. As stewards of creation, humans have a moral obligation to care for and preserve the natural world.

Key Aspects of Stewardship:

1. Environmental Ethics: The principle of stewardship has significant implications for environmental ethics. It suggests that humans are responsible for protecting the environment, conserving resources, and ensuring that the earth remains a viable habitat for future generations. Environmental degradation, exploitation of natural resources, and harm to ecosystems are seen as violations of the stewardship role that God has given humanity.

2. Sustainable Living: Stewardship also implies the importance of sustainable living—using resources in a way that meets the needs of the present without compromising the ability of future generations to meet their own needs. This principle encourages practices such as conservation, recycling, and the use of renewable energy, all of which are seen as ways to honor the Creator by caring for His creation.

3. Justice and Equity: The principle of stewardship extends beyond environmental concerns to include issues of justice and equity. It suggests that the resources of the earth should be used in a way that benefits all people, not just a privileged few. This has implications for economic justice, the

fair distribution of resources, and the responsibility to address global inequalities.

The Sanctity of Life

Another ethical principle that is deeply rooted in the doctrine of Creation Ex Nihilo is the sanctity of life. The belief that life is created by God out of nothing suggests that life is sacred and should be protected and respected at all stages.

Implications of the Sanctity of Life:

1. Opposition to Killing: The sanctity of life principle implies a strong ethical opposition to killing, whether in the form of murder, abortion, euthanasia, or capital punishment. If life is a gift from God, then taking a life is seen as an affront to the Creator and a violation of the moral order. This principle supports a pro-life ethic that values and protects life from conception to natural death.

2. Respect for Human Dignity: The sanctity of life also reinforces the concept of human dignity, suggesting that all people, regardless of their circumstances, deserve to be treated with respect and compassion. This has implications for how we treat the sick, the elderly, the disabled, and the marginalized. It calls for a commitment to caring for those who are most vulnerable and to ensuring that their dignity is upheld.

3. Nonviolence and Peace: The principle of the sanctity of life also supports a commitment to nonviolence and peace. If all life is sacred, then acts of violence and war are seen as violations of the moral order. This principle encourages the pursuit of peaceful resolutions to conflicts, the promotion of social harmony, and the rejection of violence as a means of achieving political or personal goals.

Moral Decision-Making in the Light of Creation Ex Nihilo

Moral Discernment and Divine Guidance

The doctrine of Creation Ex Nihilo suggests that moral decision-making is not solely a human endeavor but is guided by divine wisdom and principles. This belief shapes how individuals and communities approach ethical dilemmas, seeking to align their decisions with the moral order established by God.

Approaches to Moral Discernment:

1. Scriptural Guidance: For many believers, moral decision-making is informed by sacred scriptures, which are seen as divinely inspired texts that provide guidance on how to live according to God's will. The teachings of scripture are interpreted as revealing the moral order that God has established and are used to discern right from wrong in various situations.

2. Prayer and Reflection: Prayer and reflection are also important tools for moral discernment. By seeking God's guidance through prayer, individuals can gain insight into how to navigate ethical challenges in a way that honors the Creator. Reflection on one's actions and motivations, in light of the doctrine of Creation Ex Nihilo, can lead to a deeper understanding of how to live a morally responsible life.

3. Community and Tradition: Moral decision-making is often carried out within the context of a community of faith. Religious traditions provide a rich repository of ethical teachings, practices, and interpretations that help guide individuals in making moral choices. The wisdom of the community, as well as the teachings of religious leaders, can offer valuable perspectives on how to apply the principles of Creation Ex Nihilo to contemporary ethical issues.

Moral Accountability

The belief in Creation Ex Nihilo also carries with it the idea of moral accountability. If humans are created by God with a purpose, then they are accountable to God for how they live their lives. This accountability shapes how individuals approach ethical decision-making, knowing that their actions have consequences not only in this life but also in the eyes of God.

Aspects of Moral Accountability:

1. Judgment and Justice: The doctrine of moral accountability suggests that individuals will be judged by God for their actions. This belief reinforces the importance of living a morally upright life, knowing that there will be divine consequences for one's choices. The concept of divine judgment underscores the seriousness of moral decisions and the need to act justly and righteously.

2. Repentance and Forgiveness: Moral accountability also includes the possibility of repentance and forgiveness. Recognizing that humans are fallible and capable of making mistakes, the doctrine of Creation Ex Nihilo encourages individuals to seek forgiveness from God and to make amends for their wrongs. This process of repentance and reconciliation is seen as a way to restore one's relationship with the Creator and to realign oneself with the moral order.

3. Eternal Consequences: The belief in an afterlife, where individuals are held accountable for their actions, adds another dimension to moral decision-making. The doctrine of Creation Ex Nihilo suggests that

how we live in this life has eternal implications. This belief motivates individuals to strive for moral excellence and to live in a way that reflects the values of the Creator.

The Ethical Challenge of Modern Issues

Bioethics and Technology

In the modern world, advances in science and technology have created new ethical challenges that require careful consideration in light of the doctrine of Creation Ex Nihilo. Issues such as genetic engineering, cloning, artificial intelligence, and biotechnology raise complex questions about the sanctity of life, the limits of human creativity, and the ethical use of technology.

Ethical Considerations in Bioethics:

1. Genetic Engineering: The ability to manipulate genetic material raises questions about the extent to which humans should intervene in the natural order. The doctrine of Creation Ex Nihilo suggests that life is sacred and that genetic engineering should be approached with caution, ensuring that it respects the integrity of creation and does not harm individuals or the environment.

2. Cloning: Cloning, particularly human cloning, challenges traditional concepts of identity, individuality, and the uniqueness of each person as a creation of God. Ethical considerations include the potential for exploitation, the commodification of human life, and the implications for human dignity.

3. Artificial Intelligence: The development of artificial intelligence (AI) raises questions about the nature of consciousness, the role of humans as creators, and the ethical

implications of creating machines that can make decisions and potentially act autonomously. The doctrine of Creation Ex Nihilo encourages careful reflection on the moral responsibilities that come with such technological power and the need to ensure that AI is used in ways that align with ethical principles.

Environmental Ethics

The growing awareness of environmental degradation and climate change has brought environmental ethics to the forefront of moral discourse. The principle of stewardship, rooted in the doctrine of Creation Ex Nihilo, provides a framework for addressing these issues.

Environmental Ethical Challenges:

1. Climate Change: Climate change poses a significant threat to the planet and all its inhabitants. The doctrine of Creation Ex Nihilo suggests that humans have a moral responsibility to address this issue by reducing carbon emissions, conserving resources, and protecting vulnerable ecosystems. Ethical considerations include the need for global cooperation, the protection of future generations, and the promotion of environmental justice.

2. Biodiversity: The loss of biodiversity due to habitat destruction, pollution, and overexploitation is another critical issue. The principle of stewardship calls for the preservation

of species and ecosystems, recognizing the intrinsic value of all life forms as part of God's creation.

3. Sustainable Development: The challenge of balancing economic development with environmental sustainability is a key ethical issue in the modern world. The doctrine of Creation Ex Nihilo encourages a vision of development that promotes human well-being while respecting the limits of the earth's resources and ensuring that the needs of future generations are met.

Conclusion: Creation Ex Nihilo as a Moral Foundation

The doctrine of Creation Ex Nihilo provides a robust moral foundation for ethical decision-making in both personal and social contexts. By grounding moral values in the act of divine creation, this doctrine offers a framework for understanding human dignity, rights, and responsibilities. It challenges individuals and communities to live in ways that reflect the goodness of creation, respect the sanctity of life, and fulfill the moral obligations that come with being stewards of the earth.

In a world facing complex ethical challenges, the principles derived from Creation Ex Nihilo offer guidance and direction. They call for a commitment to justice, compassion, and the responsible use of resources. By aligning our actions with the moral order established by the Creator, we can contribute to the flourishing of creation and the fulfillment of our purpose as beings created in the image of God.

Existential Implications of a Created vs. Uncreated Universe

The question of whether the universe is created or uncreated—whether it was brought into existence by a divine act or has existed eternally without a creator—has profound existential implications. This distinction shapes our understanding of human identity, purpose, and the nature of reality itself. In this chapter, we explore the existential implications of living in a created universe as opposed to an uncreated one, examining how these different perspectives influence our views on meaning, morality, and the human condition.

The Created Universe: Existential Implications

Meaning and Purpose in a Created Universe

In a universe that is believed to be created, particularly under the doctrine of Creation Ex Nihilo (creation out of nothing), the existence of the universe is intentional and purposeful. This belief fundamentally shapes how individuals understand their own lives and their place in the cosmos.

Key Implications for Meaning and Purpose:

1. Intrinsic Meaning: In a created universe, meaning is not something that must be constructed by individuals; it is intrinsic to the nature of reality. The universe, having been created by a purposeful deity, is imbued with inherent meaning. This suggests that human lives are part of a broader, divinely ordained plan, where each person has a role to play within the cosmic order. The belief in a created universe gives rise to the notion that life has objective meaning, rooted in the intentions and purposes of the Creator.

2. Divine Purpose: If the universe and everything in it were created by God, then human existence is purposeful. Each individual is believed to have been created for a specific reason, with a unique role to fulfill in the divine plan. This belief can provide a profound sense of direction and motivation, as individuals seek to discover and live out their God-given purpose. The existential angst that can arise from a perceived lack of meaning is alleviated by the assurance that one's life is meaningful in the eyes of the Creator.

3. Moral and Ethical Framework: A created universe also implies a moral order established by the Creator. In this view, moral values are not subjective or relative but are grounded in the character and will of God. This provides a clear framework for ethical behavior, where moral duties and obligations are understood as part of the divine order. The

belief in a created universe encourages individuals to live in accordance with this moral order, striving to align their actions with the purposes for which they were created.

Human Identity and Dignity

The belief in a created universe profoundly influences how individuals perceive their own identity and the dignity of human life. If humans are created by God, their identity is defined not by arbitrary or external factors but by their relationship with the Creator.

Implications for Human Identity:

1. Imago Dei (Image of God): In many religious traditions, particularly in Christianity, the belief that humans are created in the image of God (Imago Dei) is central to understanding human identity. This doctrine suggests that humans possess a unique dignity and worth that is intrinsic and non-negotiable. The belief in a created universe affirms that human life is sacred, and that every person is a reflection of the divine, endowed with the capacity for reason, creativity, and moral responsibility.

2. Relational Identity: The belief in a created universe emphasizes the relational aspect of human identity. Humans are seen as inherently relational beings, created to live in communion with God, with others, and with the natural world. This relational identity shapes how individuals

understand their purpose in life, emphasizing the importance of community, love, and mutual respect. It also highlights the responsibility humans have to care for creation and to nurture relationships that reflect the goodness of the Creator.

3. Accountability and Responsibility: In a created universe, human beings are accountable to the Creator for how they live their lives. This belief instills a sense of moral responsibility, as individuals recognize that their actions have consequences not only in this life but in the eyes of God. The belief in divine judgment or an afterlife further reinforces the idea that how one lives matters, and that individuals are called to fulfill the purpose for which they were created.

The Uncreated Universe: Existential Implications

Meaning and Purpose in an Uncreated Universe

In contrast to a created universe, an uncreated universe is one that exists without a divine creator or purpose. This view, often associated with naturalistic or atheistic perspectives, suggests that the universe is a product of random processes or has existed eternally without a beginning. The existential implications of this view are markedly different from those of a created universe.

Key Implications for Meaning and Purpose:

1. Constructed Meaning: In an uncreated universe, meaning is not intrinsic but must be constructed by

individuals. Without a creator or divine purpose, life does not have inherent meaning; instead, meaning is something that humans must create for themselves. This perspective can lead to existential freedom, where individuals are free to define their own purpose and values. However, it can also lead to existential anxiety, as the burden of creating meaning falls entirely on the individual, with no external or objective source of guidance.

2. Absence of Divine Purpose: The absence of a divine purpose in an uncreated universe suggests that human existence is the result of random processes or natural laws, without any ultimate goal or direction. This can lead to a sense of cosmic insignificance, where human life is seen as a fleeting moment in the vast, indifferent expanse of the universe. For some, this realization can be liberating, as it frees individuals from the constraints of religious or traditional moral systems. For others, it can lead to feelings of nihilism or despair, as the search for meaning becomes a solitary and subjective endeavor.

3. Subjective Moral Frameworks: In an uncreated universe, moral values are not grounded in a divine order but are the product of human societies and cultures. This can lead to a more relativistic approach to ethics, where moral values are seen as subjective and contingent on social, cultural, or

personal factors. Without an objective moral order, individuals must navigate ethical dilemmas based on reason, empathy, or social consensus. This can foster a sense of moral autonomy, but it may also lead to ethical uncertainty, as there is no external standard by which to judge right and wrong.

Human Identity and Dignity

The view of an uncreated universe also has significant implications for how individuals perceive their own identity and the dignity of human life. Without a creator, human identity is seen as the result of evolutionary processes or social constructions, rather than as something divinely ordained.

Implications for Human Identity:

1. Biological Identity: In an uncreated universe, human identity is often understood in purely biological terms. Humans are seen as the product of evolution, shaped by genetic and environmental factors. This perspective can lead to a more materialistic view of human life, where identity is reduced to physical and psychological characteristics. While this view can foster a sense of continuity with the natural world, it may also diminish the sense of intrinsic worth and dignity that is central to the belief in a created universe.

2. Existential Freedom: The absence of a creator in an uncreated universe can lead to a sense of existential freedom, where individuals are free to define themselves and create

their own identity. This freedom allows for greater individual autonomy and self-expression, but it also comes with the responsibility of constructing a meaningful life in a universe that offers no inherent purpose or direction.

3. Moral Relativism: In an uncreated universe, the concept of human dignity may be viewed as a social construct rather than an objective truth. This can lead to moral relativism, where the value of human life is determined by societal norms, cultural practices, or individual preferences. While this approach allows for flexibility and adaptability in ethical reasoning, it may also undermine the idea of universal human rights and the inherent worth of every person.

The Existential Tension Between Created and Uncreated Views

The Search for Meaning

The existential tension between a created and uncreated universe is most evident in the search for meaning. While a created universe offers the assurance of intrinsic meaning and purpose, an uncreated universe challenges individuals to find or create meaning in a seemingly indifferent cosmos.

Navigating the Tension:

1. Philosophical Inquiry: Philosophers have long grappled with the tension between these two views, exploring

questions of meaning, purpose, and identity in both religious and secular contexts. Existentialist philosophers like Jean-Paul Sartre and Albert Camus, for example, embraced the idea of an uncreated universe, arguing that meaning must be constructed by individuals in the face of an absurd and meaningless world. In contrast, religious philosophers like Søren Kierkegaard and C.S. Lewis emphasized the importance of faith and divine purpose in providing meaning and direction.

2. Personal Reflection: On a personal level, individuals must navigate the existential implications of these differing views, often wrestling with questions of faith, doubt, and the search for meaning. For some, the belief in a created universe provides a sense of security and purpose, while others find meaning in the freedom and autonomy of an uncreated universe. The existential tension between these views can lead to profound self-reflection and exploration, as individuals seek to understand their place in the world and the meaning of their existence.

3. Cultural and Social Impacts: The tension between created and uncreated views also plays out on a cultural and societal level, influencing debates about ethics, morality, and the role of religion in public life. In societies where belief in a created universe is dominant, ethical systems and social norms

are often grounded in religious teachings. In more secular societies, where the uncreated view may be more prevalent, moral values and social practices are shaped by humanistic principles and reason.

Conclusion: The Existential Stakes of Creation

The question of whether the universe is created or uncreated carries significant existential implications for how we understand meaning, purpose, identity, and morality. In a created universe, life is imbued with intrinsic meaning and purpose, grounded in the intentions of a divine Creator. This view offers a framework for understanding human dignity, moral values, and the ultimate purpose of existence.

In contrast, an uncreated universe challenges individuals to find or create their own meaning in a world that offers no inherent purpose. This perspective emphasizes existential freedom and autonomy but also raises questions about the source of moral values and the significance of human life in a vast, indifferent cosmos.

Ultimately, the existential implications of a created versus uncreated universe are deeply personal, shaping how individuals view themselves, their relationships, and their place in the world. Whether one finds meaning in the belief in a divine Creator or in the freedom of an uncreated universe, the search for meaning and purpose remains a central aspect of the human experience, driving us to explore the deepest questions of existence and our place in the cosmos.

Comparative Analysis of Theological and Philosophical Arguments

The interaction between theology and philosophy has been a cornerstone of intellectual inquiry for centuries, with both disciplines seeking to understand the nature of existence, the origins of the universe, and the meaning of human life. While theology often relies on revealed truths and divine authority, philosophy typically employs reason and logical analysis to explore these same questions. Despite their different approaches, theology and philosophy have much to offer each other, and a comparative analysis of their arguments can provide a richer and more comprehensive understanding of the profound questions that have intrigued humanity throughout history. This chapter offers a comparative analysis of key theological and philosophical arguments, focusing on areas where these disciplines converge, diverge, and complement each other.

Theological and Philosophical Foundations of Creation

Theological Arguments for Creation

In theology, the doctrine of Creation Ex Nihilo—the belief that God created the universe out of nothing—serves as a fundamental tenet of many religious traditions, particularly in Christianity, Judaism, and Islam. Theological arguments for creation are deeply rooted in sacred texts and religious teachings, which assert that the universe and everything in it were brought into existence by the will and power of a divine being.

Key Theological Arguments:

1. Divine Revelation: The primary basis for theological arguments for creation is divine revelation, as recorded in sacred scriptures. For example, the Book of Genesis in the Bible begins with the declaration, "In the beginning, God created the heavens and the earth" (Genesis 1:1). This statement is taken as a direct revelation of the truth of creation, affirming that the universe has a definitive origin in the creative act of God.

2. The Cosmological Argument: Theologically, the cosmological argument for the existence of God often serves as a foundation for the belief in Creation Ex Nihilo. This argument posits that everything that exists has a cause, and since the universe exists, it must have a cause that is not itself caused by anything else. This uncaused cause is identified as God, who brought the universe into existence from nothing. The cosmological argument underscores the theological claim

that the universe is not eternal but has a beginning in the divine will.

3. The Doctrine of Creation: Theological arguments for creation often emphasize the doctrine of creation as a central element of faith. This doctrine not only explains the origins of the universe but also provides a framework for understanding the relationship between God, humanity, and the world. Theologically, creation is seen as an expression of God's love, wisdom, and power, and it establishes the foundation for the moral and spiritual order of the universe.

Philosophical Arguments for and Against Creation

Philosophy approaches the question of creation from a different perspective, often relying on reason, observation, and logical analysis to explore the origins of the universe. Philosophical arguments for creation, as well as those against it, reflect the diversity of thought within the discipline, ranging from metaphysical explorations to critiques of theological claims.

Key Philosophical Arguments:

1. The First Cause Argument: One of the most significant philosophical arguments for creation is the First Cause Argument, also known as the cosmological argument in philosophy. Similar to its theological counterpart, this argument posits that the existence of the universe requires a

first cause that is uncaused and eternal. Philosophers like Aristotle and Aquinas have developed versions of this argument, identifying the first cause as a necessary being—God. The First Cause Argument provides a rational basis for believing in a creator, even in the absence of divine revelation.

2. The Argument from Contingency: Another important philosophical argument is the Argument from Contingency, which asserts that everything in the universe is contingent, meaning that it depends on something else for its existence. Since the universe is composed of contingent entities, it must ultimately depend on a necessary being that is not contingent—God. This argument supports the idea of a created universe by emphasizing the need for a necessary being to explain the existence of contingent beings.

3. Critiques of Creation Ex Nihilo: On the other hand, some philosophers have critiqued the concept of Creation Ex Nihilo, arguing that it raises logical and metaphysical challenges. For example, the principle of "ex nihilo nihil fit" (out of nothing, nothing comes) suggests that it is impossible for something to come into existence from nothing. Philosophers like David Hume and Immanuel Kant have questioned whether the concept of creation from nothing is coherent and whether it can be reconciled with our understanding of causality and existence.

Convergence and Divergence: Theological and Philosophical Approaches

Points of Convergence

Despite their differences, theological and philosophical approaches to creation share several points of convergence. These areas of overlap highlight how both disciplines contribute to a deeper understanding of the origins of the universe and the nature of existence.

Key Areas of Convergence:

1. The Existence of a First Cause: Both theology and philosophy often converge on the idea that the universe requires a first cause or an uncaused cause. Whether through divine revelation or rational argumentation, both disciplines affirm the necessity of a being that is eternal, uncaused, and capable of bringing the universe into existence. This convergence suggests that the idea of a creator is not only a matter of faith but also a conclusion that can be reached through reason.

2. The Contingency of the Universe: Another area of convergence is the recognition that the universe is contingent and not self-sustaining. Both theological and philosophical arguments emphasize that the universe's existence depends on something beyond itself, whether that is understood as God in theological terms or a necessary being in philosophical

terms. This shared understanding supports the view that the universe is not eternal and requires an explanation for its existence.

3. The Moral and Ethical Implications of Creation: Both theology and philosophy acknowledge that the concept of creation has significant moral and ethical implications. The belief in a created universe, whether understood theologically or philosophically, provides a foundation for concepts such as human dignity, moral responsibility, and the sanctity of life. These shared ethical principles underscore the importance of creation as a basis for moral values and behavior.

Points of Divergence

While there are areas of convergence, theology and philosophy also diverge in significant ways, particularly in their approaches to understanding creation and the implications of their arguments.

Key Areas of Divergence:

1. Revelation vs. Reason: One of the primary differences between theology and philosophy is the source of knowledge and authority. Theology relies heavily on divine revelation as the foundation for its claims about creation, while philosophy depends on human reason and observation. This difference in epistemology leads to different methods of

inquiry and can result in divergent conclusions about the nature of the universe and the existence of a creator.

2. The Nature of Causality: Theological and philosophical approaches to causality can also diverge. While both disciplines may accept the need for a first cause, theology often emphasizes God's transcendent and immanent nature, seeing God as both the creator and sustainer of the universe. Philosophy, however, may focus more on the logical structure of causality, exploring whether it is possible to have an infinite regress of causes or whether the concept of a first cause is coherent within a purely metaphysical framework.

3. The Problem of Evil: The problem of evil presents a significant divergence between theological and philosophical approaches to creation. Theologically, the existence of evil is often addressed through doctrines such as free will, the fall, and the eventual redemption of creation. Philosophically, the problem of evil is seen as a challenge to the coherence of the concept of an all-powerful, all-good creator. Philosophers like Hume and Leibniz have engaged in extensive debates about whether the existence of evil can be reconciled with the idea of a benevolent creator, leading to different conclusions in theology and philosophy.

Complementary Insights: The Interplay of Theology and Philosophy

The Value of Interdisciplinary Dialogue

The interplay between theology and philosophy offers valuable insights that neither discipline can fully achieve on its own. By engaging in interdisciplinary dialogue, theologians and philosophers can deepen their understanding of creation and address the limitations of their respective approaches.

Complementary Insights:

1. Philosophical Clarification of Theological Concepts: Philosophy can help clarify and refine theological concepts by subjecting them to rigorous logical analysis. For example, philosophical discussions of causality, time, and existence can shed light on theological doctrines such as Creation Ex Nihilo, helping to resolve apparent contradictions or ambiguities. This philosophical engagement can make theological claims more coherent and accessible to those outside the faith community.

2. Theological Enrichment of Philosophical Inquiry: Theology, in turn, can enrich philosophical inquiry by offering insights from divine revelation and religious experience. Theological perspectives can provide a deeper context for philosophical questions, such as the nature of the good, the purpose of existence, and the ultimate meaning of life. By

incorporating theological insights, philosophy can address existential questions that transcend purely rational analysis.

3. Ethical Implications and Practical Applications: The interaction between theology and philosophy can also have practical implications for ethics and moral decision-making. Theological principles, such as the belief in the inherent dignity of human beings, can inform philosophical discussions of human rights, justice, and social ethics. Conversely, philosophical rigor can help theology develop more robust and universally applicable ethical frameworks that can be used in diverse cultural and religious contexts.

Bridging the Gap: Integrative Approaches

Several thinkers have sought to bridge the gap between theology and philosophy, developing integrative approaches that draw on the strengths of both disciplines. These approaches often aim to provide a more holistic understanding of creation, one that acknowledges both the limitations and the contributions of theology and philosophy.

Examples of Integrative Approaches:

1. Thomas Aquinas: One of the most influential figures in bridging theology and philosophy is Thomas Aquinas, whose work Summa Theologica

represents a synthesis of Aristotelian philosophy and Christian theology. Aquinas argued that reason and revelation are complementary, with philosophy providing natural truths that are accessible to all, and theology offering revealed truths that complete and perfect human understanding. His integration of the First Cause Argument with the doctrine of Creation Ex Nihilo remains a cornerstone of Christian thought.

2. Paul Tillich: Paul Tillich, a 20th-century theologian and philosopher, also sought to integrate theology and philosophy, particularly through his concept of the "ground of being." Tillich argued that God is not a being among other beings but is the very ground of existence itself. This philosophical approach allowed Tillich to bridge the gap between existentialist philosophy and Christian theology, offering a way to understand God's relationship to creation that resonates with both philosophical and theological audiences.

3. Alvin Plantinga: Alvin Plantinga is a contemporary philosopher who has worked extensively on the relationship between philosophy and theology, particularly in the area of epistemology and the philosophy of religion. Plantinga's work on the rationality of religious belief and the problem of evil has contributed to a renewed dialogue between these disciplines, demonstrating that philosophical inquiry can support and enrich theological claims.

Conclusion: The Ongoing Dialogue Between Theology and Philosophy

The dialogue between theology and philosophy is an ongoing and dynamic process, one that continues to shape our understanding of creation, existence, and the ultimate meaning of life. While these disciplines approach the question of creation from different perspectives, their interaction offers a richer and more nuanced view of the universe and our place within it.

By comparing and integrating theological and philosophical arguments, we can gain a deeper appreciation for the complexity of the questions surrounding creation. This comparative analysis highlights the importance of interdisciplinary dialogue, where theology and philosophy work together to explore the mysteries of existence and to address the profound questions that have captivated humanity for centuries.

As we continue to engage with both theology and philosophy, we are reminded that the search for truth is a shared endeavor, one that benefits from the insights and contributions of multiple perspectives. Whether through faith, reason, or a combination of both, the exploration of creation remains a central aspect of human inquiry, guiding us toward a deeper understanding of the universe and our place within it.

285

CHAPTER 09

BRINGING THEOLOGY AND PHILOSOPHY

Common Ground and Divergent Views

The exploration of creation, existence, and the nature of reality has long been a focal point for both theology and philosophy. While these two disciplines approach these questions from different perspectives—one grounded in divine revelation and faith, the other in reason and empirical inquiry—they share several common concerns and, at times, arrive at overlapping conclusions. However, they also diverge in significant ways, leading to rich and complex debates that have shaped intellectual thought for centuries. This chapter examines the common ground and divergent views between theology and philosophy concerning the doctrine of creation, focusing on areas where these disciplines align, as well as where they fundamentally differ.

Common Ground Between Theology and Philosophy

The Question of Origins

Both theology and philosophy grapple with the question of origins: How did the universe come into existence? Why is there something rather than nothing? Despite their differing methods, both disciplines seek to answer these foundational questions, often finding common ground in the search for a first cause or an ultimate explanation for existence.

Key Areas of Common Ground:

1. The Concept of a First Cause: A central point of agreement between theology and philosophy is the concept of a first cause, or an uncaused cause, that brought the universe into existence. In theology, this first cause is identified with God, the Creator, who brings forth the universe ex nihilo (out of nothing). In philosophy, especially within the framework of the cosmological argument, the first cause is understood as a necessary being that explains the existence of the contingent universe. Both perspectives agree that the chain of causality must originate with a being that itself is not caused by

anything else, thereby grounding the existence of everything that follows.

2. The Principle of Sufficient Reason: Another area of common ground is the principle of sufficient reason, which holds that everything that exists must have a reason or cause for its existence. This principle is fundamental to both theological and philosophical inquiries into the nature of the universe. In theology, the sufficient reason for the existence of the universe is found in the will and purpose of God. In philosophy, the principle drives the search for a rational explanation of the universe, often leading to the conclusion that there must be an ultimate cause or necessary being.

3. The Search for Meaning: Both theology and philosophy are deeply concerned with the search for meaning in human life and the universe. The question of whether the universe has an inherent purpose or whether meaning must be constructed by individuals is a central theme in both disciplines. Theology typically posits that meaning is intrinsic to the created order, given by God, while philosophy explores whether meaning can be found through reason, ethics, and existential inquiry. Despite their different approaches, both disciplines recognize the importance of addressing the existential questions that arise from the human experience of living in a vast and often mysterious universe.

The Nature of Reality

The nature of reality—what it is, how it can be known, and what constitutes ultimate reality—is another area where theology and philosophy find common ground. Both disciplines seek to understand the fundamental structure of the universe and the principles that govern it, whether through divine revelation or rational inquiry.

Key Areas of Common Ground:

1. Metaphysical Inquiry: Both theology and philosophy engage in metaphysical inquiry, exploring the nature of being, existence, and reality. In theology, metaphysics often involves understanding the nature of God, the relationship between Creator and creation, and the ultimate purpose of existence. In philosophy, metaphysical inquiry includes questions about the nature of substance, causality, and the possibility of a reality beyond the physical world. Both disciplines share a commitment to exploring these deep questions, even if they sometimes arrive at different conclusions.

2. The Concept of Transcendence: The idea of transcendence—the existence of something beyond the physical world—is common to both theology and philosophy. In theology, transcendence refers to the nature of God as existing beyond time, space, and the material universe. In

philosophy, transcendence can refer to the existence of abstract entities (such as numbers or moral values) or the possibility of a reality that is not reducible to physical phenomena. Both disciplines recognize that there may be aspects of reality that transcend human understanding and empirical observation, leading to a shared acknowledgment of the limits of human knowledge.

3. Ethical Foundations: The grounding of ethics in a higher reality is another area of common ground. Theology often grounds ethics in the divine will or the nature of God, arguing that moral laws are expressions of the Creator's intentions for humanity. Philosophy, particularly in traditions such as natural law theory, also seeks to ground ethics in the nature of reality, arguing that moral principles are not arbitrary but are rooted in the structure of the universe. Both disciplines seek to understand how ethical behavior aligns with the fundamental nature of reality, even if they offer different explanations for the source of moral values.

Divergent Views Between Theology and Philosophy

The Role of Revelation vs. Reason

One of the most significant areas of divergence between theology and philosophy is the source of knowledge and authority. Theology often relies on divine revelation as the foundation for its claims about the universe, God, and moral values, while philosophy depends on human reason, logic, and empirical observation.

Key Areas of Divergence:

1. Epistemology: In theology, knowledge is often derived from sacred texts, religious traditions, and divine revelation. Theological claims are based on the belief that God has revealed truths about the universe, human nature, and morality that are accessible through faith and spiritual insight. Philosophy, in contrast, prioritizes reason and empirical evidence as the primary means of acquiring knowledge. Philosophical inquiry is often skeptical of claims that cannot be supported by logical argumentation or empirical data, leading to a fundamental difference in how each discipline approaches the question of truth.

2. The Nature of God: Theology and philosophy also diverge in their understanding of the nature of God. In theology, God is typically understood as a personal, omnipotent, omniscient, and benevolent being who is actively involved in the world and human history. This understanding is based on religious teachings and scriptures that describe God's nature and actions. In philosophy, particularly in the tradition of deism or certain forms of theism, God may be conceived as a more abstract, impersonal force or principle that is responsible for the creation of the universe but does

not necessarily intervene in its operations. This divergence reflects the different epistemological approaches of the two disciplines.

3. The Problem of Evil: The existence of evil and suffering in the world is a major point of divergence between theology and philosophy. Theologically, the problem of evil is often addressed through doctrines such as free will, the fall of humanity, and the possibility of redemption. Philosophers, however, frequently challenge the coherence of these explanations, questioning whether the existence of an all-powerful, all-good God can be reconciled with the presence of evil in the world. This debate highlights the differing assumptions and methodologies of theology and philosophy in addressing complex and troubling aspects of reality.

The Relationship Between Faith and Reason

The relationship between faith and reason is another area where theology and philosophy diverge, particularly in how they approach the question of belief and the justification of religious claims.

Key Areas of Divergence:

1. Faith as a Basis for Knowledge: In theology, faith is often seen as a legitimate basis for knowledge, particularly in matters of religious belief. Faith is understood as a trust in divine revelation and the truths revealed by God, which may

not always be accessible or verifiable through reason alone. Philosophy, however, typically requires that beliefs be justified by reason, logic, and evidence. This difference leads to divergent views on the justification of religious beliefs, with theology placing greater emphasis on the role of faith, while philosophy demands rational justification.

2. The Limits of Reason: Theology and philosophy also differ in their views on the limits of reason. Theologically, it is often acknowledged that reason has its limits and that certain truths, particularly those related to God and the divine, are beyond human comprehension and must be accepted on faith. Philosophy, on the other hand, tends to emphasize the power of reason to explore and understand the world, even if it recognizes that some questions may remain unresolved. This divergence reflects differing attitudes toward the capacity of human reason to grasp ultimate truths.

3. The Nature of Religious Experience: The role of religious experience in justifying belief is another point of divergence. Theology often holds that religious experiences, such as mystical encounters or revelations, are valid sources of knowledge about the divine. Philosophy, however, may be more skeptical of such experiences, questioning their reliability and interpreting them as psychological or cultural phenomena rather than as genuine encounters with the divine.

This difference underscores the varying degrees of emphasis placed on subjective experience versus objective analysis in theology and philosophy.

Bridging the Divide: The Potential for Integration

The Complementary Nature of Theology and Philosophy

Despite their differences, theology and philosophy have the potential to complement and enrich each other, offering a more holistic understanding of the universe, human existence, and the divine. By acknowledging their respective strengths and limitations, these disciplines can engage in a productive dialogue that bridges the divide between faith and reason.

Key Areas for Integration:

1. Philosophical Theology: Philosophical theology represents an area where the methods of philosophy are applied to theological questions, resulting in a more rigorous and systematic exploration of religious beliefs. Philosophical theology seeks to clarify, defend, and refine theological doctrines using the tools of logic, metaphysics, and ethics. This approach allows for a deeper engagement with theological concepts, making them more accessible to those who prioritize reason and evidence.

2. Theology's Contribution to Ethics: Theology offers a rich tradition of moral teachings that can inform philosophical ethics. By drawing on religious insights about the nature of good and evil, the purpose of human life, and the role of virtue, philosophy can develop ethical systems that are grounded in a broader metaphysical context. This integration can lead to a more comprehensive ethical framework that incorporates both rational principles and spiritual values.

3. The Role of Mystery: Both theology and philosophy recognize that some aspects of reality may remain mysterious or beyond full human comprehension. Theology often embraces this mystery, seeing it as a reflection of the divine nature, which transcends human understanding. Philosophy, while seeking to explore and explain as much as possible, can also acknowledge the limits of reason and the possibility of truths that are not fully accessible to human inquiry. This shared recognition of mystery can foster a sense of humility and openness in both disciplines, encouraging a more collaborative approach to exploring the deepest questions of existence.

The Ongoing Dialogue Between Faith and Reason

The dialogue between theology and philosophy is an ongoing process, one that continues to evolve as new questions arise and as each discipline encounters new challenges and opportunities. By maintaining an open and respectful dialogue, theology and philosophy can continue to learn from each other, addressing both the common ground they share and the divergent views that make their interaction so intellectually and spiritually enriching.

Future Directions for Dialogue:

1. Exploring the Intersection of Science and Religion: As scientific discoveries continue to expand our understanding of the universe, the dialogue between theology and philosophy will increasingly intersect with science. Both disciplines will need to engage with scientific findings, integrating them into their respective frameworks while also challenging and refining those frameworks in light of new knowledge. This intersection offers an exciting opportunity for theology, philosophy, and science to collaborate in exploring the nature of reality and the origins of existence.

2. Addressing Global Ethical Challenges: The global challenges of our time—such as climate change, social justice, and technological advancements—demand ethical responses that draw on both theological and philosophical resources. By working together, these disciplines can develop ethical principles and policies that are informed by both spiritual

values and rational analysis, offering holistic solutions to the complex problems facing humanity.

3. Reevaluating the Role of Faith in Public Life: In an increasingly pluralistic and secular world, the role of faith in public life is a topic of ongoing debate. Theology and philosophy can contribute to this discussion by exploring how religious beliefs and practices can coexist with secular values and how they can inform public policy in ways that respect both religious diversity and rational discourse. This dialogue can help bridge the gap between faith-based and secular perspectives, fostering greater understanding and cooperation in the public sphere.

Conclusion: Embracing Both Common Ground and Divergence

The relationship between theology and philosophy is characterized by both common ground and divergent views, reflecting the rich complexity of human inquiry into the nature of existence, the origins of the universe, and the meaning of life. By embracing both their shared concerns and their differences, theology and philosophy can continue to engage in a productive dialogue that deepens our understanding of the world and our place within it.

This dialogue is not merely an academic exercise; it has profound implications for how we live our lives, how we relate to others, and how we understand our relationship with the divine. By integrating the insights of both theology and philosophy, we can develop a more comprehensive and nuanced view of reality, one that honors both faith and reason and that recognizes the value of both revealed truths and rational inquiry.

As we continue to explore the common ground and divergent views between theology and philosophy, we are reminded that the search for truth is a shared journey—one that requires openness, humility, and a willingness to learn from different perspectives. In this spirit of dialogue, we can move closer to a deeper understanding of the mysteries of existence and the ultimate purpose of life.

The Role of Creation Ex Nihilo in Interdisciplinary Dialogue

The doctrine of Creation Ex Nihilo—the belief that God created the universe out of nothing—occupies a central place in theological discourse. However, its significance extends beyond theology, influencing and engaging with a variety of academic disciplines, including philosophy, science, ethics, and the arts. The concept serves as a pivotal point for interdisciplinary dialogue, offering a framework for exploring questions of existence, origins, meaning, and morality. This chapter examines how Creation Ex Nihilo plays a critical role in fostering dialogue between different disciplines, highlighting the ways in which it informs and enriches discussions across various fields of inquiry.

Creation Ex Nihilo in Theological and Philosophical Discourse

Bridging Theology and Philosophy

One of the most significant contributions of Creation Ex Nihilo is its ability to bridge the gap between theology and philosophy. As a doctrine that deals with the origins of the universe, it invites philosophical inquiry into the nature of existence, causality, and the concept of nothingness. This intersection provides a fertile ground for dialogue between theologians and philosophers, each bringing their unique perspectives to the table.

Key Contributions to Interdisciplinary Dialogue:

1. Metaphysical Foundations: In philosophy, metaphysical discussions about the nature of being and existence often intersect with the theological concept of Creation Ex Nihilo. Philosophers are concerned with questions such as, "Why is there something rather than nothing?" and "What is the nature of the first cause?" These questions resonate deeply with the theological claim that God created the universe out of nothing, leading to fruitful

exchanges between philosophical reasoning and theological doctrine.

2. Causality and Contingency: The doctrine of Creation Ex Nihilo also engages with philosophical discussions about causality and contingency. The idea that the universe is contingent upon a transcendent cause (God) challenges philosophers to consider the limits of naturalistic explanations and the possibility of a necessary being. This dialogue helps to refine philosophical concepts and provides theologians with a robust intellectual framework for articulating the doctrine of creation.

3. Existential Implications: Both theology and philosophy grapple with existential questions about the meaning and purpose of life. Creation Ex Nihilo offers a theological perspective on these questions, suggesting that meaning is rooted in the intentional act of a Creator. Philosophers, in turn, explore whether meaning can be derived from a contingent universe or whether it requires an absolute foundation. The dialogue between these perspectives enriches both disciplines, offering deeper insights into the nature of existence.

Creation Ex Nihilo and the Sciences

Engaging with Cosmology and Physics

The doctrine of Creation Ex Nihilo also plays a significant role in dialogues between theology and the sciences, particularly in the fields of cosmology and physics. As these sciences seek to understand the origins and structure of the universe, they encounter questions that resonate with theological concerns about creation.

Key Contributions to Interdisciplinary Dialogue:

1. The Big Bang Theory: The Big Bang Theory, which posits that the universe began from an initial singularity approximately 13.8 billion years ago, provides a scientific framework that aligns in some ways with the concept of Creation Ex Nihilo. Both suggest that the universe had a beginning, though the Big Bang Theory is grounded in empirical observation while Creation Ex Nihilo is a theological doctrine. The dialogue between these perspectives allows for a more comprehensive understanding of the universe's origins, incorporating both scientific and theological insights.

2. Quantum Cosmology: Quantum cosmology explores the early moments of the universe, where quantum effects dominate. Some interpretations of quantum mechanics suggest that the universe could have emerged from a quantum vacuum, challenging the idea of creation from nothing as traditionally understood in theology. This has led

to discussions about the nature of "nothingness" and the potential for interdisciplinary collaboration in understanding the universe's beginnings. Creation Ex Nihilo serves as a theological counterpart to these scientific theories, prompting theologians and scientists to consider the implications of quantum cosmology for the doctrine of creation.

3. The Anthropic Principle: The Anthropic Principle, which observes that the universe's physical constants are finely tuned to allow for the existence of life, invites dialogue between theology and science about the possibility of design or purpose in the universe. Creation Ex Nihilo provides a theological framework for understanding this fine-tuning as the result of a purposeful Creator, while scientists explore naturalistic explanations. This interdisciplinary exchange fosters a deeper exploration of whether the universe's structure is a product of chance, necessity, or design.

Creation Ex Nihilo in Ethics and Moral Philosophy

Informing Ethical Theories and Moral Values

The doctrine of Creation Ex Nihilo also has significant implications for ethics and moral philosophy. By grounding human existence in a divinely created order, it provides a basis for understanding human dignity, moral responsibility, and the nature of good and evil. This theological perspective intersects with ethical theories in philosophy, contributing to interdisciplinary discussions about the foundations of morality.

Key Contributions to Interdisciplinary Dialogue:

1. Human Dignity and Rights: The belief that humans are created in the image of God (Imago Dei) underpins the concept of human dignity and inherent rights. This theological claim has influenced philosophical discussions about the nature and source of human rights, leading to debates about whether these rights are grounded in religious beliefs, natural law, or social contracts. Creation Ex Nihilo reinforces the idea that human dignity is intrinsic and universal, contributing to the development of ethical frameworks that protect and promote human rights.

2. Environmental Ethics: The principle of stewardship, derived from the belief that the world was created by God and entrusted to humanity, has informed discussions about environmental ethics. This theological perspective aligns with philosophical concerns about sustainability, conservation, and the ethical treatment of non-human life. Creation Ex Nihilo encourages an interdisciplinary approach to environmental issues, bringing together theological principles of stewardship with scientific understanding of ecosystems and ethical theories about the moral status of nature.

3. Moral Accountability: The doctrine of Creation Ex Nihilo suggests that humans are accountable to God for their actions, providing a theological foundation for moral responsibility. This idea intersects with philosophical discussions about free will, moral agency, and the nature of ethical obligations. By engaging with these philosophical concepts, theology offers a perspective on moral accountability that is grounded in the relationship between Creator and creation, contributing to a more nuanced understanding of ethics.

Creation Ex Nihilo and the Arts and Humanities

Inspiring Creative Expression and Cultural Reflection

The doctrine of Creation Ex Nihilo has also inspired creative expression and cultural reflection in the arts and humanities. As a concept that addresses fundamental questions about existence and creativity, it resonates with artists, writers, and scholars who seek to explore the human condition and the mysteries of the universe through their work.

Key Contributions to Interdisciplinary Dialogue:

1. Art and Creativity: The idea that God created the universe out of nothing has inspired countless works of art that explore themes of creation, existence, and divine creativity. Artists have drawn on the imagery and symbolism

of Creation Ex Nihilo to express their visions of the cosmos, humanity, and the divine. This theological concept enriches artistic expression by providing a framework for understanding creativity as a reflection of the divine act of creation.

2. Literature and Mythology: In literature, the theme of creation from nothing has been explored in various forms, from mythological narratives to philosophical novels. Writers have used the concept of Creation Ex Nihilo to grapple with questions of identity, purpose, and the nature of reality. This dialogue between theology and literature allows for a deeper exploration of how creation myths and narratives shape cultural understandings of existence and the human experience.

3. Philosophical Reflection in the Humanities: Scholars in the humanities, particularly in fields such as philosophy, religious studies, and cultural studies, have engaged with Creation Ex Nihilo as a concept that influences and reflects broader cultural and intellectual trends. This interdisciplinary dialogue allows for a critical examination of how theological ideas intersect with secular thought, contributing to a richer understanding of the ways in which creation myths and religious beliefs shape human culture.

The Challenges and Opportunities of Interdisciplinary Dialogue

Navigating Differences and Finding Common Ground

While Creation Ex Nihilo offers a rich framework for interdisciplinary dialogue, it also presents challenges due to the differing methodologies, assumptions, and goals of various disciplines. However, these challenges also provide opportunities for deeper engagement and mutual enrichment.

Key Challenges and Opportunities:

1. Differing Epistemologies: One of the primary challenges in interdisciplinary dialogue is the differing epistemologies of theology, philosophy, and science. Theology often relies on divine revelation and faith, while philosophy emphasizes reason and logic, and science depends on empirical evidence and observation. Navigating these differences requires a willingness to engage with alternative ways of knowing and to seek common ground where possible. Creation Ex Nihilo provides a focal point for these discussions, inviting participants to consider how different epistemologies can contribute to a more comprehensive understanding of the universe.

2. Interpreting "Nothingness": The concept of "nothingness" in Creation Ex Nihilo is another area of

potential tension. In theology, "nothing" refers to the absence of any pre-existing matter, from which God creates the universe. In science, particularly in quantum cosmology, "nothingness" may refer to a quantum vacuum or a state of potentiality rather than absolute nothingness. This difference in interpretation can lead to misunderstandings, but it also offers an opportunity for dialogue about the nature of reality and the limits of human understanding.

3. Ethical Implications: The ethical implications of Creation Ex Nihilo, particularly in relation to human dignity, environmental stewardship, and moral accountability, provide a rich area for interdisciplinary exploration. However, these discussions can be complicated by differing ethical frameworks and cultural perspectives. The challenge is to find ways to integrate theological insights with philosophical and scientific approaches to ethics, creating a dialogue that respects diverse viewpoints while seeking common values and principles.

Conclusion: The Enduring Significance of Creation Ex Nihilo in Interdisciplinary Dialogue

Creation Ex Nihilo plays a vital role in fostering interdisciplinary dialogue, offering a theological concept that resonates across a wide range of academic fields. By engaging with this doctrine, scholars, scientists, philosophers, and artists can explore fundamental questions about existence, origins, meaning, and morality from multiple perspectives. This interdisciplinary dialogue not only enriches our understanding of Creation Ex Nihilo but also contributes to a more holistic view of the universe and our place within it.

As we continue to explore the role of Creation Ex Nihilo in interdisciplinary dialogue, we are reminded of the importance of openness, curiosity, and respect for different ways of knowing. By embracing the challenges and opportunities of interdisciplinary engagement, we can deepen our understanding of the mysteries of creation and develop a more integrated and meaningful approach to the questions that have shaped human thought for millennia. In this way, Creation Ex Nihilo serves as a bridge between disciplines, fostering a dialogue that is as rich and diverse as the creation it seeks to understand.

CHAPTER 10

CREATION EX NIHILO AND THE FUTURE

Future Directions in Theological and Philosophical Research

The doctrine of Creation Ex Nihilo—the belief that God created the universe out of nothing—has been a cornerstone of theological and philosophical inquiry for centuries. As we look toward the future, this concept continues to hold significant potential for further exploration and development. The dynamic interplay between theology, philosophy, science, and other disciplines suggests that new questions and challenges will arise, leading to deeper understanding and more nuanced perspectives. This chapter examines future directions in theological and philosophical research related to Creation Ex Nihilo, highlighting key areas where further investigation is likely to yield important insights.

Theological Research: Expanding the Doctrine of Creation

Reinterpreting Creation in Light of Contemporary Challenges

One of the most pressing future directions in theological research on Creation Ex Nihilo involves reinterpreting the doctrine in response to contemporary challenges. As the world faces new ethical, environmental, and existential questions, theologians will need to revisit and possibly reformulate traditional understandings of creation to address these issues effectively.

Key Areas for Theological Research:

1. Creation and Environmental Ethics: As concerns about climate change and environmental degradation become increasingly urgent, theologians will need to explore how the doctrine of Creation Ex Nihilo informs and inspires a robust environmental ethic. Future research may focus on how the idea of creation out of nothing can underpin a theology of stewardship, emphasizing humanity's responsibility to care for the earth as God's creation. This could involve developing new theological frameworks that integrate ecological concerns with traditional teachings on creation.

2. Interfaith Dialogue on Creation: In a globalized world, interfaith dialogue is essential for promoting understanding and cooperation among different religious traditions. Future theological research may explore how the concept of Creation Ex Nihilo can serve as a bridge in interfaith discussions, particularly with religions that have different creation narratives. By engaging with diverse perspectives, theologians can deepen their understanding of creation and contribute to a more inclusive and global theological discourse.

3. Theodicy and the Problem of Evil: The problem of evil remains one of the most challenging issues in theology, particularly in relation to the doctrine of Creation Ex Nihilo. Future research may focus on developing more nuanced theodicies that account for the existence of suffering and evil in a world created by a good and omnipotent God. This could involve integrating insights from contemporary philosophy, psychology, and social sciences to offer a more comprehensive response to the problem of evil within the context of creation theology.

Integrating Science and Theology

The relationship between science and theology has been a fertile ground for dialogue, and this is likely to continue as scientific discoveries and technological advancements raise new questions about the nature of the universe and the origins of life. The doctrine of Creation Ex Nihilo provides a theological framework that can engage with these developments in meaningful ways.

Key Areas for Theological Research:

1. Cosmology and Theology: As cosmology continues to explore the origins and structure of the universe, theologians will need to engage with these scientific findings to refine and expand their understanding of Creation Ex Nihilo. Future research may focus on how recent discoveries, such as the nature of dark matter, dark energy, and the multiverse hypothesis, can be interpreted theologically. This could lead to new insights into the nature of God's creative act and the ongoing relationship between the Creator and creation.

2. Theology of Evolution: The compatibility of evolutionary theory with the doctrine of Creation Ex Nihilo remains a topic of debate within theology. Future research may explore how these two perspectives can be reconciled, offering a theology of evolution that acknowledges both the scientific understanding of life's development and the theological belief in a purposeful creation. This could involve rethinking the role of divine action in the process of evolution

and developing a more integrated view of creation that embraces scientific knowledge.

3. Artificial Intelligence and Creation: The rise of artificial intelligence (AI) presents new challenges and opportunities for theological reflection. Future research may investigate how the doctrine of Creation Ex Nihilo informs our understanding of human creativity and the ethical implications of creating intelligent machines. Theological inquiry in this area could explore the nature of human uniqueness, the moral status of AI, and the potential for AI to participate in God's creative purposes.

Philosophical Research: Rethinking Metaphysical and Ethical Implications

Revisiting Metaphysical Concepts

Philosophical research on Creation Ex Nihilo has traditionally focused on metaphysical questions about existence, causality, and the nature of nothingness. As philosophical thought continues to evolve, there are new opportunities to revisit these concepts in light of contemporary debates and emerging ideas.

Key Areas for Philosophical Research:

1. The Nature of Nothingness: The concept of nothingness remains a central issue in discussions of Creation Ex Nihilo. Future philosophical research may explore new

ways of understanding nothingness, particularly in relation to developments in quantum mechanics and cosmology. This could involve examining the metaphysical status of "nothingness" in different philosophical traditions and considering how these perspectives intersect with contemporary scientific theories about the origins of the universe.

2. The First Cause and Cosmological Arguments: The First Cause argument has long been a staple of philosophical discussions on creation. Future research may focus on refining and critiquing this argument in light of new philosophical and scientific insights. This could involve exploring alternative models of causality, such as those suggested by quantum mechanics, and considering whether the concept of a first cause is still necessary or coherent in the context of a modern understanding of the universe.

3. Contingency and Necessity: The relationship between contingency and necessity is another key area for future philosophical research. Philosophers may investigate how the doctrine of Creation Ex Nihilo relates to contemporary debates about the nature of contingent beings and the existence of a necessary being. This could lead to new approaches to the problem of contingency and the search for a coherent metaphysical framework that accommodates both

the contingency of the universe and the necessity of a first cause.

Ethical Implications and Global Challenges

The doctrine of Creation Ex Nihilo also has significant ethical implications, particularly in relation to contemporary global challenges. Philosophers can contribute to these discussions by exploring how the concept of creation informs and shapes ethical principles and decision-making.

Key Areas for Philosophical Research:

1. Global Ethics and Justice: In an increasingly interconnected world, the need for a global ethic that addresses issues of justice, human rights, and environmental sustainability is more pressing than ever. Future philosophical research may explore how Creation Ex Nihilo can provide a foundation for such an ethic, emphasizing the interconnectedness of all beings within a divinely created order. This could involve developing ethical theories that integrate respect for creation with commitments to social justice and human flourishing.

2. Human Dignity and Technological Advancement: As technological advancements, such as genetic engineering and AI, challenge traditional notions of human identity and dignity, philosophers will need to revisit these concepts in light of Creation Ex Nihilo. Future research may focus on

how the belief in a divinely created humanity informs our understanding of human dignity and the ethical limits of technological innovation. This could lead to new philosophical approaches to bioethics, AI ethics, and the moral status of emerging technologies.

3. Philosophy of Religion and Secular Ethics: The dialogue between religious and secular ethical systems continues to be a vital area of philosophical inquiry. Future research may explore how the doctrine of Creation Ex Nihilo can engage with secular philosophies that seek to ground ethics in human reason, autonomy, or naturalism. This could involve examining whether the concept of creation provides unique insights into moral obligations, the nature of the good, and the relationship between religion and ethics in a pluralistic society.

The Interdisciplinary Future of Creation Ex Nihilo

Engaging with Emerging Disciplines

As new academic disciplines and fields of inquiry emerge, there are increasing opportunities for interdisciplinary research on Creation Ex Nihilo. Theological and philosophical perspectives can contribute to these fields, offering insights that enrich and deepen the understanding of creation across multiple contexts.

Key Areas for Interdisciplinary Research:

1. Neuroscience and Consciousness: The study of consciousness and the human mind is an area where theology, philosophy, and neuroscience intersect. Future research may explore how Creation Ex Nihilo informs our understanding of consciousness as a created phenomenon. This could involve examining the relationship between the brain and the soul, the nature of free will, and the theological implications of neuroscientific discoveries about human cognition and behavior.

2. Environmental Humanities: The environmental humanities is an emerging field that integrates ecological concerns with cultural, historical, and ethical perspectives. Future research on Creation Ex Nihilo within this context may focus on how the doctrine shapes our understanding of the natural world and our responsibilities toward it. This interdisciplinary approach could lead to new insights into the relationship between creation theology, environmental ethics, and cultural narratives about the earth and its ecosystems.

3. Digital Humanities and Theology: The rise of digital humanities offers new opportunities for theological research on Creation Ex Nihilo. Scholars may explore how digital technologies can be used to study and communicate the doctrine of creation, particularly in relation to historical texts, artistic representations, and cultural expressions. This could

involve developing digital tools and platforms that facilitate interdisciplinary research and public engagement with theological concepts in a digital age.

Conclusion: Charting the Future of Creation Ex Nihilo Research

The future of theological and philosophical research on Creation Ex Nihilo is rich with potential, offering numerous opportunities for deepening our understanding of this foundational doctrine. As new challenges and questions emerge, scholars will need to revisit and expand traditional interpretations, engaging with contemporary science, ethics, and interdisciplinary perspectives.

By exploring the implications of Creation Ex Nihilo in light of modern developments, theologians and philosophers can contribute to a more integrated and comprehensive view of creation that speaks to the concerns of the 21st century. This ongoing research will not only advance academic discourse but also provide valuable insights for addressing the pressing issues of our time, from environmental sustainability to the ethical use of technology.

As we look toward the future, the doctrine of Creation Ex Nihilo will continue to serve as a vital touchstone for theological and philosophical inquiry, inspiring new ways of thinking about the origins of the universe, the nature of existence, and the meaning of human life. Through this exploration, we can better understand the profound mystery of creation and our place within the cosmos, fostering a deeper appreciation for the creative act that brought everything into being.

Potential Impact on Emerging Fields (e.g., Artificial Intelligence, Cosmology)

As the doctrine of Creation Ex Nihilo—the belief that God created the universe out of nothing—continues to influence theological and philosophical thought, it also holds significant potential for shaping emerging fields such as artificial intelligence (AI) and cosmology. These fields, which are at the forefront of scientific and technological innovation, raise new questions and challenges that intersect with traditional theological concepts. This chapter explores the potential impact of Creation Ex Nihilo on these emerging fields, examining how the doctrine can inform, challenge, and be reinterpreted in light of new developments in AI, cosmology, and related areas.

The Impact of Creation Ex Nihilo on Artificial Intelligence

Theological and Ethical Implications of AI

Artificial intelligence (AI) is rapidly transforming various aspects of society, from industry and healthcare to communication and decision-making. As AI technologies become more sophisticated, they raise profound questions about the nature of intelligence, creativity, and autonomy—questions that are closely related to the theological concept of Creation Ex Nihilo.

Key Implications for AI:

1. Human Creativity and Divine Image: The doctrine of Creation Ex Nihilo emphasizes that human beings are created in the image of God (Imago Dei), which includes the capacity for creativity and innovation. As humans create increasingly complex AI systems, theological reflection on what it means to be made in the divine image becomes more pertinent. Future discussions may focus on whether AI, as a product of human creativity, reflects this aspect of the divine image, and what this means for the moral and spiritual status of AI entities.

2. Ethics of AI Creation: The creation of AI systems raises ethical questions about responsibility, autonomy, and the potential for harm. Theological insights from Creation Ex Nihilo can contribute to these discussions by emphasizing the moral responsibilities that come with the power to create. Just as God's act of creation is seen as purposeful and inherently good, human creators of AI must consider the ethical implications of their creations, ensuring that AI systems are

designed and used in ways that promote human flourishing and align with moral values.

3. AI and the Concept of Personhood: As AI systems become more advanced, there are ongoing debates about whether they should be granted some form of personhood or moral consideration. The doctrine of Creation Ex Nihilo, which affirms the unique status of human beings as created in God's image, can inform these discussions by providing a theological perspective on what constitutes personhood and whether AI can or should be considered persons in any meaningful sense.

Theological Engagement with AI and Machine Learning

The rise of machine learning and AI also challenges traditional theological concepts, prompting theologians to engage with these technologies in new ways. Creation Ex Nihilo provides a framework for exploring the implications of AI from a theological perspective.

Key Areas of Theological Engagement:

1. The Nature of Intelligence: AI technologies force a reexamination of what it means to be intelligent. Theological discussions of intelligence have traditionally been tied to the human soul and the capacity for reason, creativity, and moral judgment—attributes that are believed to reflect the divine

image. As AI systems increasingly exhibit these attributes, theologians will need to explore whether and how these systems relate to the divine image and what distinguishes human intelligence from artificial intelligence.

2. AI and Theological Anthropology: The development of AI prompts a rethinking of theological anthropology—the study of human nature and identity. If AI systems can mimic or even surpass human cognitive abilities, theologians must consider what makes humans unique as beings created by God. This could involve revisiting doctrines such as the Imago Dei, free will, and the soul, and exploring how these concepts apply in a world where machines can perform tasks once thought to be uniquely human.

3. AI in Worship and Religious Practice: The integration of AI into religious practice is another emerging area of interest. From AI-driven spiritual apps to robotic clergy, the use of AI in worship and religious rituals raises questions about the role of technology in faith communities. Theological reflection on Creation Ex Nihilo can contribute to discussions about the appropriateness of AI in sacred contexts, the authenticity of AI-mediated religious experiences, and the potential for AI to assist or even replace human roles in worship.

The Impact of Creation Ex Nihilo on Cosmology

Theological Reflections on the Universe's Origins

Cosmology, the scientific study of the origins and structure of the universe, has long been a field where theology and science intersect. The doctrine of Creation Ex Nihilo, which asserts that the universe was created by God out of nothing, continues to provide a theological framework for engaging with cosmological discoveries and theories.

Key Implications for Cosmology:

1. Big Bang Theory and Creation Ex Nihilo: The Big Bang Theory, which posits that the universe began from an initial singularity, has been interpreted by some theologians as compatible with the doctrine of Creation Ex Nihilo. As cosmologists continue to refine the Big Bang model and explore the earliest moments of the universe, theological engagement with these findings can deepen our understanding of the relationship between scientific and theological explanations of the universe's origins. Future research may focus on how new discoveries in cosmology, such as the nature of dark matter and dark energy, can be integrated into a theological framework that upholds the concept of creation from nothing.

2. Multiverse Theory and Theological Challenges: The Multiverse Theory, which suggests the existence of multiple or even infinite universes, presents a challenge to traditional

theological views of creation. If our universe is just one of many, what does this mean for the uniqueness of creation and the role of God as Creator? The doctrine of Creation Ex Nihilo will need to be reexamined in light of these cosmological theories, with theologians exploring whether and how the concept of divine creation can accommodate the possibility of a multiverse.

3. Theological Cosmology and Fine-Tuning: The fine-tuning of the universe—the observation that the physical constants of the universe are precisely calibrated to allow for the existence of life—has often been cited as evidence of design. Theological cosmology, informed by Creation Ex Nihilo, can contribute to ongoing discussions about the implications of fine-tuning for our understanding of God's creative purposes. This could involve exploring whether fine-tuning supports the idea of a purposeful creation and how this relates to theological concepts such as providence and divine action.

Cosmology and the Future of Creation Theology

As cosmology continues to advance, it will inevitably raise new questions that challenge and enrich theological understandings of creation. The doctrine of Creation Ex Nihilo remains a vital part of this dialogue, offering a theological perspective that can engage with cutting-edge scientific theories.

Key Areas for Future Theological Reflection:

1. Quantum Cosmology and the Nature of Time: Quantum cosmology, which applies quantum mechanics to the early universe, suggests that our understanding of time and causality may need to be rethought. The doctrine of Creation Ex Nihilo, which traditionally posits a temporal beginning to the universe, will need to engage with these new models of time. Theologians may explore how creation can be understood in a quantum context, where time may not be linear or where the distinction between past, present, and future becomes blurred.

2. The Eschatological Implications of Cosmology: Cosmology not only addresses the origins of the universe but also its ultimate fate. Theological reflection on Creation Ex Nihilo can contribute to eschatological discussions about the end of the universe, particularly in relation to concepts such as the resurrection, the new creation, and the final judgment. As cosmologists explore scenarios such as the heat death, the Big Crunch, or the Big Rip, theologians will need to consider how these scientific theories relate to the eschatological promises found in religious texts.

3. Cosmology and the Doctrine of Creation Continua: The idea that God's creative work is ongoing, rather than confined to a single moment in the past, is an important theme in contemporary theology. As cosmology uncovers the dynamic processes that shape the universe, theologians may explore how Creation Ex Nihilo can be understood as part of a broader doctrine of continuous creation (creatio continua). This could involve rethinking the relationship between the initial act of creation and the ongoing development and evolution of the cosmos.

The Role of Creation Ex Nihilo in Other Emerging Fields

Interdisciplinary Engagement with Ethics, Technology, and the Humanities

Beyond AI and cosmology, the doctrine of Creation Ex Nihilo has the potential to impact a wide range of emerging fields, from ethics and technology to the humanities. As these fields evolve, theological and philosophical reflection on creation can provide valuable insights and guide ethical decision-making.

Key Areas of Interdisciplinary Impact:

1. Bioethics and Genetic Engineering: The field of bioethics, particularly in relation to genetic engineering and biotechnology, raises questions about the limits of human

creativity and the moral responsibilities of creators. Creation Ex Nihilo can inform discussions about the ethics of "playing God" and the implications of altering the fundamental aspects of life. Theological reflection on the sanctity of creation and the purpose of human existence can guide ethical frameworks for emerging biotechnologies.

2. Digital Humanities and the Theology of Creation: The digital humanities, which explore the intersection of technology and the humanities, offer new opportunities for engaging with the doctrine of Creation Ex Nihilo. Scholars may explore how digital tools and platforms can be used to study, communicate, and reinterpret theological concepts, particularly in relation to creation. This interdisciplinary approach can foster new ways of understanding and expressing the creative act, both in traditional religious contexts and in the broader cultural sphere.

3. Environmental Ethics and Sustainability: As global concerns about environmental sustainability grow, the doctrine of Creation Ex Nihilo can play a crucial role in shaping environmental ethics. The belief that the world is a created gift from God can inspire a theology of stewardship that emphasizes the importance of caring for the earth. Theological engagement with environmental science, policy,

and activism can lead to new ethical frameworks that address the pressing ecological challenges of our time.

Conclusion: The Future Potential of Creation Ex Nihilo in Emerging Fields

The doctrine of Creation Ex Nihilo, rooted in ancient theological traditions, continues to have profound relevance in the context of modern and emerging fields. As artificial intelligence, cosmology, and other disciplines advance, they raise new questions that intersect with traditional theological concepts, challenging scholars to rethink and expand their understanding of creation.

By engaging with these fields, theologians and philosophers can contribute to a deeper and more integrated understanding of the universe, human creativity, and the ethical responsibilities that come with the power to create. The doctrine of Creation Ex Nihilo offers a rich framework for exploring these issues, providing insights that can guide the development of new technologies, inform scientific inquiry, and inspire ethical reflection in a rapidly changing world.

As we move into the future, the interdisciplinary dialogue around Creation Ex Nihilo will continue to evolve, offering new opportunities for collaboration and discovery. This ongoing exploration will not only deepen our understanding of the doctrine itself but also enhance our ability to respond to the challenges and opportunities that lie ahead, fostering a more just, sustainable, and creative world.

The Ongoing Relevance of Creation Ex Nihilo in Contemporary Thought

The doctrine of Creation Ex Nihilo—the belief that God created the universe out of nothing—has long been a foundational concept in theological discourse. However, its significance is not confined to the realms of ancient and medieval thought; it continues to hold considerable relevance in contemporary intellectual and cultural contexts. As modern society grapples with profound questions about existence, meaning, and the origins of the universe, Creation Ex Nihilo remains a vital framework for exploring these issues. This chapter examines the ongoing relevance of Creation Ex Nihilo in contemporary thought, highlighting how it informs discussions in theology, philosophy, science, ethics, and broader cultural debates.

Creation Ex Nihilo in Contemporary Theology

Reaffirming Traditional Beliefs in a Modern Context

In contemporary theology, Creation Ex Nihilo serves as a crucial point of reference for reaffirming traditional beliefs while also engaging with modern challenges. The doctrine continues to provide a coherent narrative for understanding the relationship between God and the world, grounding theological reflections on divine omnipotence, sovereignty, and the nature of existence.

Key Areas of Relevance:

1. Theological Anthropology: The belief that humans are created by God out of nothing underpins many aspects of theological anthropology. It affirms the intrinsic worth and dignity of every human being, rooted in the divine act of creation. In an era where questions of identity, purpose, and human rights are increasingly pressing, Creation Ex Nihilo provides a foundation for understanding the unique status of humanity as made in the image of God (Imago Dei). This doctrine continues to inspire theological reflections on the nature of human beings, their purpose, and their relationship with the Creator.

2. Divine Sovereignty and Providence: Creation Ex Nihilo emphasizes God's absolute sovereignty over creation, asserting that the universe exists solely because of God's will and power. In contemporary theology, this concept remains central to discussions about divine providence—the belief that God continues to sustain and guide creation according to a divine plan. As theologians address issues such as the problem of evil, environmental stewardship, and the meaning of history, the doctrine of Creation Ex Nihilo offers a vital

perspective on how God's sovereignty is manifested in the ongoing unfolding of creation.

3. Ecumenical and Interfaith Dialogue: The doctrine of Creation Ex Nihilo is a shared belief across various Christian denominations and has parallels in other religious traditions, such as Judaism and Islam. This common ground provides a basis for ecumenical and interfaith dialogue, allowing different faith communities to engage in meaningful conversations about the nature of God, the origins of the universe, and the ethical implications of creation. In a world marked by religious pluralism, Creation Ex Nihilo continues to be a touchstone for theological discussions that seek to build bridges between diverse religious perspectives.

Engaging with Contemporary Theological Movements

Creation Ex Nihilo also remains relevant as contemporary theology engages with new movements and challenges, such as liberation theology, feminist theology, and ecological theology. These movements often reinterpret traditional doctrines in light of current social and environmental concerns, and Creation Ex Nihilo plays a key role in these reinterpretations.

Key Areas of Engagement:

1. Liberation Theology: In liberation theology, the doctrine of Creation Ex Nihilo is often reinterpreted to emphasize God's preferential option for the poor and oppressed. The belief that all people are created by God and endowed with dignity and worth provides a theological basis for advocating for social justice, human rights, and the liberation of marginalized communities. Creation Ex Nihilo supports the idea that the existing social order is not divinely ordained but can be transformed in accordance with God's creative purposes for justice and equality.

2. Feminist Theology: Feminist theologians have engaged with Creation Ex Nihilo by critiquing traditional patriarchal interpretations of creation and offering alternative readings that emphasize the equality and agency of women. The doctrine is reexamined to highlight the inclusive and relational aspects of creation, challenging gender hierarchies and affirming the full humanity of women as created in the image of God. Creation Ex Nihilo thus remains relevant in contemporary debates about gender, power, and the role of women in religious communities.

3. Ecological Theology: The ecological crisis has prompted theologians to revisit the doctrine of Creation Ex Nihilo in the context of environmental ethics and sustainability. The belief that the world is a gift from God,

created out of nothing and entrusted to humanity, inspires a theology of stewardship that calls for the protection and preservation of the environment. Contemporary ecological theology draws on Creation Ex Nihilo to argue for the sacredness of the natural world and the moral responsibility to care for creation in ways that reflect God's creative intentions.

Creation Ex Nihilo in Contemporary Philosophy

Addressing Metaphysical and Existential Questions

In contemporary philosophy, Creation Ex Nihilo continues to be a significant concept for addressing metaphysical and existential questions about the nature of reality, causality, and the meaning of existence. Philosophers engage with this doctrine to explore the implications of a universe created out of nothing and to examine the coherence of traditional arguments for the existence of God.

Key Areas of Relevance:

1. Metaphysical Foundations: The doctrine of Creation Ex Nihilo raises important metaphysical questions about the nature of being and the origin of the universe. Philosophers continue to debate whether it is possible for something to come from nothing and what this implies about the nature of reality. These discussions often intersect with philosophical inquiries into the concepts of necessity,

contingency, and the nature of causality, making Creation Ex Nihilo a vital point of reference in contemporary metaphysics.

2. The Problem of Causality: Creation Ex Nihilo challenges traditional philosophical notions of causality, particularly the principle that everything must have a cause. The idea that God created the universe without any pre-existing material raises questions about the nature of divine causality and the relationship between cause and effect. Contemporary philosophers engage with these issues, exploring whether the doctrine can be reconciled with modern understandings of causality or whether it requires a rethinking of causal principles.

3. Existential and Nihilistic Concerns: In existential philosophy, questions about meaning, purpose, and the absurdity of existence are central themes. Creation Ex Nihilo offers a counter-narrative to nihilistic interpretations of the universe, asserting that existence is purposeful and grounded in the creative act of a transcendent God. Philosophers who explore existential concerns may find in Creation Ex Nihilo a framework for understanding the possibility of meaning and purpose in a seemingly indifferent or chaotic world.

Intersecting with Contemporary Philosophical Debates

Creation Ex Nihilo also intersects with various contemporary philosophical debates, offering insights and challenges to current trends in philosophy. These intersections highlight the ongoing relevance of the doctrine in addressing the philosophical concerns of the 21st century.

Key Areas of Intersection:

1. Philosophy of Religion: In the philosophy of religion, Creation Ex Nihilo continues to be a central topic of discussion, particularly in debates about the existence of God, the nature of divine attributes, and the problem of evil. Philosophers of religion engage with this doctrine to explore whether it provides a coherent and compelling explanation for the existence of the universe and to address challenges posed by atheistic and agnostic perspectives. The ongoing relevance of Creation Ex Nihilo in these debates underscores its importance as a foundational concept in the philosophy of religion.

2. Process Philosophy: Process philosophy, which emphasizes the dynamic and relational aspects of reality, presents an alternative view to the traditional doctrine of Creation Ex Nihilo. Process philosophers often critique the idea of creation out of nothing, proposing instead that the universe is in a constant state of becoming and that God is intimately involved in the ongoing process of creation. The

dialogue between Creation Ex Nihilo and process philosophy offers valuable insights into the nature of God, the universe, and the relationship between time and eternity.

3. Analytic Philosophy: In analytic philosophy, discussions about the nature of existence, possible worlds, and modal logic often intersect with the doctrine of Creation Ex Nihilo. Analytic philosophers may explore the implications of creation for concepts such as necessity, possibility, and the existence of multiple worlds. These discussions contribute to a deeper understanding of how Creation Ex Nihilo fits within contemporary analytic frameworks and how it can be used to address philosophical problems related to existence and causality.

Creation Ex Nihilo in Contemporary Science

Engaging with Scientific Theories and Discoveries

The ongoing relevance of Creation Ex Nihilo is also evident in its engagement with contemporary scientific theories and discoveries. As science continues to explore the origins of the universe, the nature of time and space, and the possibilities of life beyond Earth, the doctrine of Creation Ex Nihilo provides a theological perspective that complements and challenges scientific understandings.

Key Areas of Relevance:

1. Cosmology and the Big Bang Theory: The Big Bang Theory, which posits that the universe began as a singularity and has been expanding ever since, is often seen as compatible with the doctrine of Creation Ex Nihilo. The idea that the universe had a beginning aligns with the theological claim that God created the universe out of nothing. As cosmologists continue to investigate the nature of the early universe, theological reflections on Creation Ex Nihilo can offer insights into the significance of a universe with a temporal beginning and the implications for understanding the nature of time and causality.

2. Quantum Mechanics and the Nature of Reality: Quantum mechanics, with its counterintuitive principles and probabilistic nature, raises profound questions about the nature of reality and the role of the observer. The doctrine of Creation Ex Nihilo can contribute to discussions about the relationship between the quantum world and the macroscopic universe, particularly in relation to the concept of nothingness and the emergence of something from nothing. The ongoing dialogue between theology and quantum physics highlights the relevance of Creation Ex Nihilo in addressing the mysteries of the quantum realm.

3. Astrobiology and the Search for Extraterrestrial Life: The search for extraterrestrial life and the study of

astrobiology raise new questions about the scope of creation and the possibility of life beyond Earth. The doctrine of Creation Ex Nihilo provides a theological framework for understanding the potential existence of other life forms as part of God's creative work. Theological reflections on the implications of discovering extraterrestrial life, the uniqueness of Earth, and the universality of God's creative purposes are becoming increasingly relevant in light of advancements in space exploration and astrobiology.

The Role of Theology in the Science-Religion Dialogue

The ongoing relevance of Creation Ex Nihilo is further highlighted by its role in the broader dialogue between science and religion. This dialogue seeks to bridge the gap between scientific explanations of the universe and theological interpretations of creation, fostering mutual understanding and respect.

Key Areas of Dialogue:

1. Complementarity of Science and Theology: The doctrine of Creation Ex Nihilo underscores the complementarity of science and theology in exploring the origins of the universe. While science provides empirical explanations of the processes and mechanisms that govern the cosmos, theology offers a deeper understanding of the

ultimate causes and purposes behind these processes. The ongoing dialogue between science and theology, informed by Creation Ex Nihilo, contributes to a more holistic view of reality that integrates both scientific and spiritual insights.

2. Ethical Implications of Scientific Discoveries: Scientific advancements, particularly in fields such as genetics, artificial intelligence, and environmental science, raise ethical questions that intersect with theological concerns about creation. The doctrine of Creation Ex Nihilo provides a moral and spiritual foundation for addressing these questions, emphasizing the responsibility of humanity to use scientific knowledge in ways that honor the Creator and respect the integrity of creation. This ethical dimension of Creation Ex Nihilo remains relevant as society navigates the challenges and opportunities presented by modern science.

3. Public Engagement and Education: The ongoing relevance of Creation Ex Nihilo extends to public engagement and education, where the doctrine can be used to foster a deeper appreciation for both science and theology. By integrating the concept of creation into educational curricula and public discourse, theologians and scientists can encourage a more informed and respectful dialogue between these two fields. This engagement helps to bridge the perceived divide

between science and religion, promoting a more nuanced and integrated understanding of the world.

Creation Ex Nihilo in Contemporary Culture

Shaping Cultural Narratives and Worldviews

The doctrine of Creation Ex Nihilo continues to influence contemporary culture, shaping narratives and worldviews that address questions of existence, meaning, and identity. As society grapples with the complexities of modern life, Creation Ex Nihilo provides a foundational narrative that informs cultural expressions and public discourse.

Key Areas of Cultural Influence:

1. Art and Literature: Creation Ex Nihilo has long been a source of inspiration for artists and writers, and it continues to shape contemporary cultural expressions. From visual art to literature, the concept of creation out of nothing is explored in various forms, often as a metaphor for human creativity, transformation, and renewal. Contemporary works of art and literature that engage with themes of creation, chaos, and order reflect the ongoing relevance of Creation Ex Nihilo in the cultural imagination.

2. Media and Popular Culture: In popular culture, the doctrine of Creation Ex Nihilo is often referenced in discussions about the origins of the universe, the nature of God, and the meaning of life. Films, television shows, and

other media frequently explore themes related to creation, existence, and the cosmos, drawing on both scientific and theological narratives. The presence of Creation Ex Nihilo in popular culture highlights its enduring relevance as a concept that resonates with the human experience and continues to spark curiosity and wonder.

3. Public Discourse on Science and Religion: The doctrine of Creation Ex Nihilo also plays a role in public discourse on the relationship between science and religion. As debates about creationism, evolution, and the origins of the universe continue to unfold in the public sphere, Creation Ex Nihilo provides a theological perspective that can engage with scientific explanations while affirming the spiritual significance of creation. This ongoing relevance is evident in discussions about education, public policy, and the role of religion in society.

Conclusion: The Enduring Relevance of Creation Ex Nihilo in Contemporary Thought

The doctrine of Creation Ex Nihilo remains a vital and relevant concept in contemporary thought, influencing theology, philosophy, science, and culture. As society continues to explore the profound questions of existence, origins, and meaning, Creation Ex Nihilo offers a framework for understanding these issues from a theological perspective that is both ancient and ever-renewing.

In theology, Creation Ex Nihilo continues to inspire reflections on human dignity, divine sovereignty, and the nature of creation, while engaging with contemporary movements and challenges. In philosophy, the doctrine provides a foundation for addressing metaphysical and existential questions, contributing to ongoing debates about the nature of reality and the possibility of meaning. In science, Creation Ex Nihilo offers a complementary perspective to scientific explanations of the universe, fostering dialogue between science and religion and guiding ethical decision-making in light of new discoveries.

Finally, in culture, Creation Ex Nihilo shapes narratives and worldviews that resonate with the human experience, inspiring art, literature, media, and public discourse. Its ongoing relevance is a testament to its power as a concept that speaks to the deepest concerns of humanity, offering a vision of a universe that is both mysterious and meaningful, grounded in the creative act of a transcendent God.

As we move forward into the future, the doctrine of Creation Ex Nihilo will continue to play a crucial role in shaping how we understand the world and our place within it, guiding us toward a deeper appreciation of the mysteries of existence and the creative power that brought everything into being.

CONCLUSION

SUMMARY OF KEY INSIGHTS

The doctrine of Creation Ex Nihilo—the belief that God created the universe out of nothing—has been explored throughout this work in various theological, philosophical, scientific, and cultural contexts. This concept, while rooted in ancient traditions, continues to hold profound significance in contemporary thought. The following summary highlights the key insights derived from the exploration of Creation Ex Nihilo across these diverse fields, emphasizing its enduring relevance and the potential it holds for future inquiry.

Theological Insights

1. Foundation of Theological Anthropology: Creation Ex Nihilo serves as a fundamental doctrine in understanding human identity and dignity. It affirms that all human beings are created in the image of God (Imago Dei) and possess inherent worth. This theological perspective underpins discussions about human rights, social justice, and the moral responsibilities of individuals and communities.

2. Divine Sovereignty and Providence: The doctrine emphasizes God's absolute sovereignty and ongoing providence in the world. It asserts that the universe exists because of God's will and continues to be sustained by divine power. This understanding informs theological discussions about the nature of God, the problem of evil, and the meaning of history.

3. Relevance in Contemporary Theological Movements: Creation Ex Nihilo has been reinterpreted in light of contemporary theological movements such as liberation theology, feminist theology, and ecological theology. These reinterpretations highlight the doctrine's adaptability and relevance in addressing modern social and environmental challenges, emphasizing themes of justice, equality, and stewardship.

Philosophical Insights

1. Metaphysical Foundations: The doctrine raises important metaphysical questions about the nature of existence, causality, and the possibility of something coming from nothing. Philosophical exploration of these concepts continues to deepen our understanding of the origins of the universe and the nature of reality, making Creation Ex Nihilo a central topic in contemporary metaphysical inquiry.

2. Challenges to Traditional Causality: Creation Ex Nihilo challenges traditional philosophical notions of causality, particularly the principle that everything must have a cause. This has led to ongoing debates about the nature of divine causality and whether the concept of creation from nothing can be reconciled with modern understandings of causality.

3. Existential and Ethical Implications: The doctrine offers a counter-narrative to existential and nihilistic interpretations of the universe, asserting that existence is purposeful and grounded in a transcendent creative act. This perspective provides a framework for addressing existential concerns about meaning, purpose, and the human condition in a seemingly indifferent universe.

Scientific Insights

1. Dialogue with Cosmology: The Big Bang Theory and other cosmological models suggest that the universe had

a temporal beginning, a concept that resonates with Creation Ex Nihilo. The ongoing dialogue between cosmology and theology continues to explore the implications of a universe with a beginning and the relationship between scientific explanations and theological interpretations of creation.

2. Engagement with Quantum Mechanics: Quantum mechanics challenges our understanding of reality, particularly in terms of causality and the emergence of something from nothing. Theological reflections on Creation Ex Nihilo provide a perspective on these challenges, contributing to discussions about the nature of nothingness, the role of the observer, and the relationship between the quantum world and the macroscopic universe.

3. Implications for Astrobiology and Environmental Science: The search for extraterrestrial life and the study of the universe's fine-tuning have raised new questions about the scope and purpose of creation. Creation Ex Nihilo informs discussions about the uniqueness of Earth, the potential existence of other life forms, and the ethical responsibilities of humanity as stewards of creation.

Cultural and Ethical Insights

1. Shaping Cultural Narratives: Creation Ex Nihilo continues to influence contemporary art, literature, and media, shaping cultural narratives about existence, creativity,

and transformation. The doctrine's themes of creation, chaos, and order resonate with the human experience, inspiring new interpretations and expressions in various cultural contexts.

2. Guiding Ethical Decision-Making: The doctrine provides a moral and spiritual foundation for addressing the ethical implications of scientific and technological advancements, particularly in fields such as genetics, artificial intelligence, and environmental ethics. Creation Ex Nihilo emphasizes the responsibility to use knowledge and creativity in ways that honor the Creator and respect the integrity of creation.

3. Public Engagement and Education: The ongoing relevance of Creation Ex Nihilo extends to public discourse and education, where it fosters a deeper understanding of the relationship between science and religion. By integrating the concept of creation into curricula and public discussions, theologians and educators can promote a more nuanced and respectful dialogue between these fields, contributing to a more informed and integrated worldview.

Future Directions

1. Interdisciplinary Research: The doctrine of Creation Ex Nihilo holds significant potential for future interdisciplinary research, particularly in emerging fields such as artificial intelligence, quantum cosmology, and

environmental humanities. As these fields continue to evolve, theological and philosophical engagement with Creation Ex Nihilo can provide valuable insights and guide the development of new theories and ethical frameworks.

2. Reinterpreting Traditional Doctrines: As society faces new challenges and questions, there is a need to revisit and reinterpret traditional doctrines in light of contemporary developments. Creation Ex Nihilo will continue to be a central point of reference in these efforts, offering a framework for understanding the origins of the universe, the nature of existence, and the meaning of human life in a rapidly changing world.

3. Ongoing Dialogue Between Science and Religion: The relationship between science and religion remains a critical area of exploration, with Creation Ex Nihilo serving as a vital touchstone for this dialogue. As scientific discoveries and technological advancements raise new questions about the universe, the doctrine provides a theological perspective that can engage with and complement scientific explanations, fostering a more holistic understanding of reality.

Conclusion: The Enduring Legacy of Creation Ex Nihilo

The doctrine of Creation Ex Nihilo continues to be a powerful and relevant concept in contemporary thought, shaping theological, philosophical, scientific, and cultural discussions about the origins of the universe, the nature of reality, and the meaning of existence. Its enduring legacy lies in its ability to provide a coherent and compelling narrative that addresses the deepest questions of human life, while also engaging with the challenges and opportunities of the modern world.

As we move forward into the future, Creation Ex Nihilo will remain a central point of reference for scholars, theologians, philosophers, scientists, and cultural commentators, guiding our exploration of the mysteries of existence and inspiring new ways of thinking about the world and our place within it. Through ongoing research, dialogue, and creative expression, the doctrine will continue to contribute to a deeper and more integrated understanding of creation, offering insights that are as relevant today as they were in the ancient past.

Reflection on the Significance of Creation Ex Nihilo for Faith and Reason

The doctrine of Creation Ex Nihilo—the belief that God created the universe out of nothing—holds profound significance for the relationship between faith and reason. This doctrine is not merely a theological assertion but a foundational concept that bridges the realms of religious belief and intellectual inquiry. It invites believers and thinkers alike to explore the deepest questions of existence, the origins of the universe, and the nature of reality. Reflecting on the significance of Creation Ex Nihilo for faith and reason reveals how this doctrine enriches both spheres, offering a unified vision of truth that encompasses both divine revelation and human understanding.

Creation Ex Nihilo as a Foundation for Faith

Affirming Divine Sovereignty and Purpose

For people of faith, Creation Ex Nihilo affirms the sovereignty and omnipotence of God. The belief that the universe was brought into existence by a divine act underscores the idea that all of reality is dependent on God's will and power. This theological assertion provides a foundation for understanding the world as a creation with intrinsic meaning and purpose, rather than as a random or purposeless phenomenon.

Key Reflections:

1. The Dependence of Creation on God: The doctrine of Creation Ex Nihilo emphasizes that everything that exists does so because of God's creative will. This underscores the complete dependence of the universe on God, not only for its origin but also for its continued existence. For believers, this

fosters a sense of trust and humility, acknowledging that all of creation is sustained by the Creator's ongoing involvement.

2. Purpose and Meaning in a Created Universe: Creation Ex Nihilo assures believers that the universe is not the result of blind chance but of a purposeful act of God. This belief provides a framework for understanding human life as part of a larger divine plan, imbuing existence with meaning and direction. It encourages faith in a God who is not only powerful but also intentional, guiding the course of history and the destiny of humanity.

3. Faith in the Unseen: The concept of creation from nothing challenges believers to have faith in the unseen and the incomprehensible. It reminds them that not all aspects of reality are accessible to human understanding, and that divine mysteries often transcend human reason. This fosters a faith that is both humble and expansive, open to the wonder and mystery of God's creative power.

Creation Ex Nihilo and the Role of Reason

Engaging with Intellectual Inquiry

While Creation Ex Nihilo is rooted in faith, it also engages deeply with the realm of reason. The doctrine invites philosophical and scientific inquiry, challenging thinkers to explore the implications of a universe that began from nothing. In this way, Creation Ex Nihilo serves as a bridge between faith and reason, encouraging a dialogue that enriches both.

Key Reflections:

1. Rational Exploration of Metaphysical Questions: Creation Ex Nihilo raises profound metaphysical questions about the nature of existence, causality, and the concept of nothingness. These are not only theological concerns but also central to philosophical inquiry. The doctrine encourages philosophers to engage with these questions, using reason to explore the possibility of a first cause, the nature of being, and the relationship between the contingent universe and a necessary creator.

2. Compatibility with Scientific Inquiry: The doctrine of Creation Ex Nihilo is not opposed to scientific investigation; rather, it complements it by addressing questions that science alone cannot fully answer. While science explores the mechanisms and processes of the universe's origins, Creation Ex Nihilo provides a framework for understanding the ultimate cause behind these processes. This encourages a harmonious relationship between faith and reason, where scientific discoveries are seen as revealing the intricacies of God's creation.

3. Critical Reflection and Theological Development: Reason plays a crucial role in the ongoing development and

refinement of theological doctrines, including Creation Ex Nihilo. Through critical reflection, theologians and philosophers can deepen their understanding of the doctrine, addressing challenges and incorporating new insights from various fields of knowledge. This process of intellectual engagement ensures that faith remains dynamic and responsive to new information, rather than static or dogmatic.

The Interplay of Faith and Reason in Understanding Creation

A Unified Vision of Truth

Creation Ex Nihilo offers a unique opportunity to integrate faith and reason, demonstrating that these two modes of knowing are not mutually exclusive but complementary. The doctrine suggests that faith and reason, when properly understood, lead to a unified vision of truth that encompasses both divine revelation and human inquiry.

Key Reflections:

1. Faith Seeking Understanding: The famous phrase fides quaerens intellectum (faith seeking understanding) encapsulates the dynamic relationship between faith and reason. Creation Ex Nihilo invites believers to deepen their faith through the pursuit of understanding, using reason to explore the mysteries of creation. This approach honors both

the certainties of faith and the insights of reason, recognizing that each can illuminate the other.

2. Reason Enriched by Faith: Reason, when informed by faith, is able to approach the ultimate questions of existence with a sense of purpose and meaning. Creation Ex Nihilo provides a context for rational inquiry that goes beyond mere analysis, offering a vision of the universe as a coherent and purposeful creation. This enriches philosophical and scientific investigations, allowing them to contribute to a fuller understanding of reality.

3. Theological Reflection and Philosophical Inquiry: The interplay of faith and reason in the doctrine of Creation Ex Nihilo encourages ongoing theological reflection and philosophical inquiry. It challenges thinkers to continuously explore the relationship between God and creation, the nature of existence, and the meaning of life. This dialogue ensures that both faith and reason remain vibrant and relevant, capable of addressing the complexities of the modern world.

Conclusion: The Enduring Significance of Creation Ex Nihilo

The doctrine of Creation Ex Nihilo remains a cornerstone of the relationship between faith and reason, offering a profound synthesis of belief and intellectual inquiry. It asserts that the universe is a creation with purpose and meaning, rooted in the will of a transcendent Creator. At the same time, it invites rational exploration of the mysteries of existence, encouraging a dialogue between theology, philosophy, and science.

In a world where questions about the origins of the universe, the nature of reality, and the meaning of life continue to challenge humanity, Creation Ex Nihilo provides a framework that integrates faith and reason. It reassures believers that their faith is not opposed to reason but is, in fact, enriched by it. Likewise, it offers to the realm of reason a perspective that transcends the limits of empirical knowledge, opening the door to the ultimate questions of existence.

As we continue to explore the implications of Creation Ex Nihilo, we are reminded that the search for truth is a shared journey—one that requires both the light of faith and the clarity of reason. Together, these two ways of knowing lead us toward a deeper understanding of the world, ourselves, and the God who brought everything into being from nothing.

FINAL THOUGHTS ON THE IMPLICATION FOR FUTURE EXPLORATION

As we conclude this exploration of Creation Ex Nihilo—the belief that God created the universe out of nothing—it's clear that this doctrine continues to be a vital and dynamic concept with profound implications for future inquiry. The intersections of theology, philosophy, science, and culture that have been examined reveal a rich tapestry of ideas and questions that invite further exploration. The implications of this doctrine for future study and reflection are vast, promising to inspire new insights, debates, and discoveries across multiple disciplines.

Theological Implications for Future Exploration

1. Reimagining Divine Action in a Modern World: As scientific knowledge expands, theologians will need to continue reimagining the ways in which divine action is

understood in relation to the natural world. Creation Ex Nihilo provides a foundational framework for exploring how God's creative power might be understood in light of contemporary cosmology, evolutionary biology, and quantum physics. The challenge will be to articulate a theology that is both faithful to the doctrine and responsive to new scientific paradigms, fostering a dialogue that respects both divine mystery and scientific inquiry.

2. Exploring the Ethics of Creation: The ethical implications of Creation Ex Nihilo are profound, particularly in the context of environmental stewardship, social justice, and technological innovation. Future theological exploration will likely focus on how this doctrine can inform ethical responses to the global challenges of climate change, biodiversity loss, and the equitable distribution of resources. Additionally, as technology continues to advance, particularly in areas like artificial intelligence and genetic engineering, theologians will need to engage with the ethical dimensions of human creativity in ways that reflect the reverence due to God's creation.

3. Interfaith and Ecumenical Dialogue: In an increasingly interconnected world, the doctrine of Creation Ex Nihilo offers a common ground for dialogue between different religious traditions. Future exploration could focus

on how this concept is interpreted across various faiths, fostering greater understanding and cooperation on shared concerns such as peacebuilding, environmental conservation, and human dignity. By engaging with diverse theological perspectives, scholars can enrich the doctrine's relevance and application in a pluralistic world.

Philosophical Implications for Future Exploration

1. Rethinking Metaphysical Concepts: The metaphysical questions raised by Creation Ex Nihilo—about existence, causality, and the nature of nothingness—remain central to philosophical inquiry. Future exploration in this area could involve rethinking these concepts in light of contemporary developments in philosophy and science. For example, philosophers may explore new models of causality that account for the complexities of quantum mechanics, or they might investigate the implications of a multiverse on traditional metaphysical assumptions.

2. Engaging with Process Philosophy and Theologies of Becoming: Process philosophy, which emphasizes the dynamic and relational aspects of reality, presents a compelling alternative to traditional metaphysical views of creation. Future philosophical exploration could involve a deeper engagement with process thought, examining how it can be integrated with or distinguished from the doctrine of

Creation Ex Nihilo. This dialogue could lead to new insights into the nature of God, time, and the unfolding of creation.

3. Addressing Existential Concerns: The existential implications of a universe created from nothing invite ongoing philosophical reflection. Future exploration might focus on how Creation Ex Nihilo can offer a framework for addressing contemporary existential concerns, such as the search for meaning in a secular age, the challenge of nihilism, and the human response to suffering and death. Philosophers could explore how this doctrine provides a basis for hope, purpose, and ethical living in the face of existential uncertainty.

Scientific Implications for Future Exploration

1. Integrating Theological and Cosmological Models: The relationship between Creation Ex Nihilo and contemporary cosmological theories, such as the Big Bang and quantum cosmology, offers fertile ground for future exploration. Scientists and theologians working together could develop more integrated models that respect both the empirical rigor of science and the theological depth of creation doctrine. This interdisciplinary work could lead to a more comprehensive understanding of the origins of the universe and the nature of time, space, and matter.

2. Exploring the Boundaries of Science and Theology: As science continues to push the boundaries of human knowledge, particularly in fields like artificial intelligence, genetic engineering, and space exploration, the doctrine of Creation Ex Nihilo will remain a key point of reference. Future exploration could focus on the boundaries between what science can explain and what remains within the realm of theological mystery. This ongoing dialogue will be crucial for maintaining a balanced perspective that honors both scientific achievement and the transcendence of divine creation.

3. Ethical Implications of Scientific Discoveries: The ethical implications of scientific discoveries, particularly those that involve the manipulation of life and matter, will continue to be an important area of exploration. The doctrine of Creation Ex Nihilo can provide a moral framework for evaluating the impact of these discoveries on human life, society, and the environment. Future work could focus on developing ethical guidelines that reflect the sacredness of creation and the responsibility of humanity to act as stewards of the world entrusted to them by God.

Cultural and Ethical Implications for Future Exploration

1. Cultural Narratives of Creation: The stories we tell about the origins of the universe and humanity shape our understanding of identity, purpose, and destiny. Future exploration could focus on how Creation Ex Nihilo is represented and reinterpreted in contemporary culture, including literature, art, and media. By examining how this doctrine is woven into cultural narratives, scholars can gain insights into its ongoing influence and the ways in which it continues to resonate with modern audiences.

2. Public Discourse on Science and Religion: The doctrine of Creation Ex Nihilo will remain central to public discourse on the relationship between science and religion. As debates about creationism, evolution, and the role of religion in public life continue, future exploration could focus on how this doctrine can contribute to a more informed and constructive dialogue. By engaging with diverse perspectives, scholars and public intellectuals can help bridge the gap between scientific and religious communities, fostering mutual respect and understanding.

3. Ethical Frameworks for a Globalized World: In an increasingly interconnected and globalized world, the ethical implications of Creation Ex Nihilo are more relevant than ever. Future exploration could focus on developing ethical frameworks that address global challenges such as climate

change, social inequality, and technological advancement. By drawing on the theological and philosophical insights of Creation Ex Nihilo, these frameworks can offer a vision of justice, stewardship, and human dignity that speaks to the needs of our time.

Conclusion: Charting the Course for Future Exploration

The doctrine of Creation Ex Nihilo, with its rich theological, philosophical, scientific, and cultural implications, offers a vast and fertile landscape for future exploration. As scholars, theologians, philosophers, and scientists continue to engage with this concept, they will uncover new insights and raise new questions that challenge and deepen our understanding of the universe and our place within it.

The future of Creation Ex Nihilo lies in its ability to adapt and respond to the ever-evolving intellectual and cultural environment, providing a foundation for exploring the mysteries of existence, the ethics of creation, and the relationship between faith and reason. By embracing the challenges and opportunities that lie ahead, we can ensure that this ancient doctrine continues to inspire and guide future generations in their quest for truth, meaning, and understanding.

As we look to the future, the implications of Creation Ex Nihilo will continue to unfold, offering new perspectives on the timeless questions of who we are, where we come from, and what our ultimate purpose might be. In this ongoing journey of exploration, Creation Ex Nihilo will remain a beacon of insight and inspiration, illuminating the path toward a deeper and more integrated understanding of the world and the divine act that brought it into being.

BIBLIOGRAPHY

This comprehensive bibliography includes a selection of theological works, philosophical texts, and scientific papers that have informed and contributed to the exploration of Creation Ex Nihilo in this work. These sources represent a broad spectrum of thought, encompassing historical and contemporary perspectives across multiple disciplines.

Theological Works

1. Aquinas, Thomas. Summa Theologica. Translated by Fathers of the English Dominican Province. New York: Benziger Bros., 1947.

- A foundational work in Christian theology, where Aquinas discusses the concept of creation and divine causality.

2. Augustine of Hippo. Confessions. Translated by Henry Chadwick. Oxford: Oxford University Press, 1991.

- Augustine's reflections on creation and God's relationship to time and the universe.

3. Barth, Karl. Church Dogmatics, Vol. III/1: The Doctrine of Creation. Translated by G. W. Bromiley and T. F. Torrance. Edinburgh: T&T Clark, 1958.

- Barth's extensive treatment of the doctrine of creation within his broader systematic theology.

4. Berkhof, Louis. Systematic Theology. Grand Rapids: Eerdmans, 1939.

- A Reformed perspective on the doctrine of creation, including discussions on Creation Ex Nihilo.

5. Bultmann, Rudolf. History and Eschatology: The Presence of Eternity. New York: Harper & Row, 1957.

- Bultmann's exploration of the relationship between history, eschatology, and creation.

6. Catherine Keller. Face of the Deep: A Theology of Becoming. New York: Routledge, 2003.

- A feminist and process-oriented interpretation of creation, challenging traditional views of Creation Ex Nihilo.

7. Moltmann, Jürgen. God in Creation: A New Theology of Creation and the Spirit of God. Translated by Margaret Kohl. Minneapolis: Fortress Press, 1993.

- Moltmann's ecological theology, which reinterprets the doctrine of creation in light of contemporary environmental concerns.

8. Rahner, Karl. Foundations of Christian Faith: An Introduction to the Idea of Christianity. New York: Seabury Press, 1978.

- Rahner's foundational work, including his thoughts on creation and the relationship between God and the world.

9. Tillich, Paul. Systematic Theology, Vol. 1: Reason and Revelation, Being and God. Chicago: University of Chicago Press, 1951.

- Tillich's integration of existential philosophy with Christian theology, including discussions on creation and being.

10. Wright, N.T. Creation, Power and Truth: The Gospel in a World of Cultural Confusion. London: SPCK Publishing, 2013.

- Wright's exploration of the theological implications of creation in the context of contemporary cultural and intellectual challenges.

Philosophical Texts

1. Aristotle. Metaphysics. Translated by W. D. Ross. Oxford: Oxford University Press, 1924.

- A key text in Western philosophy, where Aristotle explores the nature of being and causality.

2. Craig, William Lane. The Kalam Cosmological Argument. London: Macmillan, 1979.

- Craig's defense of the cosmological argument for the existence of God, rooted in the concept of creation from nothing.

3. Descartes, René. Meditations on First Philosophy. Translated by John Cottingham. Cambridge: Cambridge University Press, 1996.

- Descartes' foundational work on the nature of existence and the relationship between mind, body, and God.

4. Hick, John. Philosophy of Religion. 4th ed. Englewood Cliffs: Prentice Hall, 1990.

- An accessible introduction to the philosophy of religion, including discussions on arguments for the existence of God and the concept of creation.

5. Kant, Immanuel. Critique of Pure Reason. Translated by Paul Guyer and Allen W. Wood. Cambridge: Cambridge University Press, 1998.

- Kant's exploration of metaphysics and epistemology, with implications for the philosophical understanding of creation and causality.

6. Leibniz, Gottfried Wilhelm. Theodicy: Essays on the Goodness of God, the Freedom of Man and the Origin of Evil. Translated by E. M. Huggard. London: Routledge, 1951.

- Leibniz's discussion of creation, evil, and the nature of God's creative act.

7. Plantinga, Alvin. God and Other Minds: A Study of the Rational Justification of Belief in God. Ithaca: Cornell University Press, 1967.

- Plantinga's philosophical exploration of belief in God, including reflections on creation and divine action.

8. Sartre, Jean-Paul. Being and Nothingness: An Essay on Phenomenological Ontology. Translated by Hazel E. Barnes. New York: Washington Square Press, 1992.

- Sartre's existential analysis of being and nothingness, offering a secular perspective that contrasts with theological views on creation.

9. Whitehead, Alfred North. Process and Reality: An Essay in Cosmology. Corrected ed. Edited by David Ray Griffin and Donald W. Sherburne. New York: Free Press, 1978.

- Whitehead's process philosophy, which presents a dynamic view of reality and contrasts with traditional notions of Creation Ex Nihilo.

10. Wittgenstein, Ludwig. Tractatus Logico-Philosophicus. Translated by C. K. Ogden. London: Routledge & Kegan Paul, 1922.

- Wittgenstein's early work on the limits of language and reality, offering a unique perspective on metaphysical discussions about creation.

Scientific Papers and Texts

1. Davies, Paul. The Mind of God: The Scientific Basis for a Rational World. New York: Simon & Schuster, 1992.

- A physicist's exploration of the relationship between science and theology, including discussions on the origins of the universe.

2. Ellis, George F. R., and Stephen Hawking. The Large Scale Structure of Space-Time. Cambridge: Cambridge University Press, 1973.

- A seminal work in cosmology, exploring the structure of space-time and the implications for the beginning of the universe.

3. Greene, Brian. The Elegant Universe: Superstrings, Hidden Dimensions, and the Quest for the Ultimate Theory. New York: W. W. Norton & Company, 1999.

- Greene's accessible introduction to string theory and its implications for our understanding of the universe's origins.

4. Hawking, Stephen. A Brief History of Time: From the Big Bang to Black Holes. New York: Bantam Books, 1988.

- Hawking's famous work on the nature of time, the origins of the universe, and the limits of scientific knowledge.

5. Linde, Andrei. "The Inflationary Universe." Reports on Progress in Physics 47, no. 8 (1984): 925–986.

- A key paper on the theory of cosmic inflation, which offers insights into the early moments of the universe and the concept of creation.

6. Penrose, Roger. The Road to Reality: A Complete Guide to the Laws of the Universe. New York: Alfred A. Knopf, 2005.

- Penrose's comprehensive exploration of the physical laws that govern the universe, including discussions on the Big Bang and the origins of space-time.

7. Smolin, Lee. The Life of the Cosmos. Oxford: Oxford University Press, 1997.

- Smolin's exploration of cosmological theories, including his ideas on cosmological natural selection and the implications for the concept of creation.

8. Stenger, Victor J. God: The Failed Hypothesis—How Science Shows That God Does Not Exist. Amherst: Prometheus Books, 2007.

- Stenger's critique of theistic arguments, including discussions on the scientific challenges to the concept of Creation Ex Nihilo.

9. Susskind, Leonard. The Cosmic Landscape: String Theory and the Illusion of Intelligent Design. New York: Little, Brown, 2005.

- Susskind's defense of the multiverse hypothesis and its implications for discussions on fine-tuning and creation.

10. Tegmark, Max. Our Mathematical Universe: My Quest for the Ultimate Nature of Reality. New York: Alfred A. Knopf, 2014.

- Tegmark's exploration of the mathematical foundations of reality, offering insights into the nature of the universe and the concept of creation.

Interdisciplinary Works

1. Barbour, Ian G. Religion and Science: Historical and Contemporary Issues. San Francisco: HarperSanFrancisco, 1997.

- Barbour's examination of the relationship between religion and science, including discussions on creation, cosmology, and theological implications of scientific discoveries.

2. Clayton, Philip, and Arthur Peacocke, eds. In Whom We Live and Move and Have Our Being: Panentheistic Reflections on God's Presence in a Scientific World. Grand Rapids: Eerdmans, 2004.

- An interdisciplinary collection of essays exploring the relationship between science, theology, and the concept of creation.

3. McGrath, Alister E. Science and Religion: A New Introduction. 2nd ed. Oxford: Wiley-Blackwell, 2010.

- McGrath's introduction to the dialogue between science and religion, including discussions on creation, evolution, and the Big Bang.

4. Polkinghorne, John. The Faith of a Physicist: Reflections of a Bottom-Up Thinker. Minneapolis: Fortress Press, 1994.

- Polkinghorne's reflections on the relationship between his Christian faith and his work as a physicist, with insights into the doctrine of creation.

5. Russell, Robert John, Nancey Murphy, and C. J. Isham, eds. Quantum Cosmology and the Laws of Nature:

Scientific Perspectives on Divine Action. Vatican City State: Vatican Observatory Publications, 1993.

- A collection of essays examining the relationship between quantum cosmology, the laws of nature, and theological concepts of creation.

This bibliography represents a selection of the many works that contribute to the rich and ongoing dialogue about Creation Ex Nihilo. These sources provide a foundation for further exploration and reflection, offering diverse perspectives that continue to shape our understanding of creation, existence, and the relationship between faith and reason.

Appendix A: Key Terms and Definitions

This appendix provides definitions of key terms used throughout the discussion of Creation Ex Nihilo. Understanding these terms is essential for engaging with the theological, philosophical, and scientific concepts explored in this work.

1. Creation Ex Nihilo: A Latin phrase meaning "creation out of nothing." It refers to the belief that God created the universe without using any pre-existing materials, bringing everything into existence solely by divine will and power.

2. Divine Sovereignty: The concept that God possesses ultimate authority and power over all creation. In the context of Creation Ex Nihilo, divine sovereignty

emphasizes God's control over the universe's existence and ongoing sustenance.

3. Imago Dei: A theological term meaning "image of God." It refers to the belief that human beings are created in the image and likeness of God, possessing inherent dignity and worth.

4. Metaphysics: A branch of philosophy concerned with the fundamental nature of reality, including questions about existence, causality, and the nature of being. Metaphysical discussions often intersect with theological concepts like Creation Ex Nihilo.

5. Cosmology: The scientific study of the origins, structure, and development of the universe. Cosmological theories, such as the Big Bang Theory, often engage with theological discussions about the beginning of the universe.

6. Theodicy: A term referring to the defense of God's goodness and omnipotence in the face of the existence of evil and suffering. Theodicy is often discussed in relation to Creation Ex Nihilo, particularly in addressing why a good God would create a world that includes suffering.

7. Process Philosophy: A school of thought that emphasizes the dynamic and relational aspects of reality. It contrasts with traditional views of Creation Ex Nihilo by suggesting that the universe is in a constant state of becoming

rather than being created from nothing at a single point in time.

8. Causality: The principle that everything that happens has a cause. In discussions of Creation Ex Nihilo, causality is examined to understand how the universe could come into existence from nothing and what role God plays as the ultimate cause.

9. Quantum Mechanics: A branch of physics that studies the behavior of particles at the smallest scales, where classical concepts of causality and determinism often do not apply. Quantum mechanics raises questions about the nature of reality and the possibility of something emerging from nothing, which are relevant to discussions of Creation Ex Nihilo.

10. Anthropic Principle: A philosophical consideration that observations of the universe must be compatible with the conscious life that observes it. The Anthropic Principle is often discussed in relation to fine-tuning arguments, which suggest that the universe's physical constants are precisely calibrated to allow for life, potentially pointing to a purposeful creation.

Appendix B: Additional Readings and Resources

For readers interested in further exploring the topics covered in this work, the following additional readings and resources provide a deeper understanding of Creation Ex Nihilo and its implications across theology, philosophy, science, and culture.

Theology

1. Grenz, Stanley J. Theology for the Community of God. Grand Rapids: Eerdmans, 1994.

- An accessible and comprehensive systematic theology that includes discussions on creation and the doctrine of God.

2. McFague, Sallie. The Body of God: An Ecological Theology. Minneapolis: Fortress Press, 1993.

- A work that explores the doctrine of creation from an ecological perspective, emphasizing the interconnectedness of all life.

3. Zizioulas, John D. Being as Communion: Studies in Personhood and the Church. Crestwood: St. Vladimir's Seminary Press, 1985.

- A theological exploration of creation that emphasizes the relational nature of being, drawing on Eastern Orthodox traditions.

Philosophy

1. Copan, Paul, and William Lane Craig. Creation out of Nothing: A Biblical, Philosophical, and Scientific Exploration. Grand Rapids: Baker Academic, 2004.

- A detailed exploration of the doctrine of Creation Ex Nihilo from biblical, philosophical, and scientific perspectives.

2. MacIntyre, Alasdair. After Virtue: A Study in Moral Theory. Notre Dame: University of Notre Dame Press, 1981.

- While focused on moral philosophy, this work provides insights into the implications of metaphysical concepts, including creation, for ethics and human flourishing.

3. Swinburne, Richard. The Existence of God. 2nd ed. Oxford: Clarendon Press, 2004.

- A rigorous philosophical argument for the existence of God, including discussions on the origin of the universe and the nature of creation.

Science

1. Krauss, Lawrence M. A Universe from Nothing: Why There Is Something Rather than Nothing. New York: Free Press, 2012.

- A provocative exploration of the origins of the universe from a scientific perspective, challenging traditional notions of creation from nothing.

2. Rees, Martin. Just Six Numbers: The Deep Forces That Shape the Universe. New York: Basic Books, 2000.

- A discussion of the physical constants of the universe and their role in shaping the cosmos, relevant to fine-tuning arguments and creation.

3. Tipler, Frank J., and John D. Barrow. The Anthropic Cosmological Principle. Oxford: Oxford University Press, 1986.

- A comprehensive examination of the Anthropic Principle and its implications for cosmology and the concept of creation.

Interdisciplinary

1. Clayton, Philip. God and Contemporary Science. Edinburgh: Edinburgh University Press, 1997.

- An interdisciplinary examination of the relationship between theology and science, focusing on how contemporary scientific discoveries intersect with traditional theological concepts.

2. Fergusson, David. Creation. Grand Rapids: Eerdmans, 2014.

- A concise and insightful exploration of the doctrine of creation from an interdisciplinary perspective, engaging with both theological and scientific viewpoints.

3. Haught, John F. Science and Faith: A New Introduction. Mahwah: Paulist Press, 2012.

- An introduction to the dialogue between science and faith, with discussions on creation, evolution, and the theological implications of scientific discoveries.

Online Resources

1. Stanford Encyclopedia of Philosophy (https://plato.stanford.edu/)

- An excellent online resource for in-depth articles on philosophical topics, including entries on metaphysics, causality, and arguments for the existence of God.

2. The BioLogos Forum (https://biologos.org/)

- A resource for exploring the relationship between science and Christian faith, including discussions on creation, evolution, and cosmology.

3. The Center for Theology and the Natural Sciences (https://www.ctns.org/)

- An organization dedicated to the dialogue between theology and the natural sciences, offering resources, publications, and programs on topics related to creation and cosmology.

This selection of additional readings and resources provides a starting point for those who wish to delve deeper into the complex and fascinating discussions surrounding Creation Ex Nihilo. These works offer a range of perspectives, from theological and philosophical to scientific and cultural, ensuring that readers can explore the doctrine's implications in a comprehensive and multidisciplinary manner.